Colombia at a Crossroads

A Historical and Social Biography

Ri

wv ͟͟.com

Richard McColl

Copyright © first edition 2023 by Richard McColl and Fuller Vigil.
Copyright © second edition 2024 by Richard McColl and Fuller Vigil.
All rights reserved.
No portion of this book may be reproduced in any form
without written permission from the publisher or author,
except as permitted by U.S. copyright law.

Contents

About the author
Ackowledgements
PART 1. Overview and Introduction
  Author's Foreward
  A Chance Encounter
  Introduction
  Covid-19 and Colombia
  Colombia, a country of contradictions
PART 2. Colombia under Gustavo Petro
  Gustavo Petro – the Last South American Guerrilla by Richard McColl
  Gustavo Petro, Bogotá's uncompromising heavy metal mayor
  Petro's Presidential loss
  Petro's Presidential win
  President Petro 2022-2026
  Petro and US
  The Reality under Petro
  Colombia at a Crossroads after 30 Years of Neoliberalism in Colombia
PART 3. History and Politics
  Pre-Hispanic Period
  Spanish Conquest 1500-1549
  New Granada: Spanish Rule (1549-1808)
  Independence 1808 – 1819
  Modern Colombia: A Democracy on the edge 1903…
  Politics since 1958
  The Constitution of 1991
PART 4. Uribe, Peace, Conflict and the Evolution of the Conflict
  President Uribe
  Alvaro Uribe: The Complex Role of a Former President
  President Santos
  President Duque and his Orange Economy
  Colombia's Guerrillas
  The FARC
  Peace with the FARC
  The ELN
  Paramilitary Groups
  Narcotics Trade
  Total Peace
  Evolution of the Conflict

PART 5. The Economy, formal and informal
  The Economy: Mixed fortunes
  The Neo-Liberal Turnaround
  Extractives under Petro
  Global partnerships
  The Informal Economy
  Alternative Crops
  The drug economy
  Corruption
  Mixed prospects and Covid-19
PART 6. Colombian Culture and Society
  Culture: What does it mean to be a Colombian?
  The Population
  Music
  Sports
  Forgotten Histories
  Colombian football, and why it matters
  Carnival and festivals
  Media
  Press Freedom in Colombia
  Literature
  A Prophetic voice
  Colombian cinema
  Architecture
  Colombian Urban Context
  Fashion
  Graffiti
  Fine Arts and Crafts
  Colombian Photography
  Food and Drink
PART 7. Geography and the Land
  Overview
  Where to Go
PART 8. Further Information
  Further Reading
  Basic Health & Safety
  Key Sources
About Fuller Vigil
Also by Richard McColl and Published by Fuller Vigil

About the author

Richard McColl is a freelance foreign correspondent and consultant based between Bogotá and Mompós in Colombia. His writing has appeared in dozens of publications worldwide including the Wall Street Journal, the Globe and Mail, the BBC and Foreign Policy magazine amongst others.

He hosts a weekly podcast: Colombia Calling and is often a pundit discussing Colombian politics on international broadcast outlets and is the host of the LatinNews podcast.

He holds a diploma in Conflict Resolution and a PhD in Social and Human Sciences from the Universidad Pontificia Javeriana in Bogotá and is a trustee for the UK-based NGO, Children Change Colombia.

Fuller Vigil

Cover photo: Richard McColl reproduced with permission from Chirrete Golden.

Designer: Jose Duran.

First Edition: October 2023

This edition No2, May 2024

Copywrite: Fuller Vigil

ISBN:

Printing: Gente Nueva, Bogotá

Ackowledgements

A huge thanks to everyone at Fuller Vigil.

A special thank you to the contributing authors, Adriaan Alsema of Colombia Reports, Nicolas Forsans, Professor of Management and Director of The Essex MBA, University of Essex, Dr Andrei Gomez and Dr Peter Watson, Lecturer in the Department of Spanish, Portuguese and Latin American Studies, University of Leeds. It goes without saying that their investigations, research and affection for Colombia add something additional to this text.

Most of all, I want to thank my family for their encouragement and belief in this project which, at times, did not seem like it would see the light of day.

PART 1.
Overview and Introduction

Author's Foreward

Having reported on South America for international news outlets as a freelance foreign correspondent since 2001 and tiring of moving nomadically about the continent, I decided upon relocating to Colombia full-time in 2007. For the first few years, I contented myself with writing guidebooks, travel articles, filling the wordcounts with whimsy and superficial observations of hotel locations, reflections on the poor state of public transport and the cost of a "blue plate special," in cleaner establishments across the country. It was more of a promise to my family that I would not involve myself in writing about Colombia's fraught political spectrum and conflict and run unnecessary risks.

Colombia was and is a country in transition and this was clear from the very outset, but my goal was to promote tourism and enable the trickle-down economics from this income to effect some change on the ground in the communities. By mid-2011, my tolerance for thread-counts and hotel reviews had hit an impasse and it was time to shift into different fields in order to get the news about Colombia out there.

For five years, my aim had been to promote Colombia, almost as an on-looker and then, in the face of events so nefarious in their nature, it was evident that I could pursue this path no longer. It may have been a kidnapping, learning about the families of friends and loved ones affected by either guerrilla groups, paramilitary groups, common delinquency or unfathomable corruption, whatever the case, I cannot put my finger on the moment when things changed for me. It was likely a compilation of events taking place in Colombia that led me to deciding that I could no longer only focus on the positive and airbrush out some of the realities in the country, much of which are to be detailed in further chapters. The decision was made to continue promoting my adopted home-land but also to highlight things of importance as well, often negative.

As they say in Colombia: *"El que peca y reza empata,"* or - he who sins and prays evens the score. And that's how it's been since roughly 2012 when I embarked on an *Especialización en Resolución de Conflictos* focusing on the Colombian conflict and its causes and then, latterly, a doctorate in *Ciencias Sociales y Humanas*, both at the Pontificia Universidad Javeriana in Bogotá.

So, the aim of this book is not only to focus on Colombia's problems, politics and history, but also to celebrate her culture and society and that's is the reason it's divided into several parts.

It is not a guide book, nor a travelogue and nor is it a list of dry facts. Writing this has been a multi-year challenge and will no doubt raise ire in many circles, but the hope is to create something which is more of a summary of Colombia, something with a pulse. There will be absences and facts overlooked which are of importance to some and of less note to others, but for this, the recommended reading – despite its age - is David Bushnell's unrivalled: *The Making of Modern Colombia: A Nation in Spite of Itself* (University of California Press (February 9, 1993). There are of course dozens of academic and personal histories, both fiction and non-fiction, available from which to gain further insights into Colombia and her complexities which can be found in the chapter dedicated to further reading.

In keeping with the idea that this book has a "heartbeat", there are chapters and essays contributed by experts in their fields including: Adriaan Alsema, Nicolas Forsans, David Restrepo, Andrei Gomez Suarez and Peter Watson and each is credited in turn with their titles and roles. There is a forgotten history in Colombia recounted, curiosities, further anecdotes and some articles which have been published in the mainstream press as well, all of which, I hope, will add to the colour and depth of the book.

Given that this book has been written over a period of several years and has been delayed due to the election of Gustavo

Petro, Colombia's first leftist president, it makes sense to begin with an overview of his first years in power 2022-2024, before then plunging into the History and Politics chapter which precedes, Culture and Identity, Geography and the Land, then the Conclusion and Further Reading.

A word of advice to the reader is warranted as well. It's a herculean task to separate Colombia and Colombians from the conflict and politics and this makes writing a book of this nature a risky venture. One must remember and be very aware that the conflict has spread through every level of Colombian society and in every corner of the country is of course not without its consequences. A massive underclass of Internally Displaced People (IDPs) has been forcibly removed from their traditional homes and lands to the cities in what can only be described as a tragic mass exodus. Society here continues to suffer from the deep scars of trauma and needs constant yet sympathetic therapy, but as with everything, there are glimmers of hope, some more evident than others. For this reason, this foreword ends with an anecdote dating back to 2006.

A Chance Encounter

"Be careful here," warned Alejandra. "These places are just for drugs and prostitution."

This was nothing new.

The more time you spend in less than salubrious digs, the more you come to realise that, while these pastimes take place, they can be avoided. I am no Charles Nicholl, as detailed in his book: *The Fruit Palace: An Odyssey Through Colombia's Cocaine Underworld*, (St Martins Pr; First Edition (January 1, 1986) just another bum with a vague direction, a half-baked plan and a dozen money making ideas.

Thanking Alejandra for her kindness and arranging to meet later for a drink, I headed inside. Already dusk but still swelteringly hot, I checked into my room, threw my shirt into the corner, slapped the fan onto max and collapsed on my bed.

"*Requisa Policial*"

Hammering on my door. "Police inspection. Open the door."

In that half state of consciousness due to the merciless Caribbean humidity, I sleepwalked, reached over, flicked back the bolt and before I could put my shirt on two heavily armed agents in fatigues entered and behind them the man in charge. One policeman stood guard as if he expected me to scarper while the other tossed my mattress, pulled the stuffing out of the pillow, tipped the contents of my backpack onto the floor and then headed for the bathroom. All the while the chief looked on disapprovingly.

Making the perhaps foolhardy decision not to play the dumb gringo I started answering his questions in Spanish. Routine. "Where are you from, what are you doing?" I was not guilty of what he hoped, but certainly guilty of apathetic wanderings. All of it unspoken, but quite clearly behind his eyes was the parental and officious rebuke: "Get a job, have a shave and get the hell out of my country."

He picked up my guidebook, open at the page describing the trek to the Lost City, and fixing a probing glare directly at me said:

"I see that in your passport you have visited Colombia on several occasions, and that you speak Spanish very well. What exactly is it that you do here *Señor* McColl?"

"I have visited *Chocó, Nariño, Valle* and the *Pianguera* communities in the pacific."

Idiotic. The only word that can possibly describe the lunacy of telling him that I had visited regions distributed violently between right-wing paramilitaries, leftist guerrillas, the Government and opportunistic cartels. His eyebrows arched in surprise; perhaps he noted the foolishness of my statement. He thought he had me, and thumbing the pages in my passport more deliberately, multiple entry and exit stamps from Colombia, Peru, Bolivia, Ecuador, Paraguay and Central America he nodded an affirmation to the other agent. The two of them set about checking above the exterior lintels of the windows, behind the plumbing of the shower, places that I had not even thought of checking upon entering the room. I had heard about set-ups and the like, but I realised at this moment, if there was anything planted in here, these men would find it.

Picking up my discarded shirt, the Chief held it close to his nose and sniffed. "So, you smoke."

"No."

"This shirt smells of smoke, you are a *marijuanero*."

Such was the change of climate from the spring-like Bogotá to the concrete sauna of this Santa Marta hotel room, I was suffering. I had barely slept the night before having spent most of the previous evening closing a bar in the capital. Bags under my eyes, sweating and in an unimaginable lethargy, I cut the perfect image of a stoner. But, I could hardly believe that he was smelling my rum, sweat and smoked infused T-shirt.

The questions were coming thick and fast and I began to fear that should the policemen not find any loot that, having spent so much time on this case, they would make it worth their while with a bribe or an addition to my belongings that would leave me hopelessly stranded and floundering in a tropical cell.

"I was in *Guapi*, *Buenaventura*, and *Tumaco* while researching for an NGO."

He remained unimpressed.

"I was looking into sustainable practices and reforestation efforts as well as having the opportunity to view the nesting habits of the incredible sea turtles that make their home at *Sanquianga National Park*." I thought that by throwing out some specifics, he might start to take me seriously. Was I mistaken, or did his eyes lose a shade of their degree of inquisition and disapproval and register some interest?

"And you saw the Green Turtle?"

"Yes, I saw a mother drag herself onto the beach and lay her eggs, it was breath-taking."

The chief smiled, "I too have been there, and it is a thing of beauty." He stood up from the chair in the corner. "In Colombia, we have so much more than cocaine to offer." This statement came more as a reprimand than an observation. "We have the most amazing jungle and those turtles get to be this big, "he moved his arms, linked them in a hoop demonstrating the size of a fully-grown Green Turtle.

"I am glad you have come to see this side of things, what else do you know? The women?" he leered enthusiastically. "The *rolas*, the *paisas* and the *costeñas*?"

I could see my exit.

"My heart is broken every day by a Colombiana," he seemed pleased with this statement, I continued: "I am planning on hiking to the Ciudad Perdida in the next few days."

"This is one of the most unforgettable experiences in

Colombia; you will see remarkable birdlife, beautiful jungles, the indigenous people and the ruins of a great empire. My Colombia is very special in that she has everything."

The chief continued for a further five or six minutes, becoming increasingly enthusiastic as he spoke of the wonders of his country. He picked up my guidebook and thumbing the section on "his Colombia", dog-eared many of the pages detailing places where he felt I should spend time and if I had already been there, where I should spend more time.

He asked for a pen and noted down his number on the inside back cover of my guidebook, should I have any further problems

He smiled, we shook hands and the *requisa policial* was over, the

Passing by the front desk on my way out, I asked as to the frequency of these room searches.

"Oh yes, the last one happened ten years ago."

"And they found?"

"Cocaine, hand grenades, guns," he shrugged.

Richard McColl

Introduction

There may well have been a renaissance of sorts underway in Colombia prior to 2020. Against the backdrop of the ubiquitous on-going and habitual political strife, an increasingly beleaguered peace accord signed with the Revolutionary Armed Forces of Colombia (FARC) in 2016, record figures of coca cultivation, tumbling oil prices and economic woes, the tragedy of the Covid-19 pandemic, the rising cost of living and problems in neighbouring Venezuela: despite all these issues, things felt positive, well, more upbeat than before. How Colombia has responded to and mostly recovered from Covid-19 and its fallout in the long-term remains to be seen. The pandemic seems such a tragedy since the country had been enjoying a period of spring where hope for peace was a reality and no-longer a pipe-dream despite a government working against it, a new generation of Colombians was making their voices heard in timely, organic and democratic protests, high-profile country image campaigns were yielding results, and the ever-present old guard of politicians, landowners and oligarchs, who for so long were indubitably in charge, were now having their roles, power and positions questioned.

This sentiment and shift in attitude was nowhere more in evidence than in the Colombian capital Bogotá, when in 2019 Colombia's expanding middle class poured out into the streets, filling the city's main thoroughfares to protest at the injustices they felt they were confronting - the government's failure to fully implement the peace agreement, opposition to fracking, calls for better infrastructure, contracts free from corruption, in favour of human rights, greater access to healthcare and education – it was because they could now do so.

The 2016 signing of peace with a majority of the FARC rebels after years of negotiations in Havana, Cuba, removed a common enemy from the hearts and minds of the Colombian population.

The accords were seen internationally as the most robust of their kind, placing the victims at the heart of the negotiations and applying transitional justice in a push for reconciliation and reparation of a deeply traumatized population.

The accords cast greater transparency on what one might call the normal concerns of the middle class such as the lack of investment in infrastructure, education and access to decent healthcare. The veil was lifted, and Colombians began to focus on the causes of the armed conflict and to re-assess the situation in their country, as they were now allowed to consider the larger picture of politics, culture and society. Dozens, if not scores of cases of corruption began to see the light of day even resulting in the arrest and imprisonment of the government's anti-corruption czar. So much had previously been pushed into the shadows of the armed conflict, with people being led to believe that any and all of the ills faced by Colombia stemmed from the conflict itself.

How things have changed. And yet, they have not. Scarred into the collective memory of the members of the FARC reintegrating into society are the 418 plus comrades in arms who have been assassinated since peace was signed. As of April 2024, the Institute for Development and Peace, a Colombian think-tank (INDEPAZ)[1], had registered 1495 assassinations of social leaders and activists since the signing of the peace accord and 462 massacres since 2018. This staggering number of deaths will undoubtedly grow as the struggle for domination in the lucrative coca-growing, mining, agricultural and strategic territories continues. It's not a question of finding the person who pulled the trigger, but the overarching individual or individuals guilty of sending the message for this to be done. Yet the justice system remains backlogged and the inherent corruption for so long a scourge in Colombia, continues to affect progress.

Violence continues to boil over along the border with Venezuela as armed groups jostle for control of the smuggling corridors, and migrants from that country come and go; the department of Cauca continues to be a hot-spot for killing; the Pacific coast port cities of Buenaventura and Tumaco suffer from neglect and lawlessness, Colombia still manages to move ahead, albeit in an austere funereal pace of two steps forward, one step back. And, of course, the violence has spilled over into Ecuador as well, affecting the presidential elections in 2023 just as thousands of migrants from Cuba, Haiti, Venezuela and much futher adrift head to the northern Darien jungles to continue on the hazardous overland journey on through Central America in the hope of new lives in the United States.

The country somehow positions herself as a tourist destination par excellence for bird watchers and the intrepid traveller, for those seeking luxury in Bogotá and Cartagena or on a coffee hacienda, and people in search of something new such as the iridescent purple waters of Caño Cristales or the urban regeneration and renovation underway in Medellín.

Good news does surface from Colombia, despite at times the questionable achievements of whichever government is in power. Colombians are a happy, gracious and inquisitive people keen to ensure that you get the most from their country, however, they do recognise the failings of their homeland. The advice given here is listen to what Colombians have to say about the conditions in which they live and then hopefully you can form your own opinion as it is they who have learned to co-exist with issues in their country.

---

[1] INDEPAZ: 26 September 2016 to 26 April 2024. https://indepaz.org.co

Covid-19 and Colombia

The Colombian government registered the first "official" case of Covid-19 on 6 March 2020, but it is suspected that the virus had reached the country well before this, given the earlier outbreaks in neighbouring Ecuador and Peru. By reacting quickly and putting a quarantine in place nationwide, with Bogotá leading the way, President Iván Duque was initially lauded for his response. He called for an "intelligent isolation" to minimize damage to the economy, but the insufficient healthcare system collapsed, underfunded by years of budget cuts and corruption, revealing the unpleasant truth of inequality inherent in South American and Colombian society.

As in many countries, there was no Plan B beyond a draconian quarantine, and the result was little more than a delay of the inevitable. By August 2020, six months into the pandemic, Colombia had one of the highest per-capita mortality rates for coronavirus in the world, a fact confirmed by Johns Hopkins University after the country registered a daily average of 300 deaths over two weeks. Colombia's mortality rate for mid-August 2020 was 27.8 for every 100,000 inhabitants or 3.3 case-fatality ratio, while the country held the title for the nation with the longest period of lockdown, exceeding 170 days. By late January 2021, almost two million Colombians had been infected with the virus and the official death toll stood at 50,000. Whilst Colombia's regional neighbours were fast in rolling out and applying a vaccination program by January 2021, Colombia's efforts fell short, leaving the country well behind in terms of an effective response.

The reality of the pandemic is that, with Covid-19 in the region, the veneer of progress so often attached to South America's war on poverty was stripped bare. Instead, we saw a part of the world severely lacking in provision for the neediest, an invisible population to many devoid of the most basic things such as clean water, sanitation, a stable income, and healthcare.

During the first 10 months of the pandemic, Colombian President Iván Duque hosted an evening address to the nation, opening up a televised forum to cabinet ministers, representatives of the World Health Organization, and medical professionals to discuss government initiatives to mitigate and control the spread of coronavirus. Going under the title Prevención y Acción (Prevention and Action), the one-hour program kept millions of Colombians updated with announcements (while silencing independent news and therefore drowning out any potential criticism) although over time the show was rightly lambasted for its focus on promoting the government's agenda and it latterly suffered from pitiful viewing numbers dropping to as low as 120 viewers on YouTube[2].

After five months in which citizens were restricted in their movements, the gradual easing of the strict quarantine was substituted by Mandatory Selective Isolation, in which suspected carriers of the virus were obliged to self-isolate for 14 days. This measure allowed the national government to reactivate key economic sectors while placing much of the responsibility for preventing virus transmission on individuals. The Ministry of Health applied additional measures requested by Mayors and Governors to limit agglomerations, alcohol sales, enact curfews and rotating lockdowns. Beyond this, at the time of writing, the government seems bereft of further ideas.

By early 2023, face mask mandates were only place in public transport before becoming a thing of the past. Between January 2020 and June 2023 Colombia[3] recorded a total of 6,371,090 confirmed cases of Covid-19 and 142,794 deaths.

---

[2] El Espectador: https://www.elespectador.com/politica/el-pobre-rating-del-programa-presidencial-prevencion-y-accion-article/

[3] WHO: https://covid19.who.int/region/amro/country/co

Colombia, a country of contradictions

Colombians are passionate, patriotic and proud. Whether it's the seemingly endless parade of national holidays celebrating independence and victories at battles, the tricolour flags flying proudly or the fierce nationalism on display any time the Colombian national football team plays, Colombians are quick to show their colours.

This also manifests itself at 6am and 6pm every day when all radio stations are obliged to play the Colombian national anthem.

The anthem, "*Oh Gloria Inmarcesible* (Oh unfading glory)", was originally edited from a poem by former Colombian president Rafael Núñez and put to music by Italian opera singer Oreste Sindici. Over the years, many different versions and adaptations were made but the current 11-verse anthem (usually only the chorus and one verse are sung) was first presented to the public in 1887. It quickly became popular and was officially adopted as Colombia's national anthem in 1920.

Throughout the anthem, there are numerous references to the various parts of Colombia, with Boyacá, Cartagena, the Caribbean and the Andes all getting a mention. Pride at being Colombian and at past victories and battles for independence run through the whole song and the lyrics speak passionately about sorrow, pain and struggles but also optimistically about overcoming difficulties and the bright future of Colombia.

The lyrics and the significance of the song seem to awaken feelings of national pride and foster a true sense of Colombian-ness. And why shouldn't people feel proud to be Colombian? The spectacular beauty of the country, the rich culture, the phenomenal ability of Colombians to always see the light at the end of the tunnel are just some of the reasons why we should sing the anthem proudly, hand on heart and with the unfaltering Colombian spirit that typifies Colombian people.

"And thus, the motherland is formed".

BUT!

If we take a moment to look at the three main symbols of Colombia, the flag, the crest and the hymn, nothing comes close to the hymn in terms of its significance and indeed its mystique. So, we must unravel and question a few facets to all of these three items if we are going to deep dive into the national anthem itself and not forget that a social media campaign, "*Libertad y Orden,*" was waged in March 2023 by figures in opposition to the government of President Petro. National symbols, as always, co-opted for political effect.

Beginning with the tricolour flag, the resplendent yellow is there representing the wealth of gold in the country. Herein we can find two major problems; the first is that Colombia's gold was obviously sacked and removed by the Spanish empire at the height of their colonial aspirations, and the second, what little gold actually remains here, is in the hands of Colombia's elites and well beyond the reach of most ordinary Colombians, just showing why Colombia remains one of the most unequal countries in the region with a Gini coefficient between 0.55 and 0.6 according to a recent UNDP[4] report.

If this wasn't enough, let's take a look at Colombia's crest, a tragicomedy of symbols which no longer exist or are in the process of disappearing in this country. Amongst these symbols, perhaps the most striking is the image which adorns the base of the crest. Panamá! Is it a lament that Panamá remains on the crest or has the fact that it is there been overlooked all these years? And what should we say about the country's national bird, the majestic condor? According to recent statistics, only 40 or 50 condors remain in Colombia today, an infinitesimally small number for the animal which is one of the principle symbols of our country.

So, based on the information explored, perhaps it's clear that there's but one national symbol which can resonate – although not free from its defects – with the national identity: the Colombian National Anthem, *la Marcha Triunfal,* set to music by the Italian composer, Oreste Sindici, using verses written by Rafael Núñez, a former president.

Out of the three national symbols, the anthem is the one which we probably know least about and which has been feted in popular beliefs and half-truths over the years.

What is certain is that the anthem is interpreted, and its significance alters, according to the ideological bent of the government in power. This of course has created some confusion with respect to the original intentions of the authors and their text. What did Nuñez mean when he wrote: "*cesó la horrible noche*?" One response to this would be that it's a celebration of the end of Spanish colonization, and more contemporary times it has been used to celebrate the fall of liberal and conservative governments, and most recently, it was used to celebrate the signing of the peace accord with the FARC.

The hymn itself is made up of eleven verses which not only refer to battles for the freedom of Colombia but also others which have defined Latin America.

To some critics, the text of the national anthem reflects the parochial mentality of Nuñez and for others it could be a rallying cry to a never-ending glory, popular jubilation and something which cannot be eclipsed. Whatever the case, it is clear that the incongruity of the anthem goes far beyond the issue of it being an over-lengthy and enduring song.

The chorus of the national anthem, written in 1850, to celebrate the independence of Cartagena de Indias (1811), remarks at the infinite glory of having expelled the Spanish from Colombian lands. What we are expected to see and believe throughout the lyrics of the anthem is that the horror of Spanish colonialism has ended and that we are now living in a new, independent territory, made up of free individuals. And, that humanity, still suffering and tied up with chains, understands that this freedom is at the whim of a love for Jesus Christ who taught this from up on the cross.

And rather than solely focusing on the trumpets of war which play a sombre if triumphant tune throughout the anthem, perhaps it´s better to look at the penultimate verse, verse No10. Within these poignant lines, it is made clear to us that the true freedom of a people does not solely depend on wars of independence but on a socio-political system which is truly inclusive for each and every inhabitant in this new country. The sun, as it says, has to shine upon us all, and not just upon a special few.

One suggestion is that we pull verse ten from its obscurity towards the end of a seemingly endless anthem and bring it up to ensure it receives the exposure it deserves.

---

[4] Agence France de Developpment: https://www.afd.fr/en/extension-research-facility-inequalities-colombia

PART 2.
Colombia under Gustavo Petro

Gustavo Petro – the Last South American Guerrilla by Richard McColl

Colombian Politics Today – President Gustavo Petro

We cannot fail Colombian society. The dead deserve it. The living need it.

Today begins the Colombia of what is possible. Today begins our second chance.

From President Gustavo Petro Urrego's inaugural address 7 August 2022[5].

Following an historic election victory in a second-round run-off in June 2022, Colombia's first ever leftist president, Gustavo Petro Urrego, assumed office on 7 August 2022 before a crowd of hundreds of thousands and a packed Plaza de Bolívar. Amongst his promises, the pledge to "bring to Colombia what it has not had for centuries, which is tranquillity and peace." Having campaigned on a radical agenda to redistribute wealth, end the war on drugs and tackle the climate crisis, Petro marked a distinct break with the country's conservative politics. In short, he promised hope for Colombia, at least from the lectern. Many were wrapped up in the idea and the illusion of change.

As any observer of Colombia will tell you, President Petro faces an uphill struggle for his ambitious plans, which will find him confronting political intricacies, societal restraints and historical contexts. All of this needs to be explained with regards to Colombia's present and past. Having lived in Colombia full-time since 2007 and reported from here in previous years, there has been a distinct pattern of events which have led to this moment and can allow for an ampler view of the first year of Petro's presidency.

***

A great deal has been made of a "new pink tide[6]" in South America with the election of Luiz Inácio Lula da Silva for his third term in Brazil in 2023, President Gabriel Boric Font in Chile in 2022, outgoing Argentine President Alberto Ángel Fernández and the arrival of Javier Milei, embattled Luis Alberto Arce Catacora in Bolivia and accidental Peruvian President Dina Ercilia Boluarte Zegarra, and not including the dictatorial behaviour of Venezuela's Nicolás Maduro Moros. However, more than a shift left, this seems to be something more cyclical and a reaction, in part, to the events which occurred in each country during the Covid-19 pandemic. Certainly, the entry of Daniel Noboa as President of Ecuador in 2023 has shown that there is still substantial support for rightwing candidates.

Rather than suggest that Gustavo Petro makes up part of this "adjacent" pink tide would be to overlook and underestimate the internal machinations within Colombia which brought him to power. It's better then, to see Petro as *"the Last South American Guerrilla,"* and position him alone on this winner's podium, for, he is the last guerrilla of this type to come to power.

He makes a bold statement that his is a "government of change," presumably one to refresh the democratic system in Colombia in being the first leftist government here, but by starting out with a cabinet and close political allies made up, in many cases, with familiar faces such as Armando Benedetti[7], the first Colombian Ambassador to Venezuela in three years, a significant political chameleon and vote winner in the country's malleable Caribbean region, the respected Columbia University professor José Antonio Ocampo as finance minister – formerly finance minister and director of national planning under President Ernesto Samper (1994-1998) and agriculture minister under President César Gaviria (1990–1994). It did not end here either, the Minister of Agriculture, Cecilia López Montaño, who had extensive experience in the government of Ernesto Samper, the Minister of National Education, the centrist, Alejandro Gaviria who served under both President Álvaro Uribe (2002–2010) and was health minister for President Juan Manuel Santos (2010–2018), the Minister of Foreign Affairs, Álvaro Leyva who served as energy minister in the administration of President Belisario Betancur (1982–1986), the Minister of Defence, Iván Velásquez and political heavyweight Roy Barreras as the president of the Senate.

Many of these individuals were already known to the Colombian public, flip flopping between political affiliations and allegiances, to ensure their continued importance and status, but hardly representing a government of change, suggesting that Petro sought not only to reach across the political divide, but also to calm the markets, reassure foreign investors and steady the boat to defy his critics from day one in power. Predictably, this level-headed cabinet did not last and by the end of his first year, President Petro had made 29 changes[8].

So, perhaps when we think of change and the "new left" such as Boric in Chile, despite the obvious and public friendship enjoyed between them, there is a distinct difference.

Petro hails from a background not dissimilar to that of Brazil's Dilma Van Rousseff[9] - former president (2011-2016), impeached in 2016 and associated with corruption and deficit and once of COLINA (Comando de Libertação Nacional) and then the Vanguarda Armada Revolucionária Palmares (Palmares Armed Revolutionary Vanguard) guerrillas. Or José Alberto Mujica Cordano, formerly a high-ranking member of the Tupamaros – National Liberation Movement and who fared much better as president between 2010-2015 in Uruguay or perhaps Chile's socialist president Michelle Bachelet Jeria[10] (2006-2010 and 2014-2018), herself detained and tortured by Augusto Pinochet's DINA secret police outfit in 1975. Ousted former Peruvian president Pedro Castillo (2021-2022) and Petro were on a different plain from one another and current president Dina Boluarte – whilst giving off political vibes akin to that of a substitute teacher – ordered the indefinite return of the government's ambassador to Colombia after Petro's outburst of "twitterocracy" in criticising the transfer of power and leading Boluarte to accuse the Colombian premier of "distorting reality[11]."

Petro's rebel in the M-19 past puts him shoulder to shoulder with the aforementioned group of South American premiers in politics, style and past – rather more as the last guerrilla than the new left - and one cannot help but think that he may have been better served having been in power at the same time as one or the other them, more so at least than alongside a pragmatic yet under pressure Lula or the earnest but struggling Boric and inevitably being lumped together with the stolid and increasingly dictatorial Maduro in Venezuela. There's no love lost between Petro and Milei in Argentina either and the Colombian premier is unlikely to close his account of X (formerly twitter) any time soon.

Of course, Colombia's politics did not lend itself to a shift to the left in the 2000s with Uribismo at its zenith and with George Walker Bush in the White House. Dare we suggest it, but could Petro have come too late? What would have or could have been, had he won the 2018 competition versus Iván Duque Márquez (2018-2022)?

Who is Gustavo Petro?

Born in the Caribbean town of Ciénaga de Oro in Córdoba, 1960, Petro moved to Zipaquirá, just 45km from Bogotá at a young age. It was here, aged 17 that he became affiliated to the M-19 guerrilla group. The M-19 may have been less brutal than other rebel groups in Colombia as the second largest group in the 1980s, but it did carry out what is considered one of the bloodiest acts in the country's recent history: the 1985 siege of Colombia's national judicial building that led to a battle with the police and the military, leaving 94 people dead.

What did alias "Aureliano" – named after a character in García Márquez's One Hundred Years of Solitude – do in the M-19? Speaking to the New York Times[12], Sandra Borda, a renowned Colombian political analyst and professor at Los Andes University said:

"What's key is that he wasn't part of the main circle who made the decisions in M-19. He was very young at that moment. He didn't participate in the most important operations of the M-19, the military operations."

Petro never saw combat and is remembered by his fellow ex-guerrillas more as a thinker and political strategist than an armed revolutionary.

While the exact beginnings of the M-19[13] (Movimiento 19 Abril) are up for debate, the guerrilla group took its name from the date of a 1970 presidential election that its members believed was stolen from the National Popular Alliance (Alianza Nacional Popular, ANAPO) candidate, former dictator Gustavo Rojas Pinilla, by Conservative candidate Misael Pastrana Borrero (president from 1970-1974 and father of president Andrés Pastrana Arango 1998-2002).

Petro rejected the armed struggle in the late 1980s and while he was largely responsible for stockpiling weapons for the M-19 he was captured and tortured by the authorities in 1985 spending time in Bogotá infamous La Picota jail until his release in 1987.

He reintegrated into civilian life in 1990, when M-19 signed a peace treaty with the government but these links have made him persona non grata in many circles despite that he has worked diligently and lawfully ever since.

Far-right groups were responsible for most paramilitary crimes during Colombia's decades-long internal conflict but so were left-wing ones such as the M-19, according to the UN[14]. Many Colombians continue to associate leftist guerrilla movements with violence and instability and rightly or wrongly stigmatize any left-leaning politician as being a "guerrilla-sympathiser." For these people, the trauma lived is unshakable and the crimes of the past are unforgivable.

Context and background are important to understand attitudes towards Petro as he was a member of an organization which was responsible for scores of civilian casualties during the savage siege of the Palace of Justice in 1985, the hostage taking at the Embassy of the Dominican Republic, the kidnapping and murder of Afro-Colombian labour leader José Raquel Mercado, business leader Hugo Ferreira Neira, and oil company executive Nicolás Escobar Soto who was literally buried alive, and the kidnapping of Conservative Party leader Álvaro Gómez Hurtado. Although Petro was not directly involved in these events, memories are understandably long in Colombia.

Early political life

While active in the M-19 he held his first elected posts, first as Ombudsman of Zipaquirá in 1981, then as councillor for the city in 1984. After 16 months in jail[15], he was instrumental in the formation of the political party *Alianza Democratica M-19* (AD M-19), which replaced the guerrilla movement and participated in the 1991 assembly to rewrite Colombia's constitution. In 1991 he also became one of the first candidates from the new party to hold office when he was elected to the House of Representatives.

After finishing his term, he sought asylum in Belgium – former guerrilla fighters who were entering politics in Colombia were being assassinated. For two years he worked in the Colombian Embassy in Belgium as a diplomatic attaché for human rights.

Petro returned to the House of Representatives in 2002 when he was elected as a member of the leftist movement *Via Alterna*. In 2005 he played a role in unifying leftist parties and politicians, including the AD M-19, to create the Democratic Pole (*Polo Democratico Alternativo* – PDA). Standing for the PDA, he was elected senator in 2006 becoming one of the more admired lawmakers of the opposition party.

During Petro's time in congress he became known as an ardent critic of the government and frequently engaged in verbal warfare with then President Álvaro Uribe. He was also known as a relentless campaigner against corruption and the infiltration of armed groups into politics, playing a role in uncovering and pursuing both the parapolitics and FARC-politics scandals.

Petro's antagonistic relationship with government worsened when it became evident he was a victim of a wiretapping and surveillance campaign orchestrated by Colombia's secret service, the DAS, who were allegedly reporting back to the presidential palace.

The *parapolitica* scandal

As early as 2002, paramilitary chief Salvatore Mancuso told journalists that during that year's congressional elections the paramilitaries hoped to win 30 per cent of the seats in Congress. And after the elections, Mancuso had bragged that "the original goal of 35 per cent has been by far exceeded, and it constitutes a landmark in the history of the AUC." Three years later, in June 2005, paramilitary leader Vicente Castaño told Semana magazine "we have more than 35 per cent of friends in Congress. And by the next elections we are going to increase that percentage.16"

The term parapolitics (*parapolitica*) came into being to describe the ties between paramilitary organizations such as the now-demobilized AUC (*Autodefensas Unidas de Colombia* – United Self-Defences of Colombia), and state officials in Colombia.

Whilst an opposition Senator, Gustavo Petro denounced ties between the AUC and members of the coalition and government of then-President Álvaro Uribe going back as far as 2002, but the scandal did not break until 2006 after seized computers from demobilized paramilitary leader alias Jorge 40 revealed that the paramilitaries had signed pacts with politicians to "refound the motherland."

Few of those in Colombia's political and business sector have been brought to justice for their role in the conflict —indeed, while paramilitary testimonies have revealed the names of some 13,000[17] members of the business sector who supported massacres and displacements, criminal prosecutors have largely failed to act on that information. Meanwhile, of the paramilitaries who've confessed to crimes under the 2005

Justice and Peace Law, the number of those who've actually been convicted for conflict-related abuses is miniscule. The transitional justice system mandated by the 2016 peace accords —strongly opposed by Uribe and his supporters—is a new opportunity for Colombia to hold some of the worst human rights offenders of the conflict accountable, but only 609 "third parties"—outside supporters of armed groups—have agreed to participate in the system.

The Prosecutor General's Office announced in May 2019 that it would seek criminal charges against more than 5,000 civilians and state officials suspected of involvement in paramilitary war crimes.

This investigation did not start until after a 2016 peace deal with the FARC guerrilla group in which the government of President Juan Manuel Santos vowed to dismantle paramilitary structures that continued to exist after the demobilization of the AUC between 2003 and 2006.

Mayor of Bogotá

Elected Mayor of Bogotá from 2012 to 2016, Petro's mandate was nothing if not significant in its symbolism as a former leftist guerrilla now in effectively the second most powerful position in Colombia. Until this point, he was known for his fiery speeches from the Senate against corruption and right-wing paramilitary groups. He was soon recognized for his uncompromising stance on his cornerstone issues and also for his poor management skills, alienating allies and providing fuel for his ever-expanding list of foes.

Allegations of public service mismanagement resulted in his temporary removal from office in 2014 (Petro has said his removal was politically motivated[18]). The discord arose when, Alejandro Ordoñez[19], then Colombia's inspector-general ousted Petro and banned him from holding public office for 15 years, over an alleged mismanagement of the rubbish collection service in the capital. The Washington-based IACHR ruled that

Colombia's inspector-general violated the region's human rights charter, and insisted that Petro be allowed to serve out his term until 2016.

The story of Petro's vanquishing is an intricate, multifaceted legal process that few have mastered. However, the bottom-line is this: as Mayor of Bogotá, he took the waste collection and processing business, a multimillion-dollar enterprise, away from the hands of a close-knit, private and monopolizing conglomerate (which lined the pockets of, among others, former president Uribe's sons) and put it in the hands of the poor, the informal recyclers, the wretched of the city. This saved roughly 100 million dollars[20] a year for the city.

Tens of thousands of people demonstrated in the capital after his removal from office in December of that year. He was soon reinstated as Mayor.

Did Petro enjoy some success as Mayor of Bogotá? Like everything, it all depends on who you ask. He changed air and water from a commodity to a right and in three years, 681,801 homes were supplied with clean running water under his administration. In 2013, for the first time in recorded history no children under five died of malnutrition in the city. Through innovative social programs that include empowerment of the poorest communities, inequality in the distribution of wealth is way below national standards, which is impressive if you consider that Bogotá accounts for 24.8 per cent of Colombia's GDP[21]. The rate of homicides fell to its lowest in 30 years during his mandate.

In short, he ruffled some feathers and recognized the poor. Hardly perfect, but certainly not a lame duck that he is often made out to be.

---

[5] President Petro's inaugural address from 7/8/22 published in English by Progressive International.

[6] World Politics Review: With a Resurgent Left, What's Next for South America? 7/6/23.

[7] The challenges for Colombia's new ambassador to Venezuela, who would be Armando Benedetti, Enrique Alberto Prieto Rios PhD, Universidad del Rosario, 30 July 2022.

[8] El Colombiano: https://www.elcolombiano.com/colombia/cambios-en-el-gabinete-gustavo-petro-primer-ano-nombramientos-informe-hernan-cadavid-DH22256401

[9] The quiet rehabilitation of Brazil's ex-president Dilma Rousseff, John Martín Cullell, El Pais. 28 September 2022.

[10] Presidentes de la República de Chile, Bibliotec del Congreso Nacional de Chile BCN.

[11] Perú retira definitivamente a su embajador en Colombia tras acusar a Petro de "injerencias", El Pais, Renzo Gómez Vega, 29 March 2023.

[12] Before he was a politician, Gustavo Petro was part of an urban guerrilla group, Megan Janetsky, New York Times, 19 June 2022.

[13] Colombia: Information on the Former Guerrilla Group M-19, Resource Information Center 2003.

[14] International Criminal Court Scrutinises Paramilitary Crimes. August 27, 2008.

[15] https://www.eltiempo.com/politica/cuantos-anos-de-carcel-pago-gustavo-petro-en-epocas-de-m19-591378

[16] "Congreso, en la Mira Para," El Tiempo, March 17, 2002,

[17] WOLA: https://www.wola.org/analysis/colombia-former-president-uribe-testifies/

[18] Bogotá mayor Gustavo Petro removed by president. 20 March 2014.

[19] Ordóñez is mainly remembered for his extremely conservative Roman Catholicism, including his anti-gay stance, opposition to abortion and to same-sex marriage, (BBC Mundo, 16 de dic. 2013) themes in which he clashed directly with Petro's approach. Ordóñez rejected the contention that his religious beliefs played any part in his decision: "I am a Catholic in public life and am not ashamed of that. Such a condition is a guarantee never a threat," he argued. Ordóñez is also known for highly authoritarian actions. Semana magazine noted that in his first term Ordóñez dismissed 828 mayors and 49 governors, an average of four mayors a week and one governor per month.

[20] Alcaldía de Bogotá: http://www.bogotahumana.gov.co/index.php/noticias/comunicados-de-prensa/5567-plan-gestion-2013

[21] Banco Mundial: https://datos.bancomundial.org/indicador/SI.POV.GINI%2055.9

Richard McColl

Gustavo Petro, Bogotá's uncompromising heavy metal mayor

Interview with Mayor Gustavo Petro, 5 September 2013 by Richard McColl for Colombia Reports22.

Bogotá mayor Gustavo Petro is in London to receive an award for his administration's environmental policies, a recognition that is in stark contrast to how he is perceived in Colombia's capital.

When Bogotá awakes, the thin high-altitude air enables an uninterrupted urban panorama punctuated only with pine-covered mountains. This paradisaical image, however, vanishes once the daily commute begins and gives way to traffic-heavy thoroughfares, packed buses and an unpleasant smog hangs low permeating the city.

Keen to reverse this trend is Petro, who is pushing ahead with progressive and socially inclusive policies, not least a tangible environmental and urban regeneration plan all under his mantra of *Bogotá Humana*.

It is this strategy of *Bogotá Humana* and the work of previous administrations that has brought Gustavo Petro to London where he shared a stage with London's Boris Johnson. In an almost incongruous turn of events, given the unrest in the city in recent weeks, Bogotá has seen off competition from the likes of Buenos Aires, Paris and Singapore to win the prestigious Siemens and the C40 Cities Climate Leadership Group for work and policies employed and regarding future plans for Urban Transportation.

This triumph will hopefully enable Bogotá to remove herself from the list of cities most contaminated by sulphur dioxide as ranked by the Latin American Green City Index[23].

This seems at first glance to be a far cry from the troublesome scenarios in the pocked and defaced streets of Bogotá, but the Mayor has likened the disturbances in his city as similar to those in Paris in 2005 and London in 2012 where "a new disaffected generation" is finding a voice.

As a former leftist guerrilla attached to the M-19 group which demobilized in 1990, Petro's policies reflect his past, creating in his words, "strong political tensions."

Never one to shirk controversy, the mayor seems to court it and in July he decided to transplant his office from the stately environs of the Palacio Lievano overlooking the opulent neoclassical Plaza de Bolívar in downtown Bogotá to the working-class district of Ciudad Bolívar. He said: "the poor layers that make up the city's fabric have traditionally surrounded the mayor with enthusiastic support." This has created a mayoralty downtown with precious little cohesion.

The battle lines, if they had not been previously drawn, were now firmly established as his one clear aim is to combat the elitism and segregation that are in his words: "trying to homogenize and eliminate the differences in the city."

His aggressive position has left him with a vocal opposition, not least the former President Álvaro Uribe who he denounced for the *parapolitics* scandal which implicated an alliance between paramilitary organizations and politicians.

As a former guerrilla with experience in the struggle for political participation, Petro is in a privileged position regarding the ongoing peace talks between the Colombian government and the FARC guerrillas in Havana, Cuba.

The long running Colombian conflict has pitted various leftist groups – with the FARC being the largest and oldest – against the state for roughly 50 years in what began as an armed struggle over land.

Bogotá's mayor must be seen as representing a success story for transitional justice arguably holding the country's most powerful position behind only that of the President Juan Manuel Santos. A message to all guerrillas present at the negotiating table.

Outspoken on the subject, Petro supports a unilateral ceasefire between the guerrillas and the government but is quick to recognize that both sides are fragmented. "There are countless difficulties and complexities in organizing a truce in the Colombian situation since this is a borderless and widespread conflict." And then of course there's the issue of the guerrillas themselves: "The FARC is a derivation of a movement that muddles a social agrarian agenda with Stalinism therefore we cannot consider the FARC to be a democratic entity."

The mayor admits that he has been consulted by both the Santos administration and the FARC regarding the dialogues. A trip to Havana to participate does not seem far off.

"I am waiting for the right moment to go, not to create a media show, but to help the situation."

The mayor recognizes that any dialogue does indeed represent a strengthening of democracy in Colombia. He speaks of a violent and bloody culture of silence and assassinations stemming back only 15 years. And while political assassinations may be largely consigned to the past and Colombia has improved – he has the figures to prove this – peace in itself has been largely absent from the streets of Bogotá in the last fortnight.

Huge protests originating in the countryside held by striking farmers in opposition to various free trade agreements they see as hindering their livelihoods gathered momentum and mass support in the city. Thousands took to the streets of Bogotá culminating in riots on August 29. Much of the city, in particular some outlying districts and the colonial heart were left in tatters after vandalism and wanton violence erupted between some protesters and the riot police.

Subsequent government statements of a deliberate and malicious infiltration of the protest marches by members of the FARC guerrillas have been given short shrift by Petro and his allies.

Speaking of the president's tardy reaction to the protests, Petro said: "They were confused, the protests were a direct strike at the paradigm of this government of elites. There was huge support for the strike, as here, everyone's grandparents were farmers."

Despite the negativity engulfing Colombia and the air of cynicism expressed in the Colombian press towards the peace dialogues with the FARC, Petro remains upbeat: "it is up to the President to act boldly and help the countryside; this in itself will be opening the doors to an eventual peace in Colombia."

For now, the controversial Petro may be better received overseas than in the city he oversees. The mayor gives off the impression of revelling in a fight and adds: "the spirit of the M-19 guerrilla was likened by an Argentine journalist as being the heavy metal equivalent of all of the guerrilla groups in Colombia."

This is perhaps due to the unrelenting and uncompromising style employed in Colombian politics by Petro.

---

[22] Colombia Reports: https://colombiareports.com/gustavo-petro-bogotas-uncompromising-heavy-metal-mayor/

[23] Latin American Green City Index.

Petro's Presidential loss

In 2018, Petro ran for president again. But, the country had voted against the peace agreement with FARC in 2016 and was not ready to support a former guerrilla. It was the first time in Colombia's modern history that an openly leftist candidate reached the second round of a presidential vote, a prospect that unnerved some investors in Latin America's fourth largest economy.

"Petro represents a clearly populist project," said Andrés Molano[24], director of the Hernán Echavarría Olózaga institute of political science. "He presents himself as an outsider - an enemy of the elites - and has elaborated a messianic and anti-liberal discourse that promises a kind of revolution both politically and economically."

A distinct disadvantage to Petro was the growing crisis in neighbouring Venezuela, under the regime of Nicolás Maduro, which drove hundreds of thousands of desperate people across the border. His opponent and subsequent winner in the second-round run-off vote Iván Duque, made the most of alleging that Petro too, would plunge Colombia into a similar crisis.

With 19,511,168 votes cast, Iván Duque Márquez[25] won the contest with 10,373,080 votes to Gustavo Petro's 8,034,189. From this point, Petro began campaigning for the 2022 elections making appearances in the nationwide demonstrations against the ruling government in 2019 and 2021.

Colombia voted in a largely unknown and young president in Iván Duque, with the full backing of former president Álvaro Uribe and the promise of: "tearing the peace accord to shreds[26]," and perhaps who later came to understand that the Constitution did not permit this for a period of 12 years from its signing, and so decided to try and modify it, but in the end, just preferred to slow walk[27] and defund it. Under a Petro government, one expected that the peace accord would have been closely followed, but this of course, is mere speculation. The vote fell the way of Duque, in a large part due to people were afraid to vote for Petro rather than on arguments and proposed policies.

Petro was once again in opposition and from day one, made this point clear. He was to be the candidate for the Left in 2022.

---

[24] Reuters: https://www.reuters.com/article/us-colombia-election-petro-idUSKCN1IP22P

[25] International Foundation for Electoral Systems.

[26] Peace that antagonizes: Reading Colombia's peace process as hegemonic crisis, Richard Georgi.

[27] WOLA: Washington Office on Latin America.

Petro's Presidential win

In a contest pitting Petro against independent candidate Rodolfo Hernández who, despite originally appearing third in the opinion polls, surprised many and opened a lead of almost five percentage points over Fico Gutiérrez (Team for Colombia), who was considered the favourite to run in the second round.

It was not Hernández's raw sexuality (see below)[28] which took him into the second round, but more the right-wing Democratic Centre party's Federico "Fico" Gutiérrez failing to convince. Had Gutiérrez perhaps made a more plausible case for being the law and order candidate, then there would have been a chance, however, the winds were not in his favour after a turbulent four years of Iván Duque, massive nationwide protests in 2019 and 2021 and the Covid-19 pandemic. It seemed that the public did not want more of the same and the Democratic Centre made a poor showing in the first round.

In the absence of Fico, the Uribista and right of centre vote switched and slid seamlessly behind Hernández, a 77-year-old construction magnate and former Mayor of the city of Bucaramanga. Hernández campaigned on an anti-corruption ticket, despite being under investigation for allegedly favouring a company his son had lobbied for and was later barred from running for political office for 15 years. The sentence was overturned in July 2023. In April 2024[29] he received another ban of ten years, this time for his involvement in politics.

In the run-off, Petro garnered 50.4 per cent of the vote to beat anti-corruption outsider Rodolfo Hernández's 47.3 per cent. About 2.2 per cent of voters submitted blank votes. At 58.1 per cent, the turnout rate was the highest for the country in a presidential competition in nearly a quarter-century.

Petro rode a wave of discontent to get to the presidency. There is no doubt that the presence of Afro-Colombian Francia Márquez – a former domestic worker and award-winning environmental activist – on Petro's ticket likely helped drive support for him in the western departments of Cauca, Nariño and Choco, where he drew in more than 80 per cent of the vote.

According to a May 2022 Gallup poll, 75 per cent of Colombians said their country was headed in the wrong direction. Inequality, increasing poverty, violence, insecurity, and other issues brought wide-scale protests to the streets in recent years, and clashes with security forces left dozens dead. Petro campaigned on a call to answer those protestors and their concerns.

"First is peace, second is social justice, third is environmental justice," Petro said in his victory speech, outlining what he said will be the main tenets of his presidency. "We are going to develop capitalism in Colombia, not because we worship it, but because we must first overcome pre-modernity feudalism."

---

[28] Video from TikTok: https://www.tiktok.com/@elpaisadelax/video/7108459783757286662

[29] Procuraduría de Colombia: https://www.procuraduria.gov.co/Pages/procuraduria-sanciono-destitucion-inhabilidad-10-anos-rodolfo-hernandez-participacion-politica.aspx

Richard McColl

President Petro 2022-2026

Drawing a line beneath 16 months completed of Gustavo Petro's mandate – as we do here – reveals little and at the same time a great deal. The accusations of corruption, the political scandals, Petro's unexplained absences from meetings and obligations, the accusations, by his brother[30] that the president suffers from Aspergers continue to mount. But, were we to fall into the inevitable trap of *"whataboutism,"* couldn't we say that this is just normal governing in Colombia, and for once citizens of this country don't think their government is trying to kill them?

As Jenny Pearce, Research Professor at the London School of Economics, Department of Latin America and the Caribbean stated in the LatinNews podcast[31] (Series 1, Episode 11): "I genuinely believe that Gustavo Petro has the best interest of the common Colombian at heart. He is trying to do the right thing."

And, it's not up for debate that there have been some major positives. Early on in Petro's tenure, thanks to the governing coalition he fashioned, he was able to pass a fiscal reform package aimed at expanding social development programs that had eluded previous administrations. He has managed to keep the economy on track despite the effects of the Covid-19 pandemic and Russia's war in Ukraine. He has presided over an impressive drop in deforestation in the Amazon and nationwide, even though this can in part be attributed to armed groups such as the Estado Mayor Central[32], a group of FARC dissidents, enforcing logging bans.

Unfortunately, something Colombia-watchers would have predicted long-before his ascent to the presidency, is that Petro is a notoriously poor manager, and beyond saying the right things from the balcony of the palace in order to rabble rouse and incite his base, he is known to be ineffective in the execution of his projects.

Despite overlooked successes[33], such as a significant decrease in gun crime during his time as mayor of Bogotá, a dramatic reduction in infant mortality, drinking water for low-income families, subsidies for education and transport and investment into social security programs, amongst others, his tenure is remembered for a degree of administrative chaos and incoherency and the projects he didn't advance on.

His opponents, of which there is no shortage, will point to his failed promises on the construction of new schools, the inability to carry through an expansion of the Transmilenio public transport system and his shortcomings in completing the planned construction of thousands of homes for low-income families. What is clear is that Petro – similar to every politician, it could be argued – exaggerates a great deal and therefore provides plenty of fuel for his detractors when he fails to come through. This said, the bar is set remarkably low when it comes to politicians in Colombia and for those who have the ill-fortune of achieving the poisoned chalice that is the mayoralty of Bogotá, a thankless task if there ever is one.

And so, this brings us to the long list of promises made for his presidency. Firstly, four years is never enough to try and alter decades of mismanagement when it comes to the war on drugs, human rights, agrarian reform and land management, reforms (including labour, health, tax, pensions and beyond), which have been designed to benefit the few in the place of the many.

As previously mentioned, another cornerstone of his presidential policies is to pursue an aggressive plan of Total Peace or *Paz Total*. One must applaud the alacrity with which the project came about and within months of taking the presidency, peace talks were once again established with the ELN guerrilla group and negotiation tables established with members of the AGC or Clan del Golfo, the largest newly emerged armed group. His desire to reduce violence in the countryside prior to the local elections has left a great deal to be desired. Arguments of rewarding guerrillas and mafias for violence abound, but, in his defence, Petro is trying a different angle from which to approach peace as it is no secret that a direct armed conflict has been unsuccessful, albeit yielding wins here and there, but not delivering peace to Colombia as a whole.

President Petro, perhaps naively, thinks all armed groups are like his M-19, people who really didn't want to fight but saw injustice and felt obliged to take up arms. He doesn't understand armed groups that are multigenerational, with leaders who don't have any non-childhood familiarity with civilian life, or that are partly/mostly/wholly "political" facades for generic criminality.

To understand of the key problems with Petro's peace strategy is to look at previous "successful" campaigns. In order to bring the FARC-EP to the negotiating table former president Santos significantly ramped up military operations against the guerrillas, with a specific focus decapitating the leadership with a focus on eliminating high value FARC targets, notably those opposed to peace negotiations. Interestingly, that strategy mirrored that taken by the US in Afghanistan. Petro needs to focus on eliminating high value FARC-EMC and ELN targets, especially those in the leadership opposed to negotiating surrender, while provoding a suite of tools to successfully integrate demobilized combatants into civil society.

It seems unlikely Petro will turn things around in the next two-thirds of his term. The Constitutional Court has already clarified that Congress must pass a law to negotiate with criminal actors, but his majority there has dissipated. The lost battle to approve his health reform has cost him significant political capital. Yet the election of a new Attorney General this year has replaced the opposition of Francisco Barbosa with an ally in Luz Adriana Camargo Garzón in the search for Total Peace.

Overall, Total Peace has yielded mixed results. So far, the price seems to be time and space for some armed actors to strengthen and expand. Petro must achieve long-lasting concessions before time runs out and a new president steps in. Momentary reductions in conflict intensity and the lives saved because of it are invaluable, yet more casualties will only be delayed if conflict re-intensifies with stronger opponents after negotiations fail to yield appeasement.

The problem with Petro, and what one suspects has made his agenda more difficult to accomplish, is that he's kind of a strange person by President standards….if anyone wonders what an Antanas Mockus (former mayor of Bogotá) presidency in 2010 would have looked like, here's a clue. Petro talks way too much, including on Twitter like Trump (although more coherent), he leaves people waiting or never shows up (and then blames his staff, which he picked), and he confuses aspirational goals for the country with immediate legislative aims (or, more precisely, doesn't understand the relation between the two).

Gustavo Petro does not need a concerted media onslaught to discredit his presidency and government, it's quite possible that he is his own worst enemy when it comes to a smear campaign. Petulance on social media, thinly veiled accusations made from each pulpit and his populist bent render him a hapless target for the opposition. By April 2024, the opposition were revelling in having organised an enormous nationwide anti Petro march.

Local Elections October 2023

"The elections will become an unofficial referendum on the Petro administration and its management of the country during the first year in office. We also expect the elections to be marked by an increase in political violence, a vacuum of information due to a lack of polling and media coverage in rural areas, and additional political disarray considering Colombia's growingly fragmented party system. With so much at stake, the government is keenly aware that the electoral results will not only impact its own political standing but also shape the direction of Colombia's political trajectory during the remainder of Petro's term and are a bellwether for the outcome of the presidential election in 2026."

Colombia Risk Analysis – September 2023[34].

And they were. The result was also clear: the "government

of change" was shown to be in a perilous state. The main mayoralties and governorships were won by politicians from different sides of the political spectrum Fernando Galán in Bogotá, Federico "Fico" Gutiérrez in Medellín, Dumek Turbay in Cartagena, Alex Char in Barranquilla and Alejandro Eder in Cali, but they had one thing in common: they came from Colombia's traditional political parties or had their support. The elections marked the return of the status quo.

Protests 21 April 2024

Ostensibly billed as a protest against Petro's reforms and the current instability in the country, but organized by members of the opposition, and with no platforms for political speeches (therefore maintaining its political objectivity), this protest was the largest of kind so far.

Protesters in all of Colombia's major cities demonstrated on Sunday 21 April 2024 against President Petro's healthcare reforms and ongoing violence that undermines peace talks with guerrilla groups. Medical associations, opposition groups and even some former allies of Petro had urged Colombians to show up in protest both against reforms Petro is trying to implement, including nationalizing health services, and against violence that continues to mar the troubled peace talks with armed groups. Petro has floated the possibility of rewriting the constitution (*constituyente*) to spur social reforms that he's been unable to advance in the face of opposition by a hostile congress and conservative business groups.

Petro, as expected, was dismissive of the marches, commenting on X, said the protests were large in Medellín, Bogotá and Bucaramanga but *"weak"* in 18 other cities. *"The main goal of the marches is to shout 'Petro Out' and to topple the government,"* Petro said, calling the protests a *"soft coup"* to thwart change.

While his health reform has been shot down, Colombian senators passed his pension reform, yesterday, a rare legislative victory for the unpopular administration (The latest data, April

2024, from polling firm Datexco[35] shows Petro having a 63 per cent disapproval rating,). The measure, which now passes to the lower house, would make the government the manager of around 70 per cent of all worker contributions, while private pension funds would receive the rest.

---

[30] CNN en español: https://cnnespanol.cnn.com/2023/09/04/petro-hermano-sindrome-asperger-orix/

[31] The LatinNews podcast: https://www.thelatinnewspodcast.com

[32] Bloomberg: https://www.bloomberg.com/features/2023-colombia-amazon-mordisco/#xj4y7vzkg

[33] Razón Pública: https://razonpublica.com/un-balance-de-la-bogota-humana/

[34] Colombia Risk Analysis: https://www.colombiariskanalysis.com/

[35] W Radio: https://www.wradio.com.co/2024/03/11/opinometro-63-de-los-colombianos-desaprueba-la-gestion-del-presidente-petro/

Petro and US

Petro's call for a radical new approach toward drugs was expected to shake up relations with Washington in a country that has for decades been the region's strongest US ally, as well as its biggest supplier of cocaine. Petro blamed the drug war for the deaths of one million Latin Americans, and called for developed countries to adopt "a strong policy of preventing consumption". His inaugural speech[36] before the U.N. general assembly, with jabs directed at the Global North, may not have come as a surprise to the Biden administration, the anti-capitalism messaging nestled into a discourse on environmentalism, did not go unnoticed in hawkish circles. As of September 2023, relations remain cordial between Presidents Biden and Petro.

The spectre of Trump being nominated to lead the Republican Party into the next election and winning would be a disaster for Petro's position on the war on drugs and a reconciliation with Venezuela, just by virtue of being seen as a left-of-centre president in South America.

Venezuela

While diplomatic ties between the two nations were severed in 2019 amid a push by Colombia and the US to force out the socialist government of Nicolás Maduro, Petro has re-established diplomatic ties and opened the border for commerce. And whilst the opposition paints Petro and Maduro as being fast friends, it is clear that the Colombian premier views his opposite number in Venezuela as more of a thorn in his side than a staunch ally. An immediate request by the regime in Caracas for the extradition of Venezuelan political opponents residing in Colombia was quietly denied by the Palacio de Nariño[37] showing Petro's desire to pursue a relationship but also respect human rights.

In what has also been a sage diplomatic move, Petro has strengthened his position with the US by ensuring that his government is now a conduit for any negotiations or conversations to take place between that country and Venezuela.

The elephant in the room will always be Petro's push for Total Peace or *Paz Total* as he attempts to negotiate with all criminal groups in Colombia simultaneously. The FARC Estado Mayor Central or FARC dissidents allegedly have bases within Venezuelan territory and the ELN control and protect illegal mining in the neighbouring country in a huge swathe of land known as the Arco Minero[38].

Petro's security policy aims to promote a climate of peace by showing goodwill toward armed groups; he has directed the country's military and police to refrain from offensive actions. But the armed groups are reluctant to disarm, while security forces are hampered in their ability to protect ordinary Colombians. Even as violent crime has gone up, the online publication La Silla Vacía reported that during Petro's first year confrontations between security forces and illegal armed groups have dropped by 45 per cent.

How Petro's government plans to hammer out peace with the ELN, so involved in what is a transnational illegal crime syndicate, remains to be seen. Without the direct intervention of President Maduro and Diosdado Cabello, the best-case scenario is that Petro can resolve some of the tangled intricacies of the now largest remaining guerrilla group within Colombia. Peace talks are on-going in Cuba between the government's negotiating team and the ELN however, it is clear that, given the armed atrocities which continue to take place in Colombia's conflict hotspots, the central wing of the ELN has little control or authority over the more belligerent and economically viable factions of their group.

---

[36] Irrational war on drugs, destruction of the Amazon, expose humanity's failures, Colombia's Petro tells UN. 20 September 2022.

[37] Petro asegura que no extraditará a opositores tras un reclamo de Diosdado Cabello.

Richard McColl

[38] El Arco Minero venezolano: una política depredadora

The Reality under Petro

If Colombians and observers were hoping for significant change under Gustavo Petro, they would be disappointed. Petro seemed to offer hope in a country very much fixed in her ways and the news feed emerging from Colombia in the first years of his presidency has not been dissimilar to the messaging from past decades. Phone tapping scandals, a key witness commits suicide in a corruption case involving Laura Sarabia one of his closest political allies, accusations levied at Nicolás Petro (Gustavo Petro's son), election campaign funds coming from illicit and dubious sources, continued violence, perceived leniency towards criminal groups, inflation concerns and the cost of living crisis. Add this to the already vast reservoir of suspicion and unbridled hatred in many quarters directed at "the guerrilla president." Things do not look good.

And, given these setbacks, Colombians are increasingly pessimistic about the Petro administration. According to the latest Invamer Poll (April 2024), 70 per cent of voters believe the country is going in the wrong direction, 85 per cent believe that security is getting worse, 82 per cent believe that the cost of living is worsening, 74 per cent think the economy is getting worse, 72 per cent think corruption is getting worse, and 62 per cent believe the fight against poverty is also getting worse. It's worth noting that Juan Manuel Santos (second term) and Iván Duque, were scoring worse at the equivalent moments during their respective governments.

Barely halfway into his presidency and Petro needs a serious and significant political win. His watered-down tax reform was passed, but nowhere near to what he planned, his healthcare reform was canned and further reforms including that of labour is drifting away from him, so much so that even the Financial Times[39] published an article suggesting that the Colombian Peso's (COP) rally against the dollar is due to renewed confidence in the country for investors in that the government's reforms will not proceed. There is the neo-classical school of thought regarding economic performance which would suggest that Petro's failures increasing confidence in Colombia is far-fetched and that the Peso climbed against the US dollar due to falling inflation in the United States and the Federal Reserve pausing its rate hikes. Again, depending on where you stand politically is how you might interpret the Peso's success.

Now that the governing alliance, that Petro initially consolidated, has run into problems and several coalition parties have distanced themselves from the president, Petro no longer enjoys an absolute majority in any of the two chambers. Playing to the crowd, in a speech delivered to hundreds of supporters on Labour Day 2023, Petro warned that attempts to restrict his reforms could lead to a revolution. He also called on his supporters to "take the debate to the streets" to pressure Colombia's institutions to embrace his reforms. Petro-watchers were not surprised by the populist rhetoric and inciting from the balcony of power. He has shown a preference for Twitter (now X) over institutional channels of governance, to his own misfortune in a few cases, not least in announcing the discovery of four indigenous Huitoto children lost in the jungle, citing a very weak and ultimately incorrect source.

His promises to wean Colombia off fossil fuels is hardly revolutionary, but his messaging went well awry[40]. The reality in the case of Colombia is that it only has proven oil reserves of 2 billion barrels which is sufficient for another 7.5 years of production. If oil production is dialled up to pre-pandemic levels of around 900 thousand barrels per day then that falls to under six years. There have been no world class oil or gas discoveries in Colombia since 1993 and no major finds since 1999. The majority of Colombia's current oil and gas reserves come from enhanced recovery techniques being implemented for existing reservoirs not from new discoveries. That is impossible to sustain over the long-term. All of that means Colombia simply lacks the hydrocarbon reserves and discoveries needed to underpin any new oil and gas projects. This means the current constraints and issues impacting Colombia's oil industry are a matter of geology not policy. Clean energy needs to be phased in, requires funding and socialization but also needs to quietly suggested to companies investing in fossil fuels. It's also worth noting that 80 per cent of Colombia's energy comes from primarily hydroelectric power. His first Minister for Mines and Energy, Irene Veléz, became the target bug-bear for the Right, her manner, commentary and lack of experience in the public forum made her the favourite scapegoat and punchbag for the opposition. After scandals surrounding contracts involving her husband, Veléz resigned.

Despite all vocal opposition, Petro has said he hoped fossil fuels would make up less than 20 per cent of Colombia's exports within two decades, down from 60 per cent now.

All of this said and done, Petro has been empowering the Right with his actions and rhetoric.

The likely outcome, which appears to be coming into fruition, is a doubling down of Petro's stubbornness towards fulfilling his desire to enact change, almost at any cost, and without striking a conciliatory tone with political parties in order to facilitate his plans, but more likely to force his government into a volatile and dysfunctional three years of accusatory claims and counterclaims.

We can expect more sabre-rattling from the balcony of the Palacio Nariño, despite gains and advances in terms of human rights, land restitution to displaced small-holders, and permitting the Jurisdicción Especial para la Paz (JEP) to continue its work in clarifying some of the most dastardly and nefarious acts during the civil conflict as well as the unravelling of the Odebrecht corruption scandal, which implicates dozens if not scores of high-ranking politicians and businessmen, but there is no way of denying the feeling that this is a government in free-fall.

For Colombia and Colombians, this is not a good thing. Colombia's far right is increasingly enamoured with anti-institutional and authoritarian idealism as well as embracing radical Christianity and libertarian economic ideas. This follows other far-right candidates in Latin America who are looking to capitalize on the misgivings of the left, including Nayib Bukele in El Salvador, who subverted his country's constitution's non-re-election clause, Javier Milei in Argentina, who has promised to dollarize the debt-ridden country, and José Antonio Kast in Chile, whose party now has the majority in the constitutional re-write.

At the time of writing, there are still over two years remaining to Gustavo Petro's tenure and in his mind and on his agenda, there are almost too many issues he would like to address. His perceived arrogance, his tense relationship with the press, the brusque, reactionary and petulant management skills will leave him found wanting. Can he claw back the middle ground? It's too early to say, but the government "of change" may not be a change as we know it…yet more volatility, uncertainty and dashed illusions…a country governed by a premier prone to late night outbursts on social media.

…indeed, it seems clearer than ever that Gustavo Petro is the *Last South American Guerrilla* and perhaps a key stumbling point is that he imagines that all armed groups are like his back in the day. Can he step out of his echo chamber and become the pragmatic uniting leader that Colombians crave? His behaviour thus far suggests otherwise.

---

[39] Financial Times: https://www.ft.com/content/e6612778-2a6c-4dd7-aba5-18d1bcd0d69b

[40] Oilprice.com: https://oilprice.com/Energy/Crude-Oil/Petros-Plan-To-End-Oil-Exploration-Threatens-Colombias-Energy-Security.html

Colombia at a Crossroads after 30 Years of Neoliberalism in Colombia

Professor Nicolas Forsans[41]

Colombia's presidential elections in 2022 resulted in an unprecedented win for Colombia's left in the country's 200 years independent history, and for Gustavo Petro of the leftist coalition *Pacto Histórico*. An economist by training, Petro gained prominence in the 1980s as a leader of the M-19 radical leftist guerrilla group who later recognized armed resistance would not lead to economic prosperity and social change. A former Mayor of Bogotá, Gustavo Petro campaigned alongside Francia Márquez, Vice President on a platform of peace consolidation, social and environmental justice, and gender equality. Francia Márquez is the first Afro-Colombian to have held such a prominent role in Colombia.

Petro's victory was not unexpected. It is part of a broader trend that saw the return in 2018 of 'late progressivism' with the election of López Obrador in Mexico and Cristina Kirchner in Argentina - a trend that reminds us of the *'pink tide'* that took place at the turn of the century across the region. Since 2020, the left won elections in Bolivia, Honduras, Peru, and Brazil. Petro's win can be seen in various, closely related ways. It is a rejection of thirty years of neoliberalism that underpinned Colombia's model of economic development. It is therefore also a response to the growing process of social mobilizations that took the form of violent street protests shaking the country at the height of the pandemic in 2019 and 2021. And also, a reflection of growing mistrust for governments and institutions alike, and youth discontent - notorious in Colombia as in other countries in Latin America.

It will therefore come as no surprise that, despite being branded a role model for the region, Colombia faces deep-rooted challenges that will need addressing if the country is to unleash its potential and promote inclusive growth and prosperity - for all.

- The structural features of Colombia's economy

Classified as un 'upper middle-income economy' with a population of 51 million, Colombia is the fourth to fifth largest economy (as measured by GDP) in Latin America after Brazil, Mexico and Argentina. Urban areas are the economic engine of Colombia, accounting for about half of the national GDP growth over the past 40 years and for 85 per cent of the country's total GDP today. Colombia has a concentrated economy, with most economic activity and half of Colombia's companies located in only five cities: Bogotá (23 per cent of Colombia's GDP and 29.4 per cent of all companies), and a long way behind Medellín (5.6 per cent and 8.7 per cent respectively), Cali, Barranquilla, Cartagena and Bucaramanga.

Colombia's economic opening process began towards the end of the 1980s with the aim of internationalising the economy and diversifying the country's exports base. The reforms included the reduction in tariff barriers, the stabilisation of the economy through fiscal and monetary adjustments, and labour market reforms to make the country more attractive to foreign capital. And alongside it, the disengagement of the state from social spending began as it transferred a large part of its social policies to local or regional administrative entities, reinforcing the prevailing clientelism.

Today, Colombia has a relatively open business environment, being ranked 67th out of 190 economies for overall ease of doing business by the World Bank but higher tariff barriers than its peers and the growing number of non-tariff barriers impede the country's internationalisation. With improving security conditions in urban areas, an abundance of natural resources and an educated and growing middle-class, Colombia continues to be an attractive destination for foreign investment in Latin America, but inflows have stagnated since the end of the commodity boom in 2014.

An uneven territorial development, the persistence of an armed conflict which, despite having been set aside in 2016, still brings violence and social unrest to parts of the country, and two decades of extractives-based economic growth impede Colombia's economic and social progress.

- An uneven territorial development

Colombian territories are poorly connected, both physically and socially, with persistent gaps in the living standards between urban and rural areas, across its geographic regions (e.g., Pacific, Atlantic, Andes, Amazon) and even across departments and municipalities. It is so for many reasons, in particular weak local governance and service delivery, poor market access, weak infrastructure highly exposed to natural disasters, and inequitable land ownership and policies that discourage local investment.

Geography is also to blame. Due mainly to poor road infrastructure that must wind its way through some of the world's tallest mountain ranges, logistics costs are some of the highest in Latin America, and movement of products from the two main ports of Cartagena and Buenaventura to central locations like Bogotá and Medellín adds considerable costs.

- The conflict is over – but not quite

Meanwhile, the signing of the peace agreement with the Revolutionary Armed Forces of Colombia (FARC) in 2016 after four years of negotiation under the presidency of Juan Manuel Santos was a historic step towards ending a 50 years conflict involving left-wing rebels, right-wing paramilitaries, drug traffickers, El Ejército and the government. The conflict caused a great deal of violence, kidnappings, forced disappearances, forced displacements and half a million fatalities.

While the 2016 agreement saw the dismantling of the FARC,

with its weapons handed over to the United Nations and its reconversion as a political party, the National Liberation Army of Colombia (or ELN, in short) remained the single largest guerrilla group involved in the pursuit of the Colombian conflict. The ELN started in 1964 as a Marxist-Leninist ideological movement inspired by Cuba's revolution, which today is believed to have thousands of fighters in Colombia with a presence in neighbouring Venezuela where it operates illegal gold mines and drug trafficking routes.

But the lukewarm approach to the peace agreement by the administration of President Duque and its rejection of talks with the ELN in 2019 mean that the peace agreement was never *fully* implemented, and peace never *fully* materialized. In addition to ELN fighters, it is estimated between 2,000 and 2,500 FARC dissidents still subscribe to FARC's doctrine and are also involved in drug trafficking. The World Bank estimates that if the country had been at peace in the past two decades, per capita income in Colombia would be 50 percent higher today.

After winning the 2022 presidential elections in August, Gustavo Petro reached out to the ELN as part of his policy of *'paz total'*, and negotiations to implement long lasting peace were expected to take place towards the end of 2022.

- An unsustainable dependence on non-renewable sources of energy

The country's successes in diversifying its economic structure have been limited. Since the turn of the century, Colombia witnessed a significant increase in its exports, but the country still very much relies on the production of primary goods, both for exports and domestic consumption. Coffee growing, one of Colombia's traditional economy activity placed the country among the top exporters of coffee worldwide since the beginning of the 20th century. But in recent years the significance of coffee growing has reduced, along that of agriculture which represent around six per cent of the country's

GDP.

And so today the country relies predominantly on the exploration and extraction of non-renewable sources of energy. This is a relatively recent phenomenon. The emergence of Colombia's extractives industries (mainly oil, but also coal and gold) have accelerated economic growth and provided record investment funding for development in the 2000s, but it poses questions about the future sustainability of the country's growth model. The opening up of the energy sector in 2003, as well as the reclaiming by the state of large parts of territory from the guerrilla contributed to a significant increase in oil production, and the importance of oil and mining in Colombia's economy has increased significantly to the expense of agriculture and manufacturing. By 2018 the country was the fourth largest oil producer in Latin America, and one of the main producers of coal, making Colombia highly susceptible to commodity price fluctuations. Around half of Colombia's exports consist of oil, and coal accounts for another quarter. Between a quarter and a third of the foreign direct investment inflows to Colombia are concentrated in extractive industries.

The government of Gustavo Petro has promised to bring economic and social change to Colombia through a restructuring of the current economic model predominantly based on extractive industries (oil and mining) to a productive one (based on industrialisation and agricultural development). A decree aimed at suspending oil and gas exploration concessions, if passed, would involve a significant policy shift. However, oil and coal represent nearly half of the country's exports and are a major source of tax revenues, which means the energy transition process will be a gradual one - even possibly lasting 15 years.

- Colombia's recent economic performance

Since the turn of the century, Colombia has done better than many of its peers in a region known for the volatility of their economy. The country has indeed developed a track record for prudent fiscal management, underpinned by an improved fiscal rule since 2012 aimed at improving fiscal sustainability and consolidating the central government's structural budget deficits, a successful inflation targeting regime and a flexible exchange rate.

The past two decades have witnessed considerable progress in reducing poverty and generating economic growth. Since 2000, despite the country's internal violent conflict, Colombia had grown more than the Latin American average and had cut extreme poverty rates by half between 2002 and 2014. In total, more than six million people had left poverty and, for the first time ever, more Colombians were considered middle class than in poverty[5]. In those two decades, Colombia's unemployment rate declined markedly, from a peak of 20 per cent at the turn of the century down to 8.3 per cent by the late 2000s. Access to education had improved while Colombia's conflict had been somewhat set aside in 2016 and institutions had become stronger. Solid economic growth was buoyed by external demand for Colombia's commodity exports – at least until 2008.

- The scars of the pandemic

But the pandemic has hit Colombia hard and has left strong marks on its people. By the time Covid-19 reached Colombia in February 2020, the 'commodity boom' had long gone and economic growth had slowed down. The virus caused over 142,000 deaths, set back income growth for years and destroyed in excess of six million jobs. A significant policy response somewhat mitigated the economic effects of the pandemic through an expansion of existing and new social programmes. Nevertheless, the pandemic brought an abrupt end to twenty years of steady economic growth and successes in reducing poverty.

The pandemic has exacerbated many long-standing social challenges, including one of the world's most unequal income distributions. The young, women, Afro-Colombians, and indigenous populations were most significantly impacted by the pandemic, both in health (exposure to Covid-19 and death) and economic terms (loss of livelihoods and poverty). Employment and income losses were particularly concentrated among households with the lowest incomes, whose labour incomes declined by up to 30 per cent. About 3.5 million people became poor and many families who had managed to escape poverty in the preceding years fell back into it.

Unlike previous crises in Latin America, the pandemic caused dramatic reductions in *both* formal and informal employment. This is because Covid-19 was framed as a health issue, and governments' priority lied in reducing the spread of the virus and preserving lives – at all costs. This led to Latin America in general, and Colombia in particular, having to enforce some of the toughest and longest lockdowns in the world. Having framed the pandemic purely in health terms, governments overlooked the social and economic implications of 'locking down' for extensive periods of time, for example on the loss of education, loss of livelihoods, mental health and intra-familiar violence. Consequently, informal workers, who account for more than 60 per cent of all workers and have no access to social protection except healthcare, were the first to lose their livelihoods during the pandemic. Women have also been disproportionately affected, amplifying pre-existing employment and wage gaps between men and women. The incomes of those at the bottom of the income distribution fell three times more than for those with higher incomes. The increase in the poverty rate, by around 3.6 percentage points in 2020, was somewhat mitigated by social emergency measures which prevented four million Colombians from falling into poverty during that time.

And so today, Colombia is a country where 40 per cent of its people live in poverty and another 12.5 per cent in extreme poverty, with a large gap between rural and urban poverty. These higher levels of poverty (however measured) can be explained by the higher incidence of poverty among ethnic minorities and people displaced by the conflict, which are disproportionally concentrated in rural areas. In the largely Afro-Colombian rural department of Chocó, the poverty rate is close to 70 per cent, with 39 per cent of its population in extreme poverty. Chocó is one of the poorest regions in Colombia with a rudimentary infrastructure and high illiteracy and mortality rates. Peripheral provinces such as La Guajira and Cauca are also home to staggeringly high levels of poverty. Meanwhile, this in Colombia's five largest cities are considerably lower, around 40 per cent. Colombia is the second poorest country in Latin America after Mexico, as measured by the proportion of its people officially living below the poverty line.

While real, the recovery from the pandemic has been very unequal. The recovery took place through a boom in private consumption and led to a rebound in informal employment. Gross domestic product (GDP) rebounded 10.7 per cent in 2021 and was still projected to grow by eight per cent in 2022while the unfavourable global economic climate that brought with it high interest rates and double-digit inflation are hurting the poorest most. Despite the recovery from the pandemic, more than two million people who had fallen into poverty in 2020 were estimated to have remained poor in 2021. With some 1.4 million people exiting poverty in 2021, the national poverty rate dropped to 39.3 per cent - yet, above pre-pandemic levels. The scars of the pandemic will linger for a long time.

- Long standing social challenges exacerbated by the pandemic

As the country confronted the pandemic, it did so with unresolved challenges: low investment and slow productivity growth which act as a drag on economic growth, a strong dependence on non-renewable commodities, increasing the country's exposure to external shocks, weak competition and low levels of economic openness. And above all, staggering high levels of inequality and labour informality in Latin America, which the pandemic made worse.

The size of Colombia's informal economy is estimated to be around a third of the country's GDP. The jobs and income losses experienced by informal workers during the pandemic wiped off a decade of progress in reducing poverty while the impact of extensive school closures at the height of the pandemic is yet to result in lower income potential, especially for disadvantageous families with no access to digital technology for online education since a third of Colombians do not have access to the internet.

Colombia's economic growth and social challenges are intimately intertwined. They were revealed in full during the *'paro nacion'*, a series of violent protests that began on 28th April 2021 against taxes, corruption and healthcare reforms proposed at the height of the pandemic by the government of the time led by President Iván Duque Márquez. The protests went far beyond opposition to government reforms and revealed a clash between two narratives. On one hand, the government's narrative that praised Colombia's macroeconomic stability and economic growth in the previous two decades. On the other, a narrative grounded on the daily struggles of millions of Colombians - impoverished, working in informal jobs in precarious conditions, uncertain to provide food for their families, with no access to financial nor social security benefits other than healthcare. 40 per cent of Colombians do not own a bank account.

Those two narratives are the product of the country's model of economic development. Rooted in neoliberalism, prioritising economic growth *per se* over other considerations, this model has promoted macroeconomic stability and economic development in a region known for the failure of import-substituting policies and economic volatility. But this neoliberal model has also disproportionately benefited the elite, with the majority of Colombians left behind and not able to enjoy the proceeds of economic growth. A recent study by Universidad del Rosario reveals that young Colombians today are preoccupied by the lack of opportunities, the prospect of unemployment and the lack of security.

- Informality generates poverty and limits the role of the State

This occurs because Colombia has one of the lowest levels of labour formality among Latin American countries, with around 60 per cent of workers in informal employment. As a result, Colombia has the second-lowest average real hourly earnings in Latin America: even in countries with lower levels of GDP per capita, such as Paraguay and Peru, workers receive a higher hourly pay than in Colombia.

There is no unique definition for informal employment. A generally accepted definition of 'informal employment' is that of jobs that are not taxed, registered by the government and/or do not comply with labour regulations. The International Labour Organisation (ILO) defines informality for salaried workers as 'those whose employers do not contribute to social protection systems'. The ILO uses a different definition for the self- employed depending on the informal nature of the business or the size of the firm (less than five workers). This makes both categories not comparable, but for the sake of simplicity we refer to informal employment as every type of worker not contributing taxes nor to social security.

In Colombia, informal employment is highly segmented by socioeconomic characteristics. Young workers, migrant and rural workers typically find themselves in informal employment, as do self-employed and part-time workers. Informality and low skills are strongly connected, as are informality and education levels: workers with formal employment contracts tend to be educated at tertiary level, and those with only primary education tend to work informally.

Some sectors are more prone to employing informal workers, for example the agricultural sector, retail, hospitality and construction tend to concentrate a significant proportion of informal workers.

Unsurprisingly, poverty rates are higher among workers in informal employment and there is a strong correlation between household income and informality. Furthermore, informal workers tend to have lower and more unstable incomes, limiting their ability to save and cope with income shocks. Many workers in Colombia transit between formality and informality many times during their professional careers. This implies that some workers, even when they contribute to social protection systems for some time, usually do not fulfil the requirements to access unemployment insurance or contributory pensions. Therefore, much of the spending on social benefits fails to reach those who need it most.

What is true of workers is also true of businesses. For many businesses, informality is a response to a difficult business environment (cumbersome regulations, high cost of formal employment), and informal businesses find it impossible to access credit, limiting their productivity and growth. Therefore, informality tends to keep companies inefficiently small and their productivity low. Facing barriers to competition, they find it hard to break into new markets while formal businesses complain about unfair competition from low performing, informal competitors. Widespread informality also reduces the bases for corporate and personal income taxes, which in turn limits the quantity and quality of public services and the capacity of the public sector.

- Reforming taxation

The result is Colombia's inability to raise taxes. Although tax revenues have doubled in the past thirty years, they only account for 19 per cent of GDP, well below the 33 per cent average for OECD countries. Astonishingly, only five per cent of Colombians pay income tax. Therefore, tax revenues mostly consist of consumption taxes. OECD data show that personal income taxes currently constitute just 1.3 per cent of GDP, the lowest level of all member countries: in Mexico, the figure is 3.8 per cent, and in Spain it is 8.7 per cent. Widespread tax expenditures and tax evasion limit tax revenues, and with it what the state can do - and what it can redistribute.

The result is that tax revenues are therefore insufficient to meet social demands while preserving investment in education, health and infrastructure. Meanwhile, high taxes on formal businesses reduce investment incentives and act as a barrier for businesses to operate in a formal way. Despite a strong response to the pandemic, social benefits do little to alleviate inequalities, and most social spending goes to the non-poor, particularly in the case of pensions. As a result, Colombia has one of the highest levels of poverty, income inequality and labour market informality in the region.

The politics of tax reforms in Colombia is very complex, as witnessed during el *'paro nacional'* of 2021 when Colombians massively rejected the government's plans to increase consumption and income taxes. In the four years under President Duque, Colombia experienced a profound social transformation that was not led by the Government, but by young urban Colombians who did not share the understanding of the country of many of their parents, nor that of President Duque. And so, by the time the 2022 presidential elections came, Colombians had been crying out for change. The challenge for Gustavo Petro is to deliver on the high expectations that have been placed onto him. In less than 100 days, he successfully got Congress to approve what was possibly the most ambitious tax reform the country has known to-date. It aimed to raise twenty trillion pesos, the most ambitious in history. Sensing the urgency, the bill was presented to Parliament the day after President Petro took office.

As approved, the tax reform will end up raising about half what the government had in mind, an additional COP 20 trillion tax revenues (or US$4 billion), the equivalent of an extra 1.3 per cent of GDP in both 2023 and 2024 that will help reduce the enormous fiscal deficit of 7.1 per cent in 2022 to 4.3 per cent in 2023 that generates concerns in international markets. Those concerns contributed to the historic devaluation of the Colombian peso in the summer of 2022, breaking for the first time the US$ 5,000 bar.

Reflecting the need to transition away from non-renewable sources of energy and protect the environment, most of the additional tax revenues will come from the coal and oil sectors and will be borne by businesses. Other corporations will also pay more. On top of a 35 per cent general tax rate, the financial sector will now pay a five per cent surcharge, while hydroelectric plants will pay a three per cent surcharge. But some of the burden will also fall onto the richest households which, in Colombia, tend to pay much fewer taxes than elsewhere on the continent. Those who earn more than COP 10 million (or US$ 2,000) will contribute more taxes. Even after the reform comes into effect, Colombia's revenue from individual taxpayers will only increase to about 1.5 per cent of GDP.

Fedesarrollo, the country's most prominent think tank, estimates the tax reform would push the effective tax on profits from 36 per cent to 70 per cent for oil companies, threatening investment in a country where oil is the main source of revenue as a result of what some observers see as an 'excessive tax burden' on the corporate sector likely to damage Colombia's competitiveness.

While reforming the tax system is a step in the right direction, it will take much broader reforms to address Colombia's social challenges. The high level of informality in Colombia generates persistent, high levels of income inequalities.

- Inequalities impede prosperity and social progress

Indeed, inequalities are a long-standing feature of the Colombian economy. They are more prevalent in Colombia than elsewhere in Latin America, a region already known as the world's most unequal. Inequalities have been identified as a constraint to the country's prosperity and social progress. Therefore, addressing these inequalities has never been more urgent. Yet, it is a very complex issue, as inequalities take many different forms – they are multidimensional in nature.

Although income inequality in Colombia has declined since the early 2000s, it remains very high by international standards. World Bank data shows that, as recently as 2018, the top ten per cent of earners in Colombia held 39.7 per cent of income. That is ten times what the bottom 20 per cent of the population earns.

The country's GINI coefficient, a measurement of income inequality with zero being perfectly equal and 100 perfectly unequal, rose to 50.4 in 2018 and reached a record high of 54 per cent in the height of the pandemic in 2020. A more general measure, the human development index (HDI) created by the United Nations, ranked Colombia 88th of the 190 countries in 2021. It measures three basic dimensions of human development: long and healthy life, knowledge, and a decent standard of living. High levels of income inequality among old age population are a major concern. According to the OECD, the relative poverty rates among the elderly population are the highest out of all the age groups in Colombia, highlighting the low reach of the pensions programme, especially in the case of women and the elderly population as only workers in formal employment actively contribute to the pensions system.

The wide dispersion of income largely originates from the labour market, which is characterised by a still high unemployment rate, a dominant informal sector and a wide wage dispersion reflecting a large education premium for those with higher education.

In Colombia, formal job creation remains heavily constrained by restrictive substantial non-wage labour costs and a minimum wage which is high compared to average incomes, deterring businesses from operating more formally and excluding low skilled workers from the formal sector.

Tax reforms since 2012 have attempted to remedy the situation through cuts in non-wage labour costs, but they remain insufficient. Reducing income inequality is therefore more than ever a necessity and a key government objective. The OECD has argued in favour of policies aimed at raising educational outcomes[22] for all and enhancing training programmes in order to improve labour supply and productivity. They've also argued in favour of delinking access to social protection from worker status in the labour market in order to break the current duality in incomes and job quality, and shifting the country's fiscal policies towards more progressive rates of taxation. There are growing calls for the creation of a basic universal level of social protection made available to all Colombians, which could be funded by merging the multitude of parallel schemes for cash transfers, pensions and health, combined with a more comprehensive set of benefits that can support those who can contribute more.

- The multidimensional nature of inequalities

But in Colombia, inequalities extend to individual and political freedom, discriminations, insecurity, and a lack of access to basic public services and social goods, such as decent housing, good health and education – and opportunities.

Inequalities are also deeply rooted in Colombia's social structures and institutions. As a result, intergenerational mobility is particularly slow: it takes an average of 11 generations to rise from the bottom ten per cent to the mean income in society, as opposed to 4.5 for the OECD average. Inequalities affect particularly women, Afro-Colombians and ethnic minorities.

Female participation in the labour market has increased markedly in the past twenty years, but despite legislation to promote gender equality and the higher average educational outcome of females, gender gaps in labour market outcomes are sizeable – women participation and employment rates are lower than for men; women suffer more from unemployment and those employed receive lower wages. The largest gaps are found among those with less education, working part time or in the informal sector which tends to be over-represented by women. Afro-Colombians are among the poorest in Colombia, as are those living in the countryside.

Land inequality, which finds its origin in the 19th century when the Colombian government sold off large parts of land to pay off its debts, has long been a source of conflict in rural Colombia. This has historically resulted in very high levels of land concentration: in 1960, 0.2 per cent of farmers owned 30 per cent of all farmland in Colombia.

The issue of land inequality is part of a much broader, and much more complex socio-political structure of exclusion that locked 'campesinos' into unfair labour contracts and unequal standing against the law. The struggles of peasants for land rights often turned violent as large landowners colluded with local authorities to expropriate them from disputed land.

These confrontations resulted in the constitution of armed groups. In the 1960s, the Colombian government implemented policies that subsidised large scale industrial farming destined for export markets rather than for local consumption, and small landowners were pushed off their land and forced to emigrate to urban centres where they provided a cheap labour pool for the burgeoning industrial economy of Colombian cities.

Beginning in 1948 and culminating in a civil war fuelled by conflict between the FARC and paramilitary militias established by landowners, local elites, and drug traffickers, Colombia's 50 years long civil war has only exacerbated this inequality.

In its final report published in June 2022, Colombia's Truth Commission estimates the conflict caused around half a million fatalities, 110,000 forced disappearances, at least 50,000 kidnappings. The country has one of the highest rates of internal displacement in the world, with nearly nine million people forced off their land as of January 2022. This has resulted in the country's swift urbanization, with 75 per cent of Colombians now living in cities, and the creation of massive informal settlements in which residents lack security and basic public services. In 2016, 1.3 million households (16 per cent of urban households) lived in informal, illegal urban settlements.

Across Colombia, there are 1,517 reported informal settlements and more than 60 per cent of them are concentrated in six Colombian cities: Medellín (17 per cent of total informal settlements in Colombia), Villavicencio (11.8 per cent), Neiva (8.9 per cent), Bucaramanga (8.8 per cent), Bogotá, D.C. (8.7 per cent) and Cali (7.4 per cent). Informal settlements represent around a quarter of the built areas of Colombian cities and are now home to almost five million people.

Social instability, particularly in the countryside thus remains a constant of Colombian political life. Despite the signing of its historic peace accords with the FARC in 2016, peace remains elusive and violence, displacements, and economic insecurity continue to affect Afro-Colombians, indigenous and *campesino* communities. Gustavo Petro's ambition to achieve total peace can be transformative for the country, but it will be a tortuous process.

- Peace and Security?

The lack of safety and security has long been a significant challenge for Colombian cities, as a result of Colombia's history of armed conflict triggering violence, civil conflict and illegal activities, high inequalities, high poverty levels and the prevalence of marginalised areas and informal settlements where citizens lack access to basic services. Despite substantial improvements in security especially in cities in the past decade, insecurity is still higher in urban than in rural areas. Indeed, Colombian metropolitan areas are amongst the least safe among OECD metropolitan areas when considering the number of homicides per 100,000 inhabitants. Only some metropolitan areas in Mexico have more homicides per head of population than Colombian metropolitan areas.

Environmental, social, LGBTQ+ and human rights activists and social leaders are still particularly targeted by local armed groups – in the first ten months of 2022 alone, 171 of them were killed, according to INDEPAZ, and since the signing of the Peace Agreement with the FARC in 2016 1,298 social leaders have been killed, with the security situation remaining particularly critical in the departments of Nariño, Chocó, Cauca y Valle. The need to establish a security policy that protects the civilian population, expand the state presence and implement the mechanisms of the peace agreement with the FARC to protect social leaders and dismantle criminal organizations is as urgent and critical as ever. And despite Petro's commitment to peace and security, there is no clear road map.

Unleashing Colombia's potential to deliver long lasting peace and prosperity for all will require deep and simultaneous reforms across several policy areas, rather than the small patches of the past. Country-wide social protests in 2021 and the election of Colombia's first ever left-wing president demonstrate that Colombians not only aspire to better economic opportunities but are also crying out for a change of economic and political models that can root out discriminations and place total peace, sustainability and inclusive growth at the heart of it.

And so, Colombia is at a crossroads. Long lasting peace has never been closer, yet more elusive. It will take political will, stamina, diplomacy and a great deal of patience to change Colombia's economic and political model that root out inequalities and discriminations so embedded in the country's structures and institutions.

As 2023 draws to a close, the country is in a very different place. Colombia has benefited from strong economic growth fuelled by a post-pandemic recovery, but it has also expressed high social expectations and witnessed a 180 degree political and ideological turn just as the economy started to slow down and the global environment deteriorate, degrading key economic indicators and damaging confidence. The hopes of social progress and economic transformation that Colombian people are holding dearly are now suspended on the actions and the laws of the coalition government in a global context that could not be less favourable.

---

[41] Professor of Management at Essex Business School (EBS) and co-director of the Centre for Latin American Studies (CLACS) at the University of Essex. All rights reserved. © Nicolas Forsans

PART 3.
History and Politics

Pre-Hispanic Period

Mystery surrounds the pre-Hispanic period of the region now called Colombia, since we can only rely on a few Spanish colonial accounts for information. In recent years efforts have been made to unravel parts of this history and scientists have made great progress by attempting to undo some of the damage inflicted upon sacred areas by successive waves of marauders.

The earliest evidence of human habitation in present-day Colombia is at the El Abra site outside Bogotá in the municipality of Zipaquirá. First excavated in 1969, these remains, closely linked to the remains of hunted game such as deer and a type of extinct horse found at the Tibito site near the town of Tocancipá, are believed to be amongst the earliest in the Americas, dating from around 12,400 years ago. The idea has been mooted but as yet remains unproven that the rock dwellings at El Abra were abandoned when the inhabitants started cultivating maize and therefore needed to be closer to their crops.

On the Caribbean coast, more is known of the powerful and imposing Tayrona civilization mainly due to the fact that their direct ancestors, the Arhuacos and Koguis, still populate the area around the Sierra Nevada de Santa Marta and that many studies have been made of the nearby Ciudad Perdida, founded circa 800AD, an astonishing 650 years before Machu Picchu in Peru. Also known as Buritaca, the Ciudad Perdida is an example of a complex civilization as it is believed to have housed over 2000 people on its terraces. So advanced were the Tayrona people that they knew all about crop rotation, methods to prevent soil erosion, and produced exceptional gold and ceramic works. At its height prior to the arrival of the Spaniards, the Tayronas might have numbered between 30,000 and 50,000 individuals. By the mid 16th century however, the Tayrona civilization was largely extinct.

Located in the central highlands and spanning a period from 1000-1538CE, the Muisca started out in small independent settlements, before becoming more centralized in the 13th century. Linguistically from the Chibcha family, the Muisca came south from Central America and settled the savannahs near Bogotá (or Bacatá). With two organized Muisca communities, the Zipa and the Zaque, in a feud over land and salt mines around Zipaquirá, it was easy for the Spanish to conquer this already divided society. Strikingly adept at in crop cultivation, hunting and as goldsmiths, the Muisca are said to have been the source for the legend of El Dorado from practices and ceremonies performed at the nearby sacred lake of Guatavita. The stone edifices that mark the burial mounds and rudimentary astrological site of El Infiernito are perhaps the best-preserved Muisca ruins.

In the south of the country the most interesting and still most visible pre-hispanic culture is that of San Agustín in the department of Huila, thanks to its spectacular anthropomorphic sculptures. This culture possibly marks the northernmost outpost of the Incan empire, and was at its zenith between 100 and 800CE. There remain a great number of unanswered questions relating to the San Agustín culture, but in recent years experts have been able to divide their timeline in to three parts: the formative period between 1000BCE and 300CE defined by small agricultural villages; the classic period from 300AD to 800CE, which saw a large expansion of its population; and the most recent period from 800CE to 1600 when the population diversified their crop cycles and cultivations. What is left are the amazing sculptures that define the San Agustin people for us with their blend of deities and mythical animals. Possibly linked to the Agustinian culture of Huila is Tierradentro in the department of Cauca, known for its pre-Columbian hypogeal or burial chambers that date from the sixth to the tenth century.

Also, in the valley of the River Cauca valley are substantial reminders of other pre-Hispanic communities, including the

Quimbayas known for their gold work, the hunter gatherer Calimas who arrived in the area around 5000BCE and subsequently fell into decline around the fourteenth century. The Nariño culture from the seventh century that straddles the Colombian border with Ecuador is known for having significant contact with both the people of the Pacific and the Amazon, and were the last link with the Incas. In the Pacific, the Tumaco people who lived between 600BCE and 400CE were expert fishermen and farmers who inhabited the estuaries and inlets of the coast. The Tumaco benefited from their access to the sea and the creation of channels for agriculture, and also left behind many interesting gold artefacts.

Richard McColl

Spanish Conquest 1500-1549

Alonso de Ojeda (1465-1515), the first Spanish conquistador to set foot on Colombian soil and attempt a settlement is arguably the explorer about whom the least is known. In 1493, Ojeda accompanied Columbus on his second voyage to the New World, and travelled on his own expedition with Amerigo Vespucci to Trinidad in 1499. Ten years later, in 1509, he created the first settlement on the South American mainland at San Sebastian de Urabá. Located in the suburb of Cañaflechal on the outskirts of what is now known as Necoclí, found on the Gulf of Urabá, nothing remains of San Sebastián as it was abandoned after frequent attacks by indigenous tribes and a lack of supplies. There were only 42 survivors from the 300 men who had started out on this expedition that charted the Caribbean coast from what is now Panama, all the way down to Lake Maracaibo in Venezuela.

In 1519 Pedrarias Dávila founded Panama City, which allowed for expeditions to depart from here to topple the Incan empire in Peru and settle Colombia. The supposed model for Cervantes' Don Quixote, Gonzalo Jiménez de Quesada (1499-1579) founded the city of Santa Fe de Bogotá in 1538, and ventured into the regions of Guaviare and Orinoco in ill-fated attempts to find and secure the legendary El Dorado. Meanwhile, his rival, the German Nikolaus Federmann (1501-1542), came from Venezuela in the same quest. The then governor of Quito, Sebastián de Benalcázar (1495-1551), moved north from Ecuador and founded the cities of Cali and Popayan. Benalcázar tried to ally himself with Federmann against Quesada, but this proved unsuccessful. The three men all laid claim to the riches to be found in the region, and eventually in 1591, after a meeting between them in the savannah of Bogotá, they resolved to take the argument to the court of Carlos V king of Spain. In 1540 control of Bogotá was wrested from Quesada when Carlos V granted Benalcázar the right to rule from his seat of power at

Popayán, overseen by the Viceroyalty of Peru.

Given its geographical location, the Caribbean coast was the first to be properly settled and in 1525 by Rodrigo de Bastidas (1445-1527) founded the city of Santa Marta, the oldest permanently settled city in Colombia. In 1533 Pedro de Heredia (1520-1555) founded Cartagena (his brother Alonso de Heredia founds the strategically important riverside town of Mompós in 1537) and this city soon overtakes Santa Marta in importance, becoming the key port for trading in slaves and supplies.

New Granada: Spanish Rule (1549-1808)

Until the middle of the 16th century, the area that is now Colombia was administered by the Viceroy of Peru based in Lima. In 1549, to delegate some responsibilities to more autonomous and outlying regions, the Royal Audiencia of Santa Fe de Bogotá was created to oversee the key provinces of Popayán, Santa Marta and Guayana (current-day Venezuela).

This Royal Audiencia even had its own president, who was answerable to all powerful Lima. However, given the enormity of the territory the Viceroy in Lima had to oversee, stretching from Panama to Chile and Argentina, in the 18th century the northern Spanish possessions were split from the southern ones.

On May 29 1717, the Viceroy of New Granada was created to control the territories including Colombia, Ecuador, Venezuela, Panama, sections of western Brazil, northern Peru and as far east as Guyana. This enormous area, while managed in Santa Fe de Bogotá by a governor-president, was divided into smaller provinces, the largest of which, Popayán, extended up into present day Antioquia, the Chocó and well out into the Amazon basin.

The idea behind the establishment of the Viceroy of New Granada had its roots not only in the geographical and logistical difficulties encountered at this period, but also to administer more effectively the entry ports into the region, counter contraband and take more effective action against piracy and foreign designs on Spanish colonial territory. Again though, the geographical conundrum came into play and the Capitania General in Caracas and the Royal Audiencia in Quito, despite nominally and legally tied to Santa Fe, became more politically and regionally independent. The Viceroyalty of New Granada existed from 1717 until 1723 when it was suspended for financial reasons and returned to the authority of Lima, only to be re-established in 1739 until the winds of independence blew through the Spanish colonies.

Independence 1808 – 1819

By the end of the 18th century, the Habsburg dynasty in Spain was near to collapse. The revolutions in the United States and France fuelled the drive towards independence throughout Latin America. In New Granada, figures such as Antonio Nariño (1765-1823), who in 1794 translated The Declaration of the Rights of Man, spearheaded a new generation determined to break free of rule from Spain.

Napoleon's invasion of Spain in 1808 was nothing short of catastrophic for any Spanish desire to hold on to New Granada. On 20 July 1810 the province of Santa Fe de Bogotá declared its independence, followed by Cartagena a year later. The vacuum of power with the defeat of the Royalist forces and the struggle between the autonomous provinces created what became known as the Patria Boba or Foolish Fatherland, when no single unifying central government could be decided upon.

Gradually, New Granada eased into five years of de facto independence from Spain under the banner of the United Provinces of New Granada.

With the Napoleonic wars over, Ferdinand VII was restored to the throne and Spanish eyes were once again drawn to the Americas and their unruly outposts there. A veteran of the Peninsula War, General Pablo Morillo was charged with bringing the colonies back under control and in 1815 besieged and took control of Cartagena. In 1816 the combined efforts of the royalist sympathisers and the Spanish army marching south from Cartagena and Santa Marta and north from the strongholds of Pasto, Quito and Popayán ended with the capture of Santa Fe de Bogotá and the collapse of the independent New Granada.

It was not until August 1819 that Simón Bolívar finally managed to drive out the Spanish forces and retake the capital. Bolívar convened the Congress of Angostura (now called Ciudad

Bolívar in Venezuela), which functioned with 26 delegates until 1821. It was here that the idea for the new republic of Gran Colombia was discussed. This was to consist of all the territories that comprised New Granada, Colombia, Venezuela, Ecuador, Panama, parts of Brazil, Peru and Guyana, as well as territories in the Caribbean including the Mosquito coast in current day Nicaragua and up into Costa Rica. Gran Colombia was meant to be a cohesive, diverse and economically powerful state to compete with European nations.

At Angostura, Simón Bolívar was proclaimed President of Gran Colombia and Francisco de Paula Santander as vice president. In 1821 at the Congress of Cúcuta a formal constitution was drawn up and agreed upon; Bolívar and Santander were officially sworn into their posts, and Gran Colombia was firmly established. The new republic quickly found its feet and set aside regional differences to continue the armed struggle against imperial Spain. Bolívar dedicated himself to liberating the royalist pockets remaining in Ecuador, the rest of Venezuela, and achieving the independence of Peru.

On the strength of these victories, both Bolívar and Santander were re-elected in 1826. However, as the memories of the independence struggle faded, the conflict between federalist and centralist beliefs came to the fore. Santander had fully backed the idea of a more federalist state. This placed him at odds with Bolívar, culminating in Bolívar's abolishment of the office of vice president in 1828 when he declared himself Dictator. Despite having largely run the country in Bolívar's long absences and campaigns, Santander was forced into exile after being implicated in an assassination attempt on Bolívar.

In 1830 Gran Colombia was dissolved when Venezuela and Ecuador seceded. With the fissures in the republic all too apparent, Bolívar resigned from the presidency. With his resignation, in 1832 Santander was able to return, and was elected President, a post he held until 1837. During this period Santander proved himself to be an able administrator, balancing carefully the differences between the liberals and conservative Catholics, promoting trade with the United States and investing considerably in education.

In 1840 Santander died, Panama declared its independence (not achieved until 1903) and Colombia was plunged into civil war. Essentially, the two factions were divided between centralists or Conservatives and federalists or Liberals, the latter believing in a separation of church and state and decentralised power, while the former upheld a strong central government.

From 1849-1857 and 1861-1880 the Liberals were in power during an era marked by insurrections and civil wars. In 1856 the Granadine Confederation was created, which was pro-federalist and gave greater autonomy to the provinces. Not surprisingly, it aroused the fervent opposition of the Conservatives. Civil war raged on, until in 1863 the Granadine Confederation was replaced by the United States of Colombia.

Reprisals between Liberals and Conservatives continued until 1886, when the United States of Colombia finally gave way to the Republic of Colombia under the presidency of the Conservative Rafael Núñez (1825-1894). Núñez governed the country for 14 years, his most famous accomplishment being that of the constitutional reform that created the Republic of Colombia. A legacy of his leadership, as the centralist policies of the new constitution of 1863 only seemed to aggravate existing antagonisms, was the ferociously bloody civil war known as the Thousand Day War (1899–1902).

Widespread violence broke out after the Conservatives were accused of holding onto the reins of power following fraudulent elections in 1899. The war spread to every corner of Colombia, dividing families and furthering the economic ruin of the country already suffering from the collapse of the coffee market. The Conservatives claimed victory, but this was nominal at best since the war had brought the country to its knees and never resolved the issues between the two factions as well as leaving more than 100 thousand Colombians dead when finally, a definitive peace treaty was signed in 1902.

Colombia was broken, demoralized and further humiliated when in 1903, the region known as the Istmo or Panama, received backing from the US to become independent. This came about after the Colombian Senate had failed to ratify the Hay-Herrán Treaty to lease the zone to the United States to create the Panama Canal. The Republic of Panama was not officially recognised by Colombia until 1914.

Modern Colombia: A Democracy on the edge 1903...

This Thomson-Urrutia Treaty that effectively paid-off Colombia, cheaply and legitimised Panamá's independence, marked a new era in Colombian history. Reeling from seemingly interminable civil wars and the humiliating loss of national territory, Colombia tentatively stepped into the twentieth century. Conservative presidents held power between 1909 and 1930, and Liberals from 1930 to 1942.

At the end of World War II, the violence and political divisions in Colombia intensified once more. Many historians see the assassination of Liberal presidential candidate Jorge Eliécer Gaitán on April 9 1948 was the spark – el Bogotazo which resulted in much of downtown Bogotá being razed to the ground - to ignite the long-running fuse to the period known as *La Violencia*42 that consumed Colombia from 1948-1964 (sometimes the end date is put at 1958 with the signing of the National Front agreement, but the violence continued). In total during this period more than 200 thousand lives were lost.

La Violencia

La Violencia, as historians know it, is one of the bloodiest periods in Colombian history, which has had unprecedented effects on the country. The violence initiated during *La Violencia* has continued its spiral effects in the social, economic and political life of Colombia. Gonzalo Sánchez[43] describes this violence in his essay *"The Violence: An Interpretative Synthesis"*.

The first and most visible process of the Violence, which left the greatest impact upon the collective memory, was a mixture of official terror, partisan sectarianism, and scorched-earth policy. This aspect of the Violence affected the lives, physical safety, psychology, and possessions of hundreds of thousands of Colombians. Its images are unerasable and in good measure have given the Violence its distinctive seal. The extreme modality of this process, was, of course, murder. Extreme not only for the number of victims but also because of the indescribable torture that surrounded these murders and marked for life the entire generation that witnessed them...Atrocities involving mutilation, sexual violation, and the desecration of victims corpses, in other words, the ritual of terror, were a pathological component that accompanied most intimidation. (p89)

The period of La Violencia occurred between 1946-1958, leaving approximately 200,000 dead from both parties. In the aftermath of Gaitan's death, a period of extreme partisan violence erupted. The main causes were that the two main parties, the Conservatives and the Liberals, started fighting for power. The repression of a Conservative government and the aspirations of the poor for economic and social betterment were other factors that contributed to the violence that erupted. After almost 10 years of violence, the National Front was signed (1958-1974) which allowed the two parties to share power and alternate the presidency (p54).

Colombia's dictator

It is little wonder, given all the violence and bloodshed that, Colombia then flirted with a dictatorship. In 1953 the army officer Gustavo Rojas Pinilla (1900-1975) led the coup that ousted President Laureano Gómez. One of Pinilla's first actions was to declare an amnesty for all those who had been fighting, to try and rein in some of the violence in the countryside.

At first this appeared to work, with battle-weary figures turning in their arms, eager to return to civilian life. But after a brief respite, heavy fighting broke out once more in the area of Tolima, and Rojas Pinilla's popularity plummeted. In 1957 he stepped down, handing over power to a military junta.

The junta ruled Colombia for 15 months before bringing a power-sharing political creation designed with the aim of bringing bipartisan violence to an end. This was called the *Frente Nacional* or National Front and ran from 1958 to 1974 and during which each party, the Conservatives and Liberals, would govern for four years alternately.

It is very possible that the *Frente Nacional* agreement was a convenient remedy to the bipartisan violence of the previous decades but upon reflection its efficacy was superficial at best. There have been far-reaching consequences of the *Frente Nacional*, not least in that it produced deeper issues in Colombia such as an increase in social violence, selective repression, political exclusion, corruption and led to a major disillusionment amongst much of the population.

---

[42] Biblioteca Nacional: https://bibliotecanacional.gov.co/es-co/proyectos-digitales/historia-de-colombia/libro/capitulo11.html

[43] The Violence: An Interprative Synthesis: https://scholar.google.com/citations?user=QOZodgsAAAAJ&hl=en

Politics since 1958

The traditional Liberal and Conservative parties soon became disillusioned with Rojas Pinilla's idiosyncratic rule, which had strong elements of crowd-pleasing populism and threatened their eventual elimination. Exiled leaders from both camps began to negotiate in Spain, to work out a settlement that would make military rule unnecessary and prevent either side from ever resorting to arms again.

This rapprochement produced the 1957 Sitges agreement between ex-Presidents Alberto Lleras Carnargo and Laureano Gómez, which set up the alternating and power-sharing arrangement known as the National Front. This agreement underpinned political life right through to the late 1970s, and elements of the modus vivendi agreed at Sitges still remain in place.

Power Sharing

The National Front, which ran for four presidential terms, until 1974, succeeded in making the country governable again. Rojas Pinilla first had to be disposed of with the minimum of fuss, by means of a 'general strike' by employers and business leaders in May 1957. The framework agreement specified alternating four-year periods of office for Liberal and Conservative presidents. It also involved an equal sharing out of the spoils of office between the parties, to end the political exclusivity that had caused so much violence in the past. But the fact that this solution meant excluding all other political forces guaranteed that other forms of violence would persist.

The formal National Front arrangement ended in 1974. But the understanding that the losing side would be given a share of power lasted until 1986, when Liberal President Virgilio Barco formed a single-party administration. The only time the Conservatives were able to win in a straight fight was when the Liberals divided and opened the door to Belisario

Betancur in 1982. But Betancur was far from being a traditional Conservative; much of his political success derived from his ability to present himself as above party, a 'national' candidate who alone could solve the problems that the traditional parties had failed to tackle.

The Constitution of 1991

Betancur's promises turned out to be largely an illusion. When the Liberal former finance minister César Gaviria Trujillo was elected president in 1990 his aim was to modernise the political system. The existing constitution, that of 1886, belonged to a different world, in which the two traditional parties reigned supreme and the president had enormous powers of patronage. There was widespread disillusion, which translated into very high rates of voter abstention, often of 70 per cent or more. There had been a virtually permanent state of siege for decades, during which the executive largely ruled by decree and the military was given wide jurisdiction over security, including trial of civilians by courts martial.

In 1991 a constituent assembly was elected to draft a new document that would, Gaviria hoped, open up the political system. Symbolically, one of the assembly's three chairmen was Antonio Navarro Wolff, one of the few surviving senior commanders of the M-19 guerrilla organisation and now leader of a legal political party, ADM-19. Colombia's ethnic minorities were also represented for the first time. Debates were wide-ranging and the new constitution, approved in 1991, included some important reforms.

Its main measures were curbs on the powers of the executive and legal guarantees for individuals and minorities. The president would no longer be able to declare an indefinite state of siege and rule by decree for the whole of his term, as many of Gaviria's predecessors had done. Instead, the new constitution contemplated different levels of internal disorder, carefully defined, and placed a limit of nine months during which constitutional guarantees might be suspended. Suspects could only be held for limited periods without standing trial; at the same time, the military's right to try civilians for public order offences, widely used and abused during periods of emergency, was curtailed.

All political offices were made electable, and the grip of the main parties on the electoral system was loosened. Ethnic minorities were allocated two seats in each house of Congress, as of right, while the president could also, if he saw fit, give seats to former guerrillas who agreed to a negotiated 'pacification' deal.

Proceso 8000

Ernesto Samper Pizano won the presidential elections and governed from 1994-1998, but his presidency was dogged by the Proceso 8000 (8000 Process). The name is little more than a case number but what it revealed is the extent to which cocaine money had permeated into Colombia's politics. As the presidential election came down to the wire and it could have gone either way, Samper or Pastrana (the Conservative candidate who later became president from 1998-2002), Samper's campaign allegedly turned to the Cali Cartel, receiving cash donations in excess of six million US dollars. These donations were delivered in large paper bags normally used for birthday gifts. In a televised address to the nation, President Samper stated that if drug money made its way into his campaign's finances, it happened "behind his back". Due to a lack of evidence with which to formally accuse the president of the Proceso 8000[44], Congress voted 111 in favour of and 43 against archiving the case and the rest is history.

The Boulevardier President – Andrés Pastrana 1998-2002

By this time, a long-suffering Colombian public was prepared to bet on peace and the image of presidential hopeful Andrés Pastrana Arango in conversation with Manuel *"Tirofijo"* Marulanda[45], the commander in chief of the FARC, before the elections, was enough to swing the vote in his favour ahead of Horacio Serpa of the Liberal Party in the second round.

Pastrana's presidency is remembered for his negotiations with the two left-wing guerrilla groups FARC and ELN (and he was also heavily criticized for all the trips that he took around the world during his term), culminating in the grant of a demilitarized safe haven to the FARC guerrillas the size of Switzerland at San Vicente del Caguán in the department of Caquetá.

In 1999, he and U.S. President Bill Clinton launched Plan Colombia to fight the guerrillas with a payment by the United States of $1.6 billion over three years to the Colombian army.

An amendment quickly emphasized the plan's second function: to encourage foreign investment.

Military counterguerrilla operations cause the forced displacement[46] of more than one million people in four years. Cocaine production increased by 47 per cent[47] during that period.

---

[44] Señal Memoria: https://www.senalmemoria.co/proceso-8000-historia-politica

[45] El Tiempo: https://www.eltiempo.com/politica/proceso-de-paz/cronica-andres-pastrana-le-gano-presidencia-a-horacio-serpa-y-abrio-las-puertas-para-alvaro-uribe-546850

[46] Radio Macondo: https://www.radiomacondo.fm/noticias-nacionales/pastrana-y-uribe-los-gobiernos-con-mas-victimas-en-el-conflicto-armado/

[47] IPS Noticias: https://ipsnoticias.net/1999/11/colombia-aumento-de-narcotrafico-agrava-la-guerra-civil/

PART 4.
Uribe, Peace, Conflict and the Evolution of the Conflict

President Uribe

Coming to power in 2002 and presiding over the country until 2010, the controversial and authoritarian figure of Álvaro Uribe Vélez signalled a change in Colombia both domestically and internationally. It can be argued that his sole election platform was that of to finish off the guerrillas in Colombia and after the debacle of the Caguán peace talks under his predecessor President Andrés Pastrana (1998-2002), the war-weary nation sat up and listened. His 'democratic security' policy showed considerable progress in the minds of his supporters and Colombia's cities became safer than before and land travel within the country became possible, but at a cost.

After pushing through an amendment in 2004 to the Colombian Constitution allowing the President to run for a second term, Uribe was re-elected in 2006. His approval ratings remained high. although they began to decline after revelations of illegalities, namely the para-politics and false positives scandals (described here under "Human Rights") linking allied politicians to the right-wing paramilitaries and the disappearances and killings of thousands of humble city-dwellers later dressed as guerrillas and added to a gruesome headcount.

Operación Orion (16-17 October 2002)

Operación Orión[48] and so-called "false positives," and the overall free hand given to paramilitaries killed a lot of innocent people, even if you accept that the baseline can't be zero since the Colombian state has always killed innocent people even with zero effectiveness against actual enemies. Just look at the raid on Medellín's infamous Comuna 13 when, in October 2002, a military offensive, that successfully removed left-wing rebels from the neighbourhood, but ended up installing paramilitary groups still terrorising the area.

The military offensive has been criticized because it was carried out in one of Medellín's most densely populated areas. While the army, police, air force and paramilitary groups combated left-wing urban militias, the then approximately 100,000 residents of the shanty town were caught in the crossfire, leaving hundreds injured.

The operation became even more controversial later, when locals began telling stories of how hundreds of residents had been detained but were never tried, how dozens of neighbours were disappeared by paramilitary forces during and after the operation and how the paramilitary Bloque Cacique Nutibara (BCN) had been collaborating with the army and police to secure paramilitary control over the area.

Overall

The FARC and ELN were pushed back during Uribe's tenure, and in many parts of the country the paramilitaries faded away not (just) because of the peace agreement in Ralito but because the guerrillas did as well. This fact has surely saved a lot of lives, and probably more than were snuffed out, but most non-monstrous people would have a problem with that. The irony is that Uribe's strongest supporters, and the man himself, actually deny the reality that makes his bad side plausibly defensible when they dismiss the peace agreement with the FARC. They're basically saying they killed all those people for nothing.

One cannot doubt that Uribe's policies were a "net utility gain," as the economists would say. In expelling FARC from urban centres and overall weakening them to the point where they would sign a peace treaty under President Santos, likely saved more lives over time than were taken by the crimes of the military and paramilitaries, especially since those groups were committing crimes before Uribe. It's the age-old philosophical argument, known as "consequentialist vs. deontological" or, more commonly, "the Trolley Problem[49]": is it OK to kill a certain number of innocent people in order to save (at least in your own mind) a larger number?

No third term

Uribe then attempted to push through a further resolution to enable himself to run for a third term but this was denied by the Constitutional Court in 2010. In the decade since Uribe was in power he has maintained a high profile in Colombia and continues to be the country's most divisive politician. He was the kingmaker to his successor as president Juan Manuel Santos, then ran a close – but losing - campaign for his next presidential project, Óscar Iván Zuluaga, and finally put a successive president into place, the current premier Iván Duque Márquez.

As a Senator he led the hard-right *Centro Democrático* (Democratic Centre) party to the Colombian mainstream and worked tirelessly to weaken and discredit the 2016 peace accords with the FARC.

Half of Colombia loves him and the other half loathes him and this came to a head in August 2020 when, Uribe was placed under house arrest by the Supreme Court as he was being investigated for witness tampering in a case alleging that his lawyer paid former paramilitary leaders to deny any links between Uribe and their factions. The case is on-going and as polarizing as ever.

---

[48] Comisión de la Verdad: https://www.comisiondelaverdad.co/el-violento-engranaje-de-la-operacion-orion

[49] Merriam Webster: https://www.merriam-webster.com/wordplay/trolley-problem-moral-philosophy-ethics

Richard McColl

Alvaro Uribe: The Complex Role of a Former President

Published first on April 18, 2013 by Richard McColl, subsequently updated.

Álvaro Uribe needs to settle down comfortably into his velvety sitting room slippers, dedicate his time to critiquing leather-bound copies of political discourse, walking his dogs on the finca(s) and lending his valid opinion to the centre pages of illustrious publications belonging to international right-wing think tanks.

This image, almost a pastoral one, of Colombia's former president is about as realistic as cold fusion. The ex-president himself has displayed his reluctance to fade away into a John Major-esque existence of cucumber sandwiches, village cricket matches and lucrative public speaking engagements through his determined, often damaging and vitriolic outbursts over whatever media may lend him the soapbox.

Often described as "bookish" in the international press, presumably due to his stature, economist's build, statistician's haircut, scholarly reading glasses and in that he couldn't have been a farther cry from the supposed vanities and imagined joie de vivre so readily embraced by bon vivant that was his predecessor Andrés Pastrana, Álvaro Uribe changed Colombia.

Wherever you find yourself politically, on the right or the left, you cannot dispute this last point. Colombia was improved by the double tenure (2002-2010) of Álvaro Uribe. But, just as a tide retreats after a storm, the flotsam and jetsam of human existence has also left behind the detritus of a politically stagnant mandate bereft of ideas.

President Uribe's time had expired long before the elections in which Juan Manuel Santos was swept into office. Accusations of links to paramilitary groups and drugs cartels, illegal wiretapping and the *parapolitica* scandal not to mention the notable disregard for human rights had all dented Uribe's political machinery. While still popular at home in Colombia, his international prestige began to wane.

Now, in this his most recent outburst (at the time of writing), to reveal on twitter (X, Where he has more than two million followers to his account) the infinitesimally delicate issue of the exact coordinates of the operation to transport several high-ranking members of the FARC Guerrillas from the depths of Colombia's jungles to Havana to partake in the peace dialogues, he has jeopardized further his role in the nation's discourse. Even *Uribistas* question his credibility.

- Does Álvaro Uribe not wish for peace in Colombia?

Of course, he does. The weekly news magazine *Semana* has paraphrased sections of his memoirs *"No Hay Causa Perdida"* (No Lost Causes) in their edition 1615 where he clearly states that peace is his objective. He wants peace under his terms. We remain unsure what his "terms" actually are though.

Then why does he feel the need to be a spoiler of the current process? We can abide his vernacular referring to the FARC as "terrorists" and so on, as this has always been his wont. In fact, this is what we desire from Álvaro Uribe. We need him as a counterweight, as an unusual political bugbear on the right. But, if there is any advice that one can offer Mr. Uribe, it is that he needs to know when to reign in the bitterness as he is in dire risk of alienating his core supporter base and causing many to reassess their views and opinions of his noteworthy achievements.

With reference to this last point, it is also incredibly timely to mention that Álvaro Uribe is not the only former president openly criticizing President Juan Manuel Santos. Uribe's predecessor Andrés Pastrana is also lining up to take lily-livered swipes as well. And while there is no doubting that Colombia would not have reached this phase of dialogues with the FARC were it not for the efforts of Pastrana in San Vicente del Caguán (1999-2002, and lest you forget, the FARC was winning the rural conflict at this stage) and the eight years of bombing runs employed by Álvaro Uribe, the commentary rings a familiar tune.

There is, however, a grave difference between the elucidations of Pastrana and Uribe. Pastrana's meandering folktales allude only to himself, and of course, this was his political line as well, while, Uribe seems out to destroy. There is a war of political vanities and legacies on the line and neither stands to benefit should this process for peace with the FARC result as successful.

Said President Santos during a march for peace: "It's normal that Colombians would be sceptical after so many deceptions. But the truth is the process is going well.

"It's a difficult and complex process," he said, adding that peace could come in months if the current pace of talks is maintained.

Enabling peace with the FARC is not peace in Colombia, we know this, but it's a huge step in the right direction. We don't want Uribe to be muzzled as his opinion and calumnious assessments are of huge importance. However, the former president must understand that the political landscape within Colombia has evolved beyond that of the period of his tenure.

Colombia's bookish former president has secured his "ism", that of *"uribismo"* (the Colombian version of Thatcherism – and just as divisive) and must retire from the trenches as he is no longer suited to the needs of modern-day political discourse. But, he must remain a vital part of the political landscape, and this is inescapable.

Can we expect him to heed any level-headed words of advice?

Of course not.

President Santos

Son of the wealthy, Juan Manuel Santos Calderón was first elected President of Colombia on 7 August 2010 and re-elected in 2014, for a second four-year term. Throughout his public sector career prior to becoming president, Santos held important ministerial roles. He was Colombia's first Foreign Trade Minister, the Minister of Finance and was Minister for National Defence in the government of president Uribe.

Over the eight years of Santos, Colombia's economy underwent major transformations. For his first term, Santos inherited a booming economy from former president Uribe: the GDP was growing at approximately 4 per cent, the unemployment level reached a single digit, inflation did not surpass 3.8 per cent and foreign investments were pouring in, particularly in the petroleum industry. During Santos' first term, Colombia signed free trade agreements with South Korea, Costa Rica and the European Union. However, his tenure saw a great deal of mass strikes that affected key economic sectors, such as airline pilots, university students, farmers, teachers, truck drivers and federal employees within the judicial branch.

Nevertheless, his great gamble began in 2012, when his government started formal negotiations with the FARC and the president broke ranks with his key political ally, former President Uribe.

The negotiations with the FARC has polarized Colombia for years, leading to a contested election in 2014. In that election, Uribe's Democratic Centre Party ran on a platform against the peace talks and managed to outperform President Santos' re-election bid during the first-round lead by Óscar Iván Zuluaga, before losing to a pro-peace bloc that coalesced around Santos in the second round.

During his second term, Santos had to deal with the economic fallout caused by the collapse of global oil prices, which led to a steep devaluation of the Colombian peso, a decrease in foreign direct investment and an increase in inflation. Meanwhile, President Santos signed even more free trade agreements, with Israel and Panama.

The great gamble was of course peace with the FARC, and it paid off with thousands of combatants signing the agreement and emerging from the jungles after decades of conflict. Santos was awarded the Nobel Prize for peace.

Santos' administration was tarnished by scandals, most notably the Odebrecht corruption scheme that engulfed parts of South America and delayed important infrastructure projects in Colombia, such as regaining the navigability of the Magdalena River and completing the Ruta del Sol highway, the principal road from the interior of the country to the Caribbean coast.

Likewise, there was a substantial increase in the cultivation of illicit crops, notably coca, and violence directed toward social leaders in rural regions of the country.

Ultimately, Juan Manuel Santos left the presidential palace as one of the most unpopular presidents in Colombia's modern history. However, by many accounts, he left the country better than he found it. Once the dust settles, history will likely look kindly upon the peacemaker's great gamble for peace. What remains to be seen is how the Odebrecht scandal plays out and how Santos was involved, not to mention his knowledge of, or role in the false positives scandal whilst Minister of Defence.

Colombia vs Nicaragua

The diplomatic shrift between Colombia and Nicaragua has often seemed like the international dispute which would never go away. To keep it brief, this argument over the ownership of the archipelago and the maritime boundaries around the islands of San Andrés and Providencia has occupied politicians in both countries for decades.

In December 2001, Nicaragua formally filed a lawsuit with the International Court of Justice (ICJ) against Colombia, claiming a maritime area of more than 50,000 square kilometres, which included the San Andrés archipelago, the keys and all the maritime territory that contains them. The Nicaraguans also emphasized that the Esguerra - Bárcenas Treaty was rejected in the 1980s that the agreement went against the Nicaraguan Constitution.

In 2007, the ICJ ruled in favour of Colombia, recognizing its sovereignty over the islands of San Andrés, Providencia and Santa Catalina; but, the maritime boundary between the two nations was not defined.

Roll on to 2012 on 19 November, the ICJ ruled that the ruling it would issue would be unfavourable to both nations. It reaffirmed Colombian sovereignty over the islands of Albuquerque, Bajo Nuevo, Quitasueño, Roncador, Serrana, Serranilla and the San Andrés, Providencia and Santa Catalina archipelago. But, the ICJ declared that the maritime border would be "divided equally", leaving Nicaragua some 70,000 square kilometres of maritime territory.

In 2023, the ICJ dismissed Nicaragua's bid to gain economic rights over an area of the Caribbean Sea that lies more than 200 nautical miles (230 statute miles, 370 kilometres) from its shores.

Don't expect this issue to go away.

Richard McColl

President Duque and his Orange Economy

To reflect on Iván Duque Márquez' tenure as president (2018-2022) is to plunge into something which is both dispiriting and was predictable. Certainly, he faced one of the most challenging global tragedies in living memory of Covid-19, but even prior to this, things were not moving smoothly and there were whispers in the corridors of power that, if he was unable to reach across the political divide to members of the opposition, he may not see out his term.

We will never know; however, his position was looking increasingly fraught after the first *Paro Nacional* in 2019 and the burden on him and his performance was most definitely eased with the pandemic, allowing for Colombians and the government to focus their fears elsewhere.

Largely unknown and inexperienced, his victory in the election was based on the voters' fear and hatred of Petro, his support from Uribe and a general suspicion towards the peace accords... not arguments and coherent ideas[50], such as he suggests on every possible occasion when challenged.

Duque's desire to re-brand "culture" and "creative industries" as the *economía naranja* (orange economy), while not a dreadful idea, was often accompanied with poor timing and worse analogies, look no further than his reference to "the seven dwarves" at a UNESCO meeting in Paris[51] or his orange juice stunt at the *2021 de los Trailblazers Latinoamericanos*[52] meeting. If this wasn't enough, there is a "The Orange Economy, an infinite opportunity[53]" pamphlet published by the former president and his sidekick, Felipe Buitrago Restrepo.

More at ease showing off his skills playing keepie uppie with a football, singing vallenatos or strumming his electric guitar, when Colombia demanded stability and continuity after President Santos and the peace accords, they received someone quite the opposite.

Duque came into power as the candidate decided upon strangling the peace accords with the FARC, he and his government had failed to understand the psychological transition which the peace agreement had instilled into much of the Colombian public. No longer were people thinking of "the conflict," and the Right was lost as they still marched to this tune. The conflict still existed, of course, but the right-wing was incapable of offering other options than the *"mano dura"* with which to improve Colombia. Duque made security a pillar of his mandate.

Duque's Security Policy

Turning back the clock, Duque endorsed direct confrontation against the illegal armed groups in the country having received a Colombia at its most stable in living memory. In his first year, massacres (now called by his government: *homicidios colectivos* or collective homicides[54]) increased by 300 per cent[55].

By focusing solely on military action, failure was foreseeable as it has been shown time and time again that there is no purely military solution to Colombia's rural insecurity. Dissident groups increased in size, the number of ELN combatants grew and illegal groups became decentralized (unlike the FARC), which meant that stability is ensured after the capture or assassination of a leader and their business interests remain intact.

Duque regularly pointed to the success story of the capture and rapid extradition of alias *Otoniel* or Dairo Antonio Úsuga[56], the commander in chief of the *Clan del Golfo* (AGC) as an operation which would lead to a reduction in the killing of social and community leaders. The opposite was the case. One week after Otoniel's capture – which was a very swift and bloodless undertaking - the AGC showed the extent of their might by carrying out an armed blockade[57] and paralysing much the country. Businesses were shut, people confined to their homes at-risk of reprisals, vehicles incinerated. It was if the bad old days of the 1990s and early 2000s had returned.

In addition to a litany of missteps, children were killed in military bombing operations aimed at attacking FARC camps. Eight children were killed in an August 2019 bombing raid and the then defence minister, Guillermo Botero, resigned. The Minister had also been accused of attempting to cover up the identities and ages of those killed. Then in March 2021, a bombing raid signed off by the subsequent defence minister Diego Molano resulted in the deaths of 12 children. Molano[58] unwisely dehumanized the victims when he referred to them as: *"maquinas de guerra,"* or "war machines."

Paro Nacional 2019

By November 2019, many Colombians were frustrated and felt alienated from the political class and what was a simmering tension, boiled over into an organic set of multiple protests with different demands. President Duque had only been in power for 15 months and his approval ratings were at rock bottom, what started as a plan for labour unions to strike ballooned into more widespread actions by indigenous groups, pensioners and students. The national strike (*Paro Nacional*[59]) was initially called in October by labour unions after rumours spread about reforms and pension cuts – proposals never formally announced by the government. The strike also came as university students continued to protest against corruption and cuts in public education.

The call also came around the same time the country witnessed an uptick in violence against indigenous and social leaders, which has been blamed in part on Duque's slow implementation of the 2016 peace deal with the FARC.

Colombia is a country tired of injustice, bad governance and social inequality was the overall clamour. Anywhere between 200 thousand and one million marched in cities and towns across the country as the strike gained momentum and the government's response was to deploy 170 thousand troops.

What began on 21 November 2019 came to an end in March 2020 with the outbreak of Covid-19. Violence, looting, thousands injured and tragically, upwards of 48 people[60] (including two policemen) had been killed.

Duque's later promises were too little too late as he called for a "*Gran Diálogo Nacional61*"

in March. As it was, this "national conversation" was effective in watering down the protests as the pandemic took over. To date, there is little actual documentation of what took place, if anything, during the short-lived dialogues. No one has ever made the contents from these short-lived dialogues – if there is any – public.

Paro Nacional 2021

In April 2021, Duque proposed an increase in taxes at a time when the Covid-19 pandemic in Colombia was beginning to worsen and as various healthcare systems were failing throughout the country. The pandemic had severely hurt the Colombian economy, with 42 per cent of Colombians earning less than US$90 per month, and with one in four Colombians under the age of 28 unemployed[62]. The tax reform was also devised to reduce Colombia's increasing fiscal deficit, which had resulted in international credit rating agencies downgrading the Colombian government's bonds thus raising the cost of borrowing.

It was clear that the problems were structural and the government would not have the solutions and if they did, there would not be time to execute them.

All the while, Bogotá was no longer the flashpoint, but the southwestern city of Cali and by the second week of May, Cali was experiencing serious shortages of fuel and food. Amnesty International published "Cali: in the epicentre of repression[63]", a report describing police repression, paramilitarism, illegal detention and torture of peaceful protesters during the National Strike. In their exhaustive digital verification of audio-visual material, they confirmed that anti-riot squad ESMAD used excessive and disproportionate force. They also documented acts of urban paramilitarism by armed civilians who accompanied law enforcement.

The blame for the unrest and violence was placed on Venezuelan infiltrators from the Maduro regime, FARC dissident groups and ELN guerrilla infiltration, gang infiltration to whomever would listen.

As the protests continued, there is little doubting that criminal elements used the disorder to further their business interests, however, it became clear to the international community[64]

that there was unacceptable state violence being used against civilian protestors.

Between 28 April and 31 July 2021, the UN Human Rights Office in Colombia received 63 allegations of deaths[65] in the context of the protests. This same report also includes 60 reported cases of sexual violence allegedly committed by the police.

As the protests petered out, a battered and broken Colombia was left to pick up the pieces. The protest wave reflected deep-seated grievances affecting much of society, rooted in economic need and extreme levels of inequality that the health and economic devastation caused by Covid-19 so flagrantly exposed. Instead of listening to the demands of the thousands of people who demonstrated, the government of Iván Duque responded with repression and violence to discourage the peaceful protests and ultimately to punish those who were demanding change in the country.

Duque and Venezuela

In February 2019, Duque asserted[66] that the "dictatorship of Venezuela has very few hours left," in a photo opportunity close to the border. President Maduro, in turn, managed to tighten his control and the Colombian premier probably continues to rue his choice of words.

However, things improved…

In what may be his most important achievement, Duque's government took the unprecedented step of unilaterally granting legal status for 10 years to any refugee to have entered Colombia before January 31 2021. In what Filippo Grandi, head of the UN Refugee Agency, described as the "the most important humanitarian gesture" of the last many decades. To be sure, there were practical considerations, as Duque readily acknowledged. "We have close to a million migrants," he noted in announcing the initiative, "who are in our country whose names we don't know." For reasons of national security, public health in a time of Covid-19, law enforcement and political stability, he added, it was essential to bring all of these new arrivals out of the shadows and into the public square.

Without doubt, there was in this gesture an element of reciprocity, with memories of a time when a prosperous and functioning Venezuela welcomed tens of thousands of Colombians fleeing conflict and instability in their own country. Former defence minister Jorge Alberto Uribe (2003) described Colombia's actions as "a demonstration of humanity, solidarity and gratitude that has very little precedent in the history of the world."

Not a misunderstood statesman, but a president with no direction

Can Duque blame his misfortunes on the pandemic? Not if you consider how he squandered the first year and a half of his presidency[67]. Upon taking office, he did nothing to reduce the fiscal deficit or debt levels, which had already surpassed the dangerous threshold of 40 per cent of GDP. Once gross general government debt approached 60 per cent of GDP in 2021, Fitch downgraded Colombia's credit ratings to junk. While debt soared, the Colombian peso plummeted, losing over a third of its value against the dollar since Duque took office. Elected on a fiscally conservative platform, he governed as a tax-and-spend social democrat, thus isolating his voter base even before the pandemic began. Other emerging markets have fared similarly, but Duque failed to take any measures to protect Colombians' purchasing power from devaluation, such as allowing dollar-denominated bank accounts.

In attempt to rescue something from his floundering premiership, Duque fashioned himself as a champion for the environment, a role he continues to covet to this day. The irony has not been lost on his detractors that the president to try and re-commence aerial fumigation of coca crops with glyphosate, who presided over a period in which the largest amounts of deforestation in his home country occurred and whose government witnessed a steep increase in the killings of environmental leaders wished to be seen as an advocate for the environment.

According to a report by Global Witness[68], Colombia was found to be the deadliest country in the world with 60 deaths in total in 2022 - more than a third of all killings globally. Despite Colombia ratifying a key legally binding regional agreement in October 2022 requiring the government to prevent and investigate attacks against defenders, this figure is almost double the number of killings reported in 2021.

---

[50] Blu Radio: https://www.bluradio.com/nacion/cuando-pude-enfrentar-a-petro-le-gane-con-argumentos-y-una-defensa-solida-de-mis-ideas-duque-cb20

[51] Colombiano Indignado: https://colombianoindignado.com/duque-hace-el-ridiculo-en-paris-al-comparar-la-economia-naranja-con-los-7-enanitos/

[52] Las 2 Orillas: https://www.las2orillas.co/explicar-la-economia-naranja-con-un-jugo-de-naranja-la-ultima-ridiculez-de-duque/Trailblazers%20Latinoamericanos%20'Conectando%20Sueños%20con%20el%20Futuro'.%C2%A0

[53] The Orange Economy: https://www.google.com.co/books/edition/The_Orange_Economy/Ub-KDwAAQBAJ?hl=en&gbpv=1

[54] DW: https://www.dw.com/es/duque-en-colombia-no-hay-masacres-sino-homicidios-colectivos/a-54662098

[55] Cambio Colombia: https://cambiocolombia.com/articulo/conflicto-en-colombia/asi-ha-crecido-el-conflicto-desde-la-firma-del-acuerdo-de-paz

[56] Caracol: https://caracol.com.co/radio/2021/10/23/nacional/1635025092_911754.html

[57] France 24: https://www.france24.com/es/américa-latina/20220508-colombia-paro-armado-clan-del-golfo-otoniel-elecciones-violencia

[58] The Guardian: https://www.theguardian.com/global-development/2021/mar/11/colombia-defence-minister-children-machines-of-war-diego-molano

[59] Al Jazeera: https://www.aljazeera.com/news/2019/11/26/colombia-protests-what-prompted-them-and-where-are-they-headed

[60] Anadolu: https://www.aa.com.tr/es/mundo/al-menos-48-personas-han-muerto-en-colombia-en-35-días-de-protestas-contra-el-gobierno/2260808

[61] France 24: https://www.france24.com/es/20191126-colombia-iván-duque-invitó-al-diálogo-a-los-representantes-del-paro-nacional

[62] Science Magazine: https://www.science.org/content/article/amid-violence-and-protests-colombian-universities-seek-promote-national-dialogue

[63] Amnesty: https://www.amnesty.org/en/documents/amr23/4405/2021/en

[64] I News: https://inews.co.uk/news/world/foreign-secretary-dominic-raab-colombia-protests-1012828

[65] OHCHR: https://www.ohchr.org/en/press-releases/2022/01/colombia-must-urgently-reform-how-it-polices-protests-avoid-further-human

[66] Americas Quarterly: https://www.americasquarterly.org/article/why-colombias-president-should-change-course-on-venezuela/

[67] Derechos Humanos Colombia: https://ddhhcolombia.org.co/2021/09/21/authoritarianism-and-inequality-are-the-legacy-left-by-the-government-of-ivan-duque-marquez-human-rights-platforms/

[68] Global Witness: https://www.globalwitness.org/en/press-releases/almost-2000-land-and-environmental-defenders-killed-between-2012-and-2022-protecting-planet/

Colombia's Guerrillas

With their roots deep in the era of *La Violencia*, Colombia's rural rebel groups did not disappear overnight. In fact, many strengthened, and while political experimentation was taking place within Congress and the halls of power in Bogotá, a new equally serious threat was developing: that of the communist-inspired guerrilla. Government concerns in the early 1960s were increasingly directed towards preventing a Cuban-style inspired revolution.

1964 can be taken as a key year socio-politically since it is widely agreed that this was when the FARC guerrilla was founded. However, in order to understand the process, we should first step back into some events in the 1950s. The existing armed gangs, whether Conservative *pijaros*, Liberal guerrillas or Communist self-defence *comandantes*, recruited heavily from the unstable elements of landless or displaced populations and increasingly from the growing slums of the big cities, where the trickle of migrants had become a flood as rural depression was followed by sectarian and communal fighting. Small towns such as Ibagué in Tolima became big cities in the space of a few years as families fled from isolated rural areas. Colombia's urban population increased from 39 per cent in 1951 to 52 per cent in 1964.

The communist Fuerzas Armadas Revolucionarias de Colombia (FARC) had its origins in the Liberal self-defence guerrillas, while the Castro-ite Ejercito de Liberación Nacional (ELN), the other big armed group still in action today, was a later creation of radicalised middle-class youths dazzled by the 1958 Cuban Revolution. Their icon was Camilo Torres, a young seminarian of good family who despaired of reforming Colombia's tradition-bound society by peaceful means and took to the hills with a handful of followers. He was killed in his first encounter with the army, but the ELN and his legend lives on to this day. Other groups such as the Movimiento 19 de Abril (M-19) took up arms later but entered a culture of political violence which had its roots in earlier decades.

Contemporary Colombia has been plagued by various ills, and at one stage there were a myriad of different groups, but it seems appropriate to focus on just a few, not least the rise of the leftist inspired guerrillas such as the ELN (Ejercito de Liberación Nacional founded in 1964), the EPL (Ejercito Popular de Liberación 1967-1991) and the FARC (Fuerzas Armadas Revolucionarias de Colombia founded in 1964-2016) and the M19 (Movimiento 19 de Abril 1970-1990) all aimed at toppling the Colombian state.

The M19 and much of the FARC and EPL have now laid down their weapons and some of the former members have moved into formal politics. But there was a stage when all groups had the capacity to shock and instil a reign of terror in Colombia. The M19 were responsible for some very high profile and symbolic actions such as the theft of a sword that belonged to Simón Bolívar, the siege of the Dominican Embassy in Bogotá and then lastly the bloody siege of the Palace of Justice in 1985. Many of the former combatants moved across into the rank and file of the ELN and FARC.

Dissident factions of the former FARC and the ELN – having shown little or no real desire to negotiate peace - still remain to this day - controlling areas of land, taxing businesses and landowners and controlling important drug routes in Colombia but they are not at the same strength as previously. The ELN, which in 2023 is estimated to number more 3200 men, has grown in recent years, consolidating power in the power vacuum left behind by the FARC after the peace accord reached in 2016 and actively recruiting Venezuelans desperate for work. The group is currently involved in peace dialogues with the government of President Petro.

The FARC

A Human Rights aberration

The FARC is among the groups responsible for "continuing homicides, threats, attacks, information theft, illegal surveillance and intimidation targeting human rights defenders and their organisations in different parts of the country" (UN 3 Feb. 2011, para. 10). The report further attributes "disappearances, confinement, forced displacement indiscriminate attacks through the use of anti-personnel mines" and "acts of sexual violence" to the FARC (ibid., para. 70).

Drug trafficking

According to academics Sanín and Giustozzi[69], the FARC's involvement in "the coca business" was "very strong" and "credible" and evidence suggests the guerrillas have been "actively engaging in the protection of crops, the processing of the product, and its exportation" since the 1990s (2010, 846). This is further corroborated by Rochlin[70], who notes that a number of factors suggest the group's "significant participation in narcotrafficking," including its "clear control over areas of [coca] cultivation, its political representation of coca growers, together with its admission of involvement in this illicit and highly profitable industry" (Aug. 2010, 735). Similarly, reports are indicating that the FARC "became more and more of a drug trafficking organization, and that they sustain themselves in this way, although they remain ideological" (Mar. 2011, 11). The International Crisis Group also mention's FARC's involvement in drug trafficking through Panama, Venezuela and Brazil, as well as along the Pacific (29 June 2010, 7).

Kidnapping

In a watershed moment for Colombia's transitional justice system in May 2021, which stems from the 2016 peace agreement between the government and the FARC, former guerrillas Pastor Alape and Julián Gallo became the first former combatants to officially own up to their crimes of kidnapping. Over an hour-long live-streamed press conference, they outlined the former Marxist guerrilla's response to the first indictment unveiled in late January 2021 by the Special Jurisdiction for Peace (known by Colombians as the JEP), which indicted them and six other FARC leaders.

In their public statement and their written response, former FARC leaders accepted the majority of the conclusions presented by the JEP's Judicial Panel for Acknowledgment in its 322-page[71] document indictment on thousands of kidnappings committed between 1990 and 2012.

Members of the FARC's secretariat admitted publicly and in front of their victims that they gave the orders to kidnap at least 21,396 people throughout the country between 1990 and 2015[72], and that they failed to control their subordinates, who subjected them to all kinds of humiliations.

One of the JEP's most striking revelations was how many kidnappings had tragic endings: at least 627 victims (2,9 per cent of the total) were murdered and another 1,860 (8,7 per cent) are still registered as missing.

1998

The Revolutionary Armed Forces of Colombia, during its zenith in 1998, counted approximately on 18,000 combatants. When, in 1998 the then President Andrés Pastrana granted the FARC a safe haven at San Vicente del Caguán for peace talks, an area the size of Switzerland in south-western Colombia, it was widely believed to have been used as an opportunity to rearm, regroup and recruit further guerrilla forces. The talks themselves were a total failure and the FARC emerged more powerful and active than before.

In the latter half of the 2000s, in particular in 2008, the FARC took some severe hits, not only due to then President Uribe's (2002-2010) policies, but also due to the FARC second in command Raúl Reyes being killed in an illegal bombing raid by Colombian forces in Ecuadorian territory, the death by natural causes of the FARC leader and ideologist Manuel *"Tirofijo"* Marulanda and then the killing of FARC commander in chief Alfonso Cano in 2011. Add this to the daring rescue of the captive and former presidential candidate Ingrid Betancourt and three American contractors in Operation Check Mate (*Operación Jaque*).

The FARC guerrillas saw their territory decrease and their influence wane somewhat also with the rise of the right-wing paramilitary groups and with total public disenchantment with the guerrilla group. The time was right for peace negotiations and these came about during the government of President Juan Manuel Santos, who was later awarded the Nobel Prize for Peace for his efforts.

---

[69] Research gate: https://www.researchgate.net/publication/233315618_Networks_and_Armies_Structuring_Rebellion_in_Colombia_and_Afghanistan

[70] EPP: https://epp.ok.ubc.ca/about/contact/james-rochlin/

[71] Jep: https://www.jep.gov.co/Sala-de-Prensa/Documents/CASO%2001%20TOMA%20DE%20REHENES/Auto%20No.%2019%20de%202021.pdf?csf=1&e=16bYs0

[72] Justice Info: https://www.justiceinfo.net/en/76928-kidnappings-colombia-farc-leaders-acknowledge-full-responsibility.html

Peace with the FARC

Colombia's Twisted and Bumpy Road to Peace by Andrei Gómez-Suárez[73]

On 24 November 2016, the government of Juan Manuel Santos (2010-2018) and the Revolutionary Armed Forces of Colombia (FARC-EP) guerrilla group signed the most comprehensive peace agreement in the world to date. It took four years of negotiations in Havana, Cuba. The 310-page Final Peace Agreement (FPA) encompasses five key issues: (1) redistribution of land and modernization of the countryside, (2) broadening political participation to include the most affected regions of the armed conflict and reforms to create a fairer political system, (3) reincorporation of the FARC-EP into social and economic civilian life and their transformation into a political party (with ad hoc stipulations to grant the party participation guarantees until 2026), (4) a national program of coca crop substitution together with a criminal policy to crack down on drug-trafficking and money laundering, (5) truth, justice, reparations and guarantees of non-recurrence for the victims of the armed conflict, based on perpetrators' acknowledgements of past wrongdoings and their commitment to carry out actions to restore the social fabric, paving the way for peaceful coexistence. Implementation of these stipulations is to be monitored by different institutions, such as the United Nations, the Kroc Institute for International Peace Studies at the University of Notre Dame, and new coordination mechanisms integrated by the two negotiating parties.

Implementation of this ambitious peace accord started soon after it was signed in Bogotá's historic Teatro Colón, but the country was split into two. The road to peace had been bumpy. Since 2012, the negotiations had faced staunch opposition by former president Álvaro Uribe (2002-2010), at the time the most popular political figure in the country because of his success in weakening the FARC-EP militarily. Santos was Uribe's candidate in 2010, but the gap between them grew when Santos' policy shifted towards negotiations with the FARC-EP, instead of exclusively seeking a military victory. In 2013, Uribe created the Centro Democrático party (CD) to contest Santos' peace policy. In 2014, the CD ran against Santos in the presidential elections, but a broad pro-peace coalition gave Santos a narrow victory for a second term in office, based on a peace ticket. However, the CD won 20 per cent of the seats in Congress, and from there they continued and reinforced their opposition to the peace process. They circulated fake news, such as telling Colombians that Santos was a former commander of the FARC-EP, via the national media and multiple social media platforms, seeking to undermine public trust in the negotiations. The mainstream media gave them a platform, from which they disseminated lies about the negotiations, supposedly out of a duty to guarantee freedom of speech.

In August 2016, the negotiation parties agreed to put the peace accord to a referendum for Colombians to have the final say before starting implementation. The campaign lasted a month. Civil society committees were created in favour (Yes) and against (No) the peace accord. Civil servants and state institutions were forbidden to campaign formally. Under Uribe's leadership, the CD fired up anti-peace emotions, using slogans which simplified reality and fostered fear and anger; these included the idea that the peace accord was going to turn Colombia "castrochavista" and that the accord was going to provide impunity for crimes committed by the FARC, calling instead for "peace without impunity". They claimed that "Gender Ideology" was encrypted in the peace accord, which sought to destroy the traditional Colombian family (this was a lie: in fact, Colombia's peace accord was the first worldwide to have a gender focus which created measures to tackle the disproportionate impact of the conflict on women and LGTBI communities). 63 per cent of Colombians abstained from the polls, but 50.2 per cent of those who voted, rejected the peace accord. Thus, the idea of a comprehensive peace was shattered into pieces and implementation ground to a halt. Santos and the FARC-EP re-opened negotiations, received 60 proposals of amendment from the No-promoters, and drafted the FPA which included 58 of these 60 proposals. It was approved by Congress on 30th November 2016, and implementation began on 1 December.

Santos spent his last eighteen months in power defending the FPA against its detractors, many of them in Congress. With a weakened pro-peace political coalition, implementation of the FPA was trapped in the run-up to the 2018 presidential elections. During this time, previously incredulous allies of the peace process, such as former vice president Germán Vargas Lleras, became staunch critics of the FPA. As a result, many stipulations contained in the FPA, such as 16 congressional seats for communities from war-torn regions were rejected by Congress. However, the disarmament of the FARC-EP and its transformation into a political party was fulfilled in record time. In July 2017, the UN certified completion of the decommissioning of weapons, and transferred the containers keeping the arms to secure locations in Colombia and abroad, to be used to make three commemorative monuments - in Colombia, Cuba, and the US. Colombian artist Doris Salcedo, winner of 2019 Nomura Art Award, was commissioned to make the one in Colombia. On 10 December 2018, she inaugurated "Fragmentos", a "counter-monument" 500 meters from the Casa de Nariño, Colombia's presidential palace. Neither the FARC nor the Colombian president attended the opening.

By then, the Fuerzas Armadas Revolucionarias de Colombia-Ejército del Pueblo had mutated into the Fuerza Alternativa Revolucionaria del Común Party (Alternative Revolutionary Force of the Commons, FARC), launched in the iconic Plaza de Bolívar amongst 15,000 attendees in September 2017. This opened the path for the participation of the FARC Party in the 2018 parliamentary and presidential elections. Rodrigo Londoño, alias Timoleón Jiménez, former commander in chief of the FARC-EP, was invested as the presidential candidate of the FARC Party; his political slogan was "Timo, President with the force of common people." His campaign lasted until March 2018, when he withdrew from the contest because of the lack of security guarantees. Demonstrations and attacks against him in many cities showed that many Colombians were not ready for reconciliation, despite public apologies by FARC-EP commanders for their acts of atrocity in towns such as Bojayá, Apartadó, Granada and Cali, and Londoño's own words apologising to all victims in September 2016, on the occasion of the signing of the first, rejected peace accord in Cartagena. Colombians were deeply angry with the FARC-EP, and their anger was projected onto the FPA and its implementation.

Iván Duque, a young bureaucrat, former employee of Santos, was chosen by Uribe to join the CD in 2013. With no experience in politics, Duque was elected Senator in 2014. In 2016, he was one of the most prominent spokesmen of the CD in the staunch campaign against the peace accord, and in the renegotiation after the Referendum. In December 2017, Duque was elected as the CD's presidential candidate, and then in March 2018, a broad political coalition, including the CDP and the Conservative Party, chose him as their leader. Duque's political coalition centred the 2018 election campaign on the idea of reforming the FPA. In June 2018, Duque won the presidency, beating Gustavo Petro, a former M-19 guerrilla member who had been mayor of Bogotá. The CD triumphed thanks to their projection of the spectre of "Castrochavismo" onto Petro, the fact that traditional political elites such as Vargas Lleras aligned with them, and substantial vote-buying in the Atlantic coast and elsewhere. On 7 August 2018, Duque was invested as president of Colombia. By then, according to the Kroc Institute's monitoring reports, 23 per cent of the FPA's stipulations had been fully implemented, and the Constitutional Court had ruled that the next three administrations were obliged to implement the peace agreement.

The first half of the Duque administration was disastrous for peacebuilding in Colombia. 216 ex FARC-EP members signatories of the FPA were assassinated between December 2016 and July 2020, 75 per cent during Duque's presidency. 2019 saw the highest number of human rights violations since 2008. Duque convened the National Commission of Security Guarantees, created by the FPA, twice, to deal with this challenge. The reform of the political system and the broadening of political participation beyond that of the FARC Party ground to a halt. The stipulations regarding land redistribution and modernization of the countryside, and the program for coca crop substitution have faced serious delays; to the extent that Kroc's fourth report warns that it is likely that these reforms will not be implemented in the 15-year timeframe established in the FPA. The transitional justice institutions, agreed in point five, suffered staunch opposition by the government.

Duque not only tried to cut their budget, but also attempted to reform the Special Jurisdiction for Peace (JEP), the institution in charge of holding perpetrators of grave human rights crimes on both sides of the conflict accountable. The CD also became the biggest party in Congress in congressional elections in 2018, and continuously tried to derail implementation too, though a broad pro-peace coalition managed to keep it on track. However, Duque's coalition found new partners among traditional elites, building a majority to approve bills going against the FPA. In this worrying context, the coordination mechanisms between the FARC Party and the government stopped working, and the parties grew further away than ever.

In June 2020, Kroc's fourth report summarized the state of implementation as follows: the general implementation of FPA stipulations had advanced six per cent in 2019, which means that overall only 25 per cent of stipulations had been fully implemented since the signing of the peace agreement, two per cent during the Duque administration. Even this two per cent was mostly due to the work of institutions with autonomy from the government, such as the Special Jurisdiction for Peace and the Truth Commission.

The future for sustainable peace in Colombia is uncertain. The obstacles in implementation have fractured the FARC, deepened civil society's distrust in the state, and radicalized the political agendas of armed actors.

Iván Márquez, the former chief negotiator of the FARC, returned to the armed struggle in August 2019. Meanwhile, Colombia's last remaining guerrilla group, the National Liberation Army (ELN) expanded in various regions of Colombia, the army began to return to counterinsurgency tactics and body count incentives, a perverse practice of the past, and paramilitary groups together with criminal groups flourished, working together to control drug-trafficking routes and protect the economic interests of a variety of legal and illegal actors across the country. According to the Conflict Analysis Resource Centre, political violence increased 55 per cent in the first semester of 2020, compared to the same period in 2019.

However, in the unfolding of what seems to be a new phase of the armed conflict, there is still hope. Multiple pro-peace civil society organizations have defended the FPA with great creativity, and have in fact lobbied for a negotiated solution to the armed conflict since the 1980s. The winds of change brought by the Santos-FARC negotiations reinvigorated these organizations and brought to life new initiatives, and together they have sought to reach broader sectors of Colombian society.

Transnational civil society network Embrace Dialogue[74] (or Rodeemos el Diálogo in Spanish) holds weekly "peace breakfasts" to help Colombians discover the power of a culture of dialogue based on six principles: respect, honesty, solidarity, co-responsibility, honesty and self-criticism, which together offer opportunities for a renewed moral imagination.

Defendamos la Paz is a powerful political platform in which leaders of different parties, including the FARC Party, and diverse sectors of society, carry out mass political demonstrations in favour of peace, showing Colombians that it is possible to work together despite different ideologies for a country without political violence. These are just two examples of the potential for peaceful change in Colombia.

The road to peace is not straightforward, but it is worth walking, if Colombia can discover it before the end of the journey.

---

[73] Andrei Gomez-Suarez is the author of Genocide, Geopolitics and Transnational Networks (Routledge, 2015) and El Triunfo del No (Icono, 2016). He has published widely on the armed conflict in Colombia and the peace process between the government and the Revolutionary Armed Forces of Colombia (FARC).

[74] Rodeemos el Dialogo: https://rodeemoseldialogo.org/

The ELN

The *Ejército Nacional de Liberación* or the National Liberation Army is another Colombian left-wing group which was formed in 1964 by intellectuals inspired by the Cuban revolution and Marxist ideology. It should be seen as more politically motivated than the FARC, to begin with, initially staying out of the illegal drugs trade on ideological grounds.

The ELN reached the height of its power in the late 1990s, carrying out hundreds of kidnappings and hitting infrastructure such as oil pipelines. By 2016, the ELN's ranks had declined from around 4,000 to an estimated 1,500 to 2,000, suffering defeats at the hands of the security forces and paramilitaries.

Recently though, with the troubles affecting Venezuela, the ELN's ranks have grown with desperate nationals of that country joining up in need of work. In order to raise money, in recent years ELN units have become involved in the drugs trade, often forming alliances with criminal gangs. The group is on US and European lists of terrorist organisations. Shortly after the FARC entered into peace talks with the Colombian government in November 2012, the ELN leader said that his group was also interested in negotiating a deal with the government.

The group was rebuffed by President Santos, who said it needed to show actions rather than words before it could sit down at the negotiating table. In what was perhaps a cynical move by President Santos at the time, in the days preceding the second-round vote in the 2014 presidential elections, the government leaked "news" that the ELN was prepared to come to the negotiating table. Colombians, buoyed by successful on-going talks with the FARC voted in favour of a government pursuing peace and President Santos won the elections by a narrow margin.

Talks with the ELN did begin but were, on again off again, in the Ecuadorian capital of Quito, under the patronage of then Ecuadorian President Rafael Correa (2007-17). The ELN is highly decentralized, and does not have the strict military hierarchy that facilitated a relatively smooth demobilization of the FARC in 2017.

Each of the ELN's war fronts has a high level of autonomy and tell the Central Command what to do rather than the other way around. The January 2019 terrorist attack on a police school in Bogotá exemplifies how the autonomy of regional units can undermine peace talks conducted by the Central Command at any time.

The claim made by the government of President Iván Duque that the Central Command was responsible for this bombing completely ignores the bottom-up nature of the ELN and should be questioned. This attack, that killed 22 police cadets, was allegedly carried out by a unit of the Eastern War Front, which is commanded by *"Pablito,"* one of the ELN's most cynical members who would believe that almost any peace deal implies submission to the centralized power structure of the State. Talks broke down irreparably and there were no negotiations planned during Duque's tenure.

With the election of Petro as president, his cornerstone policy of *Paz Total* was swung into action with alacrity and within months, negotiations were agreed. By mid 2024, seven rounds of dialogues had taken place. Questions remain on whether there can be a full and sustainable peace with the ELN since each faction is autonomous and reports show that the ELN has significant authority over both legal and illegal mining projects throughout Venezuela…why would an organization involved in such a lucrative industry willingly give up this income?

Reality of Peace Negotiations with the ELN

The ELN's leadership, who are old and haven't been in combat situations for many years, arguably has no particular interest in a peace agreement. The Petro government's strategy should be to make the ceasefire something that the ELN's rank-and-file could get used to, to the point where the leadership can't easily restart the war.

It is difficult to see a key commander such as Pablito agreeing to a peace deal and demobilizing which will force him to give up a large and lucrative set of illicit operations in Colombia and Venezuela. For, as long as Venezuela is a safe haven for the ELN the group will exist and continue engaging in lucrative illicit activities such as coca cropping, cocaine trafficking, petroleum theft, illegal gold mining, extortion and kidnapping.

Most wouldn't bet on success but why not try it? It's not as if the ELN has been under relentless pressure such that a cease fire would give them space to recover. They are a disciplined group with the modest goal of survival--no hubris about territorial control or a parallel state, which is what made the FARC vulnerable to Uribe. That makes them harder to deal with both militarily and via negotiations, but holding the latter to a standard of success that the former hasn't come close to meeting seems a little tendentious to me. And why not indulge the ELN in its fantasy that involving "civil society" would being allies to the table rather than people who think they're nuts?

Initially the ELN planned to overturn the Colombian state, install a socialist government and collectivize the means of production. The group is based on the Cuban nationalist revolutionary model used by Castro and the ELN's founders were trained in Cuba by the Castro regime.

By 1975 the ELN had been effectively neutralised by the Colombian military and was no longer able to defeat the Colombian state militarily nor instigate a broad societal revolution. At heat time it adopted a lower key guerrilla model aimed at sewing violence and intimidation to force social change.

Since then the ELN has gradually morphed into an organised criminal group with the political leadership becoming increasingly distant from the commanders on the ground where profits became more important than revolutionary ideology.

That saw parts of the ELN splinter with the more radical ideologically driven undertaking acts independently of commanders in Colombia and the leadership in Havana. At this time the ELN is largely irrelevant but the Colombian military and police have proven incapable of defeating the group.

What will likely happen if there is a peace agreement and demobilization various ELN elements in Colombia will continue their "struggle", which will be funded by coca cropping, extortion, kidnapping and illegal gold mining, with no ideological direction much like various FARC dissident groups.

Colombia has tried through to win a guerrilla war with the ELN and it hasn't worked — not since 1975 if we're talking specifically about the ELN. How can a group that doesn't recognise the government and that claims that it does not want to enter politics, actually serious negotiate a lasting and sustainable peace?

Petro, at the very least is trying a different method, even if optimism towards it is limited.

Paramilitary Groups

Started initially by landowners intent on defending their property and grouping together these fragmented paramilitary groups, over time, found that they could better finance themselves with a slice of the lucrative cocaine trade. The AAA (American Anti-Communist Alliance) founded in 1978 and disbanded in 1979 allegedly had its roots and strong ties within the Colombian Armed Forces. CONVIVIR from 1994-1998 was a formally created government supported neighbourhood watch scheme that gradually corrupted and moved into paramilitary activities before being disbanded.

"In 1989, Human Rights Watch75 wrote that although we could not prove that Colombia's military high command directly ordered paramilitaries to commit atrocities, it should be obvious that their response to these atrocities "to close ranks and avoid and frequently to obstruct any serious investigation" compromised their obligation to uphold the rule of law. We concluded that the failure to investigate and prosecute military officers who have joined with paramilitaries to commit murders and mass murder indicated, at the very least, that their superiors had chosen to tolerate these crimes."

The AUC (United Self Defence Forces of Colombia) was formed in 1997 and became the umbrella group for all paramilitary actions before nominally surrendering its arms in an agreement forged with the government of Álvaro Uribe.

The most substantial rise in paramilitary massacres during the conflict took place between 1996 and 2003, accounting for 5057 victims. This period alone represented 69.58 per cent of all victims from such events in the paramilitary conflict up to 2012. At the department level, Antioquia bore the brunt of paramilitary violence during this observed period, suffering 2232 murders in massacres between 1980 and 2012. It was followed by Santander (526), Cesar (494), Bolivar (456), Norte de Santander (455), Magdalena (399), Valle del Cauca (386), Meta (325), Cauca (275), and Cordoba (253). Antioquia alone accounted for 30.74 per cent of the victims of massacres committed by paramilitary groups in that period, along with Santander (7.26 per cent), Cesar (6.8 per cent), Bolivar (6.3 per cent), Norte de Santander (6.9 per cent), Magdalena (5.5 per cent), Valle del Cauca (5.3 per cent), Meta (4.5 per cent), Cauca (3.8 per cent), and Cordoba (3.5 per cent). Those ten departments encompassed 79.71 per cent of the massacre victims recorded between 1980 and 2012[76].

In December 2002, the AUC declared a unilateral cease-fire, thus meeting a significant pre-condition for entering into formal peace talks with the Colombian government. Negotiations commenced in July 2003 in the town of Santa Fe de Ralito (Córdoba). Shortly thereafter, the Colombian government announced that it had reached an agreement with AUC leaders that would result in the demobilization of its members by the end of 2005.

The first demobilization occurred in November 2003 when 855 members of the Cacique Nutibara Bloc, which operated in Medellín laid down their arms. The Bananero, Cundinamarca, Catatumbo, and Calima blocs also demobilized by the end of 2004, totalling approximately 4,000 paramilitaries since the first demobilization in late 2003. Subsequent demobilizations occurred through 2004 and into 2005.

Members of the AUC have been tried and found guilty of heinous crimes such as massacres including *Operación Orion*77(2002), El Salado (1997) and more, employing death squads, drugs running and torture and many of its former members have been extradited to the United States on various charges. In 2020, one of the most feared paramilitary commanders, Jorge 40 (Rodrigo Tovar Pupo), who oversaw the Bloque Norte of the armed group and controlled regions from Santander in central Colombia all the way into the Guajira department, finished his sentence in the US and was returned to Colombia.

While the AUC supposedly started as a counterbalance to the left-wing guerrilla groups, it became a criminal group[78] in its own right charging for protection and extorting from civilians and the issue of demobilizing but remaining armed, has caused significant problems. In 2007[79] it was revealed that the international fruit company Chiquita brands had been paying the AUC to protect its interests in Colombia.

In 2006 the bulk of the AUC laid down their weapons in an agreement reached with President Uribe and demobilised but this by no means signalled the end of paramilitary activities as smaller less focussed groups sprung up in the vacuum. The biggest and most effective of the groups to appear after the demobilization of the AUC were at first the Águilas Negras.

The Águilas Negras, like their offspring including the Pelusos, the Urabeños, the Puntilleros, the older Ejército Popular de Liberación (EPL) the Gaitanistas also known as the Clan del Golfo have all been implicated in drug trafficking, extortions, racketeering, murder, disappearances and kidnappings.

Targeted violence has increased dramatically in strategic area of the country including border regions with Venezuela, the department of Cauca and the Pacific coast port cities of Buenaventura and Tumaco as groups seek to gain important footholds. There have been reports that these newly formed criminal gangs (Bacrim in the Spanish acronyms or GAO *grupos armados organizados*) and the FARC dissidents have been working with the Sinaloa and Nuevo Jalisco cartels from Mexico.

The AGC, Gaitanistas or Clan del Golfo

As of 2024, the Clan del Golfo (AGC) is Colombia's most powerful drug trafficking organization, a force with control over a massive swathe of the country and the most important routes for moving cocaine to the United States. Danilo Rueda, Petro's government's peace commissioner, said Colombia does not consider the AGC to be "political" because its goal is not to "subvert the constitutional order." In a statement, he described the group's influence as a type of criminal "governance" for social control and the "protection and generation of wealth." But governance, he said, does not classify a group as a political entity.

According to Colombian authorities and human rights defenders, the AGC has cemented its control through forced displacement, extortion, killings of police officers and recruitment of minors. They say it profits from illegal mining and dominates the country's drug distribution networks by supplying cocaine to Mexican cartels although their claim is that they only tax the cartels.

To maintain control over AGC territory, the group, numbering more than 6000, employs an army of *"sicarios,"* or hitmen, who carry out acts of violence, including murders, assaults, kidnappings, torture, and assassinations against competitors and those deemed traitors to the organization, as well as their family members. The AGC has murdered and assaulted Colombian law enforcement officers, Colombian military personnel, rival drug traffickers and paramilitaries, potential witnesses, and civilians. The group uses violence to promote and enhance the reputation, and position of the AGC with respect to rival criminal organizations; preserve, protect, and expand the AGC's power and territory; finance the AGC's operations and enrich its leaders through the collection of drug debts; maintain discipline among its members and associates; and protect AGC members from arrest and prosecution by attempting to silence potential witnesses and retaliating against law enforcement authorities and those assisting law enforcement.

---

[75] Human Rights Watch: https://www.hrw.org/legacy/summaries/s.colombia9611.html

[76] https://doi.org/10.3390/socsci13020112

[77] Comisión de la Verdad: https://www.comisiondelaverdad.co/el-violento-engranaje-de-la-operacion-orion

[78] Oil Price: https://oilprice.com/Energy/Crude-Oil/Ecopetrol-Guerillas-and-Death-Squads-The-War-for-Colombias-Oil.html

[79] Insight Crime: https://insightcrime.org/news/demobilized-disarmed-colombia-paramilitaries-continue-extorting/

Narcotics Trade

Unfortunately, coffee is not Colombia's most recognized national product and the international cocaine industry has brought an ill-fame to the country. In the 1980s the most famous name in international narco-terrorism culture can only be that of Pablo Escobar (1949-1993) who ran the Medellín cartel and instilled fear on the streets of that city before being gunned down on a city rooftop in his native city. Carlos Lehder, Escobar's only surviving associate was released from prison in the US in June 2020 and according to reports, by virtue of his father's German nationality, decided to live out his remaining years there.

During Escobar's terrible reign, he was directly responsible for the assassination of presidential candidate Luis Carlos Galán in 1989, car bombing campaigns against newspapers, the bombing of a commercial airliner and the Palace of Justice siege orchestrated by the M19.

The Medellín cartel however was not alone in its nefarious activities and the rival Cali cartel run by the Orejuela brothers was just as astonishing in its cruelty and violence and was called by one US law enforcement agent, "the biggest, most powerful crime syndicate".

As a result of this rivalry between the Medellín and Cali cartels, a paramilitary group known as Los Pepes, a name derived from the Spanish phrase *"Los Perseguidos por Pablo Escobar"* ("The Persecuted by Pablo Escobar"), was started.

They waged a small-scale war against the Medellín Cartel in 1993, which ended the same year following the death of Escobar. Then there was the MAS (Muerte a Secuestradores or Death to Kidnappers) which was created alongside the Cali drug cartel and dissidents from Los Pepes. MAS was supported by drug cartels, US corporations, politicians and wealthy landowners. In 1984, the Association of Middle Magdalena Ranchers and

Farmers (ACDEGAM) was created to handle the logistics and public relations of MAS and to act as a legal front for them. Anyone who was against the interests of ACDEGAM was attacked by MAS. MAS killed hundreds of Union Patriotica members, a political party with ties to the FARC, and M-19 allied party members of the Democratic Alliance. It also killed community leaders, elected officials and farmers. According to a news source, it was also responsible for disappearances.

Currently there are still cartels in operation in Colombia, albeit less extravagant and less visible to those in the 1980s but equally as powerful and internationally renowned. Given the enormous financial gains associated with the cocaine trade it remains unlikely that this trade will ever peter out and as one cartel head is assassinated, captured or extradited another quickly springs up in his place.

Until the peace accords with the FARC which culminated in 2016, successive governments had agreed to aerial fumigations of the coca cultivations. One of the terms in the peace accord was that aerial fumigation be prohibited. As of mid 2020, fumigations were still suspended although the government of President Duque sought to renew the process in a hat-tip to the requirements being asked of him by President Trump and his new phase on the war on drugs. President Petro ensured that any use of aerial spraying of glyphosate to eradicate coca was totally outlawed.

Unfortunately, The United Nations Office on Drugs and Crime (UNODC)[80] said that potential coca production had risen by 24 per cent since 2021. The area planted with coca bushes rose by 13 per cent, and the biggest increase was recorded in Colombia's border areas.

Almost two-thirds of the coca crops are found in the provinces of Nariño and Putumayo, which border Ecuador, and in Norte de Santander, on the Venezuelan border.

Unfortunately, the illegal trade in coca is not going anywhere and continues to cause major problems in Colombia. The area planted with coca bushes in Colombia reached a record high in 2022, an annual UN report says.

The United Nations Office on Drugs and Crime (UNODC) said that potential coca production had risen by 24 per cent since 2021 and then in September 2023, Bloomberg[81] published an article claiming that cocaine is set to overtake oil as Colombia's principal export. While the figures may cut corners, there is always cause for concern with regards to this industry and how headlines of this nature might affect the relationship between the US and Colombia.

---

[80] UNODC: https://www.unodc.org/colombia/es/el-cultivo-de-coca-alcanzo-niveles-historicos-en-colombia-con-204-000-hectareas-registradas-en-2021.html

[81] bLOMMBERG: https://www.bloomberg.com/news/articles/2023-09-14/cocaine-is-set-to-overtake-oil-to-become-colombia-s-main-export#xj4y7vzkg

Total Peace

Total Peace, a cornerstone of President Gustavo Petro's government policy.
Can Colombia's President Achieve 'Total Peace'?

Gustavo Petro wants to solve 70-odd years of conflict in his four-year term. Here are the obstacles he'll face.

By Richard McColl for Foreign Policy magazine

November 8, 2022

Riding a wave of optimism and high favourability ratings in his first three months in office, Gustavo Petro, Colombia's first leftist president, wants to solve 70-odd years of conflict in his four-year term. At least, this is his high-risk, high-reward plan of *paz total*, or total peace.

Petro, an economist and former guerrilla fighter, has set his sights on signing peace agreements with as many of the 26-armed groups active in Colombia as possible. For many Colombians, the idea of lasting peace in a country so accustomed to conflict is unthinkable. But now that the National Liberation Army (ELN), one of the country's oldest and largest guerrilla groups, has announced that peace dialogues with the Colombian government will commence as early as November, total peace may not seem as outlandish as it once did.

On Oct. 26, Colombia's Congress approved the Petro administration's plan for total peace, allowing the government to negotiate with illegal armed groups. Petro's plan, which rests on the premise that peace should be state policy, aims to address the interrelated problems of armed groups, drug trafficking, coca cultivation, illegal mining, land ownership, and environmental degradation. Among the plan's minutiae are promises that the government will suspend the capture of members of armed groups and offer benefits, such as reduced sentences and a guarantee of no extradition, to members who reveal information on narcotrafficking routes and hand over earnings from illegal sources, such as cocaine trafficking.

Similar to the 2016 peace accords with the Revolutionary Armed Forces of Colombia (FARC), Petro plans to put the communities most affected by the conflict and the presence of armed groups at the centre of negotiations. His administration has proposed a "fund for peace" to ensure there is lasting and sustainable investment in those regions—something noticeably absent during the term of former President Iván Duque, who was elected in 2018 on the premise of "ripping the 2016 peace accords to shreds."

Duque's plan was to pursue "peace with legality," ramping up militarization to secure peace. His government was not able to tear up the accords, but it did make them less effective. As data collected by the Institute for Development and Peace Studies, a Colombian think tank, shows, insecurity and violence in the country increased over his term. In 2018, Duque inherited a Colombia that had seen 95 percent of the FARC's 13,000 combatants sign the peace agreement, turn over their weapons, and reintegrate into society; when he left office, 30 different FARC dissident groups—made up of former FARC guerrillas who declined to sign the agreement—had spread across the country, controlling much more territory than they had at the start of his term.

The question now is whether Petro's government, unlike his predecessor's, can achieve cease-fires with all groups involved. Analysts have their reservations. "It's extremely ambitious," said Kyle Johnson, a co-founder and researcher at the Conflict Responses Foundation, a research organization in Bogotá. While local armed groups might get involved, he said, it's unlikely the big ones, such as the ELN, or FARC dissidents will completely demobilize. "You can come to agreements with the leadership, and they'll bring along a large chunk [of members] but not everyone," he said. Likewise, Sergio Guzmán, the director of the consultancy Colombia Risk Analysis, worries about Petro "overpromising and underdelivering."

Domestically, Petro's government will face three major challenges in reaching total peace. First, it will need to guarantee that the most at-risk sectors of Colombian society, such as the inhabitants of territories controlled by armed groups, can gain access to basic human rights such as health care, running water, and education. Investing in these communities would reduce the number of Colombians joining armed groups out of desperation from a lack of opportunities. But an implementation of this size across Colombia's complex topography and poor infrastructure would require a huge budget and political will, which will be tough for a coalition government.

Second, the government will have to negotiate with all armed actors, including ELN guerrillas, dissident FARC guerrillas, drug cartels, and post-paramilitary groups (offshoots from the paramilitary groups formed in the 1990s and 2000s) such as the Clan del Golfo. The government will have to offer a variety of different concessions, such as political participation, to the politically minded ELN, as well as guarantees of no extradition to groups heavily involved in contraband.

Already, Petro's many detractors, such as the opposition Democratic Centre party, doubt the motives of the 10 groups that have so far announced intentions to negotiate, suggesting that the government's plan rewards criminals with impunity and will lead to further lawlessness. The opposition points to the ELN as a perfect example of this, since the guerrilla group has negotiated unsuccessfully with as many as seven different presidents.

Third, the government will need to reform the police and the armed forces. For years, Colombians have associated both institutions with human rights abuses and brutality. Public perception of security forces worsened after police killed 47 civilians during nationwide protests in 2021, as the nongovernmental organization *Temblores* reported. But it's the military, in particular, that is in desperate need of an overhaul. The armed forces have continued to remain bogged down in the metrics of the past, measuring success by captured guerrillas, kills, and hectares of coca plantations eradicated.

Petro has made it clear that the military's successes will now be measured by "lives saved." He wants to transform the military into a force that keeps Colombians safer from exploitation and harm, reduces assassinations by mafias and armed groups, and protects and supports the families that grow coca but have signed up to switch to growing legal crops.

Yet there is considerable scepticism that Petro can make significant changes to the country's security forces, which are suspicious of the president's past. "Look at who Petro is. He has the burden of being a former combatant," Guzmán said, referring to Petro's time as a member of the M-19 guerrilla movement.

Petro's pick for defence minister, the jurist Iván Velásquez, has only set off more alarm bells within the police and the military. Velásquez, who is tasked with restructuring both institutions, is known in Colombia for coordinating investigations into links between paramilitary groups and members of the Colombian Congress between 2006 and 2012 and then later heading the International Commission Against Impunity in Guatemala. It's only natural that the military and police eye him with suspicion. Yet, in a press conference on Oct. 31, Velásquez stated that active military members should be involved in peace negotiations since they understand the nature of the conflict on the ground. This olive branch suggests that the government may have a chance at assuaging the concerns of high-ranking members of the armed forces, but it will be an uphill battle.

Outside of Colombia, there's the issue of neighbouring Venezuela. Under President Nicolás Maduro, the Venezuelan government has given ELN guerrillas tacit approval to control vast swaths of land inside Venezuela, since they provide security for the regime in those regions, and to oversee lucrative illegal mining projects in the country. If an ELN demobilization includes forces on Venezuelan soil—which would be necessary for its success—Bogotá will need the support of Caracas to negotiate with those forces and verify that they are sticking to the agreement.

Last week, a meeting between Petro and Maduro—the first high-level meeting between the two countries in six years—resulted in a joint statement to work together on peace, commercial interests, the shared border, and environmental security. Yet, after years of distrust and the countries not having a diplomatic relationship, this declaration can only be seen as a starting point for reconciliation between the two.

Furthermore, any negotiation with Venezuela raises suspicions in international circles. As Guzmán put it, "Venezuela has no place in the international community." In October, U.S. Secretary of State Antony Blinken met with Petro on a visit to Colombia. Ostensibly, the visit was to express U.S. support for a more complete fulfilment of the 2016 peace agreement, but the "failed" war on drugs, as Petro has called it, and the issue of Venezuela were at the fore behind closed doors.

Certainly, achieving total peace will be difficult. As Jorge Mantilla, an expert on organized crime and conflict at the Bogotá-based Ideas for Peace Foundation, said, "Perhaps we should call it '*paz posible*' and not '*paz total*'?"

But even if it turns out to be a total failure, there is inherent value in the fact that, after four years of a security policy so often limited to militarization, Colombia is once again banking and betting on peace, seeking to address the underlying issues of instability and inequality in the country.

As Vera Grabe, a former politician and one of the founders of M-19, who is now working for the Peace Observatory, a Colombian organization promoting human rights, told *Foreign*

Policy: "We used to live in a desert where peace didn't exist. At least there are doubts—before, there was nothing. There is a possibility to end the conflict in Colombia as peace is, once more, a central point of debate."

***

Which Groups Are Included in 'Total Peace'?

Colombia's past 60-plus years of armed conflict and peace accords have yielded a complicated, ever-changing panorama of actors and conflict dynamics.

Total Peace, following the legal framework under which Petro can maneuver to establish peace talks, divides groups between politically motivated groups and criminal groups. This distinction is muddled but holds weight when it comes to assessing the incentives an armed group considers to disarm. Does the armed actor seek particular policy concessions that it feels are largely unachievable through democratic means? Does it seek to overthrow the state? Or does it seek profit through violent control of illicit economies, only motivated by a negotiated settlement that allows it to enjoy its spoils in peace while paying a marginal part of its due sentence?

Total peace gave two groups political status: The ELN (*Ejército de Liberación Nacional*) guerrilla and the EMC (*Estado Mayor Central* ex FARC dissidents). Negotiations between the government and each of these two groups hold to this day, despite multiple impasses.

Negotiations with the ELN have been historically and characteristically difficult. Historically, attempts in 1975, 1998, 2008 and 2017 have been shaped by the ELN's recalcitrance towards political and military concessions, refusing to end targeted kidnappings, and perpetrating terrorist attacks during negotiations. Characteristically, the ELN is formed by multiple fronts that act with less of a hierarchical chain of command, which increases the risk of some fronts refusing to demobilize under a peace agreement.

The EMC (*Estado Mayor Central*) is composed of FARC dissidents who rejected disarmament under the 2016 peace accord. With a national presence and more than 3,500 combatants, the EMC grew to become a federation of fronts led by former mid-tier FARC commanders and fed by young, poor, rural youths. Nowhere near the size or cohesion of the former FARC, the EMC is still the largest and most structured of its remnants.

Left out of Total Peace negotiations was the *Segunda Marquetalia*, a group formed by FARC commanders who had demobilized but returned to arms after feeling cheated by the government's lackluster implementation of the 2016 peace accord.

On the other hand, the Gulf Clan, or AGC (*Autodefensas Gaitanistas de Colombia*), the country's largest criminal organization, created by former paramilitaries, has unsuccessfully tried to position itself as a politically motivated group to access greater concessions through peace talks. Negotiations faltered after the government failed to pass a legal framework under which it could offer favorable conditions for the AGC leaders to surrender under.

Similarly, the Pachenca, or ACSN (*Autodefensas Conquistadoras de la Sierra Nevada*), a smaller criminal organization also created by former paramilitaries, has more vocally sought political recognition and maintained talks with the government.

Finally, Total Peace brokered talks and truces between the colliding Shottas and Espartanos gangs in the Pacific port city of Buenaventura, between 16 gangs of Medellín and the Aburrá Valley, and between six gangs in the city of Quibdó.

Thus, Total Peace has sought to negotiate and pacify the groups most responsible for violence across Colombia — the ELN, EMC, AGC, and ACSN. Negotiations with the ELN and EMC are ongoing and have made relative progress, while negotiations with the AGC and ACSN have failed to take off and the military has resumed offensive operations.

How has 'Total Peace' affected security?

Total Peace's bilateral and unilateral ceasefires have undoubtedly de-escalated fighting between armed groups and the state, according to data from the Special Jurisdiction for Peace (JEP). In 2023, attacks against security forces dropped 47 per cent, while the number of security forces murdered and wounded also fell by 33 per cent and 39 per cent, respectively. Fighting amongst armed groups slightly fell by 2 per cent, reversing the upward trend of recent years.

Civilians have also experienced a respite from Colombia's worsening security situation in the past few years: Mass forced displacement in 2023 dropped by 47 per cent, the number of forcibly displaced individuals fell by 31 per cent, and confinements dropped by 51 per cent from 2022 to 2023. The murder of social leaders fell by 25 per cent. There are disparities when it comes to 2023 homicide data from government sources: while the National Institute of Forensic Science reports a 5 per cent increase in the number of homicides, the police report a 2 per cent reduction in the past year.

However, JEP data also showed that kidnappings and reported extortions have increased by 78 per cent and 11 per cent, respectively. Considering that extortions are rarely reported, increases in extortion are likely to be higher and more costly to business owners, which is coherent with field interviews. Similarly, attacks against productive infrastructure like oil and gas pipelines, electrical towers, and hydroelectric plants have increased by 62 per cent. These attacks are a way to push extortions onto the companies that operate them while stealing resources. The number of reported non-state actor checkpoints has also increased by 23 per cent.

These worsening kidnapping and extortion statistics point to tightening social and economic control of civilian populations living under the presence of armed actors allowed to govern with little pushback in the name of negotiated peace and reduced violence. Yet the JEP study cited here shows no spatial correlation between extortion increases in most areas controlled by the EMC and ELN, which could point to formal peace negotiations positively affecting these metrics if reports are to be trusted.

Is 'Total Peace' possible?

Total Peace's initial goal of negotiating peace with all armed actors seems far removed and far-fetched. While negotiations with the politically motivated ELN and EMC have advanced albeit stuttering along the way, there is no legal framework to carry out the intended negotiations with criminal groups like the AGC. Other FARC remnants such as the *Segunda Marquetalia*, the *Coordinadora Guerillera del Pacífico,* and the *Comandos de Frontera* have not been granted political status, and they refuse to participate in formal negotiations while classified as criminal groups.

Why would an armed group lay down their weapons if the state cannot protect them from the threat of death or recruitment by other armed actors? Why reach policy agreements if they can be undermined, strangled or defunded by a new president in 2026?

Evolution of the Conflict

2016 to current date

Human Rights

Despite an initial overall decline in the period immediately after the 2016 peace accord signing with the FARC guerrillas, conflict-related violence has taken new forms and serious abuses continue. In 2019, civilians in affected parts of the country suffered serious abuses at the hands of National Liberation Army (ELN) guerrillas, FARC dissidents, and paramilitary successor groups. Human rights defenders, journalists, indigenous and Afro-Colombian leaders, and other community and social activists have faced death threats and violence. The government has taken insufficient steps to protect them. Violence associated with the conflicts has forcibly displaced more than 8.1 million Colombians since 1985. In 2017, the Colombian government initiated formal peace talks with the ELN. But in January 2019, shortly after the ELN exploded a car bomb at a police academy in Bogotá, the government of President Iván Duque ended the peace talks.

Human rights abuses have not been limited to the guerrilla group, Colombia's armed forces actions in the so-called "false positives," scandal threw light on a particularly predatory practice. Many of the military's victims during the 2002-2008 period were what have come to be known as "false positives." Soldiers stand accused of abducting civilians—or even paying criminal groups to abduct them—then killing them and presenting their bodies as those of armed-group members killed in combat. During this period, military personnel were receiving both moral and material rewards for high body counts. While the UN and human rights groups had been warning publicly of the rise in "false positives" since early 2004, the practice did not halt until the September 2008 revelation that more than a dozen men missing from a poor Bogotá suburb had been lured with the promise of employment, taken hundreds of miles away, killed, and presented as dead combatants. In May 2019, the New York Times ran with a story that Colombian weekly news magazine *Semana* had passed on: army chief Gen. Nicacio Martínez and his commanders were reviving "body counts" as a principal measure of the army's effectiveness. Rather than measure territorial security or governance, high ranking officers decided to require unit commanders to sign forms committing themselves to a doubling of "*afectaciones*"— armed-group members killed or captured—in their areas of operations. This then raised concerns about creating incentives for "false positives" to resurface once again.

In short, Colombia has a great deal to confront when it comes to human rights.

How does a country come to terms with ongoing impunity for past abuses, barriers to land restitution for displaced people, limits on reproductive rights, and extreme poverty and isolation faced by indigenous communities? Indigenous, Afro-Colombian, journalists and other community activists continue to be targeted with threats and attacks. Indepaz[82] has

reported that perpetrators have killed thousands of social and community leaders since 2016.

---

[82] Indepaz: https://indepaz.org.co/

PART 5.
The Economy, formal and informal

Richard McColl

The Economy: Mixed fortunes

Veteran Colombian economist Eduardo Sarmiento has been reporting on the Colombian economy for *El Espectador*, a Bogotá daily newspaper, for many years. In one recent analysis he pointed up the discrepancy between recent targets set by the World Bank, IMF, OECD and the government treasury on one side, and the reality of economic results on the other. Economic growth forecasts for mid-2019 were set at 3.6 per cent, but results for the first quarter of 2019[83] released by DANE[84], the government statistical office, showed industrial productivity slumping to a paltry 0.2 per cent, a 3 per cent rise in unemployment to 9.3 per cent, and a trade deficit exceeding US$3.6 billion. Due to the pandemic, Colombia fell into a deep recession of -8.0 per cent, however the ANDI (Asociación Nacional de Empresarios de Colombia) expects the country to bounce back in 2021 with a 5.0 per cent growth. By 2023, the economy grew on 0.3 per cent in the second quarter (a 2.7 per cent point drop on the first quarter figure of 3.0 per cent[85]), its lowest since the crisis in 2020 leading Petro to call on the central bank to reduce interest rates.

Twenty-five years ago, Sarmiento was commenting on a similar mismatch. The difference then was that DANE reported a booming 30 percent annual growth in exports, of some US $1.4 billion. This seemed to contradict the reality of a growing trade deficit and an appreciation of the Colombian *peso* - a development which had provoked howls of rage from Colombian exporters, who complained that their goods were becoming uncompetitive in world markets. Sarmiento suggested that many of the exports reported were fictitious, fabricated in order to justify inflows of capital derived from drug exports. The foreign trade ministry disagreed, claiming that better international prices for coffee, oil and minerals had boosted revenues, helped by booming new exports such as coal, flowers and tropical fruits.

Today, the mismatch is between financial expectations and results, whereas in the past it was a choice between truth or fiction. Either way, the moral is that things don't always turn out as they are hoped or planned, which is truer in Colombia than in many countries.

A school report on the current performance of the Colombian economy might read *'Should do better'*. In its defence, Colombia has been busy fighting a guerrilla war and drugs cartels for the last half century; it is hampered by a weak infrastructure, partly due to its topographical extremes; and it has one of the highest poverty levels and wealth gaps in South America, not to mention the aftermath of the pandemic. Nevertheless, Colombia is the world's fourth largest producer of coal, the fourth largest oil producer in Latin America, the second largest coffee exporter in the world, and has abundant natural gas reserves, gold and emeralds. It has joined numerous trade groups in recent years, including the Pacific Alliance and the OECD.

So, it is fair to ask: why *isn't* the Colombian economy doing better?

China

The biggest problem facing Colombia at this time is the growing and highly corrosive influence of China, which is using its economic might to build considerable influence in Latin America to the detriment of the U.S. and traditional regional economic and diplomatic ties.

Beijing is an authoritarian regime which has little regard for its client states other than stripping them of the natural resources it requires regardless of the environmental, social, community, economic and political damage it causes. Successive hard right administrations from Uribe to Santos to Duque openly courted Beijing and FDI from China, at such a level that it deeply concerned pre-Trump and post-Trump Washington to such an extent, particularly after Duque committed to Beijing's Belt and Road Initiative, that the Biden White House sent a secret diplomatic mission to Bogotá to ask Duque to withdraw from that commitment and dial down Chinese investment in Colombia.

That appears to have had little tangible success with China focused on bolstering economic and political ties in the Andes with the latest coup being Beijing signing a free trade agreement with the right-wing Lasso (2021-2024) administration in Ecuador.

The coffee economy

In the colonial period, Colombia was an economic backwater, and after independence from Spain it was held back by a primitive transport system, isolation and insolvency. By the late 1830s annual exports were still only worth an average of about US$3 million, and 75 per cent of those were of gold, destined mainly for Britain. Most of the population - 1.6 million in 1835 - were engaged in subsistence agriculture.

Until the mid-nineteenth century, tobacco was Colombia's main agricultural export when the Spanish monopoly was abolished in 1850 and it was replaced by quinine and coffee. Fresh opportunities provided by free trade led to rapid development from then onwards, with the growth of coffee cultivation and exports encouraged by demand in the expanding urban markets of Europe and the USA. This was also when the country's first proper bank was formed.

The process known as the Antioqueño Colonisation was launched from the old colonial city of Medellín, founded in 1616. But its centuries' long slumber was not disturbed until, pushed by demographic pressures, settlers began to clear the trees along the western slopes of the Central Cordillera in the early nineteenth century, occupying what is now known as Viejo Caldas: the present-day departments of Caldas, Risaralda and Quindío. The settlers grew food crops for subsistence to begin with, and later coffee for export. Until then, gold mining and dredging and diving for pearls in the River Aburrá had been the region's only economic activities. The city of Manizales, which was to become one of the centres of the coffee business, was founded in 1848. Other coffee centres such as Ibagué, Pereira (1863) and Armenia (1889), grew rapidly with the expansion of the industry.

Coffee was the first export crop for which Colombian landowners made big investments in land preparation, technology and infrastructure. Growth really took off from 1910 onwards, although coffee already accounted for about half Colombia's exports by the end of the nineteenth century (by 1924 it was 80 per cent). Production grew from 114,000 bags (60kg) in 1874 to 1 million in 1913 and 5.1 million in 1943.

Big estates were gradually replaced as the main centres of production by family farms established on newly-colonised land in Antioquia and other parts of the Central and Western Cordilleras of the Andes. Coffee growing was too labour-intensive for big estates to be able to compete. By 1904 there were more than 600km of railways to take the coffee to ports, but Antioquia's take-off really happened after the railway from Medellín down to the Magdalena at Puerto Berrío was completed in 1914. By the mid-1930s the total length of track had quadrupled.

It was a tough business, and from this heroic period derives the paisas' countrywide reputation for rugged self-reliance and entrepreneurial acumen. These talents were manifested in the diversification of local capital into new industries in Medellín from the end of the nineteenth century onwards, following the classic import substitution route. Coffee exports gave the initial impetus to manufacturing industry, creating both the capital surplus and the market for the first factories in Medellín.

Today, coffee-growing is the main source of income for some 550,000 farmers and their families in Colombia. By contrast, nobody knows exactly how many live off coca and poppy cultivation. In 2011, the United Nations Office for Drugs and

Crime estimated that some 80,000 families were involved in coca production. Since then, despite successive governments' efforts to incentivise the production of legal and sustainable alternatives, probably many more remain tied to the drugs trade. The two phenomena are connected: the fall in coffee prices, particularly sharp since late 2018, has driven large numbers of growers off the land, not to mention the seasonal pickers who depend on a prosperous coffee sector for employment.

Long before the current price collapse, since the 1990s or earlier, an unknown number of farmers and pickers have been leaving the traditional coffee regions of Antioquia and Viejo Caldas to find better paid work in the boom coca-growing areas in the jungles and plains of eastern and southern Colombia: Guaviare, Vichada, Putumayo and Caquetá. It's not hard to understand the temptation. Weight for weight, one kilo of coca paste is worth around as much as 340 kg of coffee or 1,000 kg of bananas. The far easier shipment of compact coca paste from the isolated coca plantations over rough roads is an added attraction.

Coffee growers who stayed in the industry vented their frustrations over the crisis with a short-lived strike in mid-July 1995. A militant organisation known as the *Unidad Cafetera Nacional,* supported by some 80 per cent of growers, blocked roads in about 100 districts of the coffee-producing heartland to back up demands for government help with some US$300 million worth of debts the small and medium-sized growers had run up with the banks, and to protest against successive reductions in the price the producers receive for their beans from the *Federación Nacional de Cafeteros.*

The coffee sector's problems are caused predominantly by two main factors: firstly, world prices, which declined soon after the collapse of the International Coffee Agreement in 1989 and, despite subsequent agreements, have fluctuated widely since. Secondly, diseases, particularly *broca,* a coffee berry-boring beetle, which was partly blamed for the country's worst-ever coffee harvest in 2010. Producers complain that the lack of money and technical assistance have helped the disease to spread.

The government introduced an emergency plan for the coffee sector in May 1995, involving subsidies totalling US$237.5 million, and said it could do nothing more. Dissatisfied with this response, coffee growers called further strikes, which have become regular occurrences still today, with workers demanding greater subsidies to compensate for the lower global prices.

Coffee crops before 1989, when they accounted for about 60 per cent of Colombia's export revenues, averaged around 18 million bags. In 1994, only 11 million bags were produced, nevertheless still earning nearly 24 per cent of Colombia's export income. Since then the crop has stayed at about the same low level, though exports rose by some 2.6 per cent in January 2019 over the same period in the previous year, with 4.8 million bags sold. The land area cultivated for coffee has shrunk by some 20 percent, partly in response to the falling prices but also due to migrant coffee workers moving on. Despite this shrinkage, output has remained steady over the last two decades, thanks to improved productivity and technological innovations. According to latest OECD figures, coffee represented 6.9 per cent of total exports, worth US$2.7 billion, making it the country's third biggest earner.

Faced with the growing militancy of its coffee growers and dwindling prices on the world market, the Colombian government joined forces with Central American countries and Brazil in July 1995 to cut exports in an attempt to stabilise the price. Colombia, the world's biggest producer of mild (arabica) coffee, led the campaign to withhold coffee from the market, arguing that speculators in the consumer countries were driving the price down. Whereas Brazilian coffee is mass produced very economically, arabica coffee, also produced by Guatemala, Costa Rica and Honduras, costs more to produce on a smaller scale, putting it at a commercial disadvantage. Despite this, world coffee prices have continued to fall. Market speculation has also continued, as has oversupply, particularly from Brazil, the world leader. Crop diseases remain a problem, exacerbated by rising temperatures in the mountainous plantation regions, due in part to climate change, according to recent studies.

Nevertheless, some economists have forecast a modest resurgence of Colombian coffee prices. The FNC (*Federación Nacional de Café*), the Colombian coffee growers' association, has called for coffee to be released from the C-Price system, the global coffee pricing benchmark, for continued government subsidies, and for coffee roasters to adopt Fair-Trade practices to allow producers a more equitable return.

Economic Successes

Until the late 1990s, Colombia enjoyed one of the longest uninterrupted periods of economic growth with relative price stability in Latin America. During the 1980s in particular, it averaged a 3.7 per cent annual growth rate, compared to 1.1 per cent registered by the other countries in the region.

Breaking away from its previous dependence on coffee, Colombia diversified its economy, developing its mining and non-traditional industries, such as flowers, tropical fruits and textiles. It was the only Latin American country not to suffer a debt crisis during the 1980s, when other governments were defaulting or frantically trying to renegotiate the loans they had accumulated during the petrodollar madness of the preceding decade.

Colombian governments have become particularly adept at handling sudden massive inflows of export revenues, followed by equally sudden scarcities. Unlike Brazil, where inflation became endemic even as the economy was booming, Colombian finance ministers became skilled at neutralising the potential inflationary effects of such booms; the windfall profits of the coffee boom of the late 1970s was a case in point, and the maintenance of relative price stability since the country became awash with drug money is another.

Colombian governments have traditionally been interventionist: the Conservative administrations of the nineteenth century had a corporatist outlook that involved the protection of monopolies, while the Liberal governments that have dominated the country since the National Front agreement of 1958 have also regulated the economy closely, controlling some basic industries (oil and steel, for example), subsidising prices of consumer goods and exports alike, particularly non-traditional ones, and intervening heavily on the exchange markets to defend the currency and price stability. Import substitution was built on ready access to cheap official credit and high protective tariffs.

This strategy was quite successful for a long time. Colombia maintained a steady growth rate despite the ups and downs of its principal products, and it never had to resort either to heavy borrowing or to the rescheduling of debts that followed in its wake after the Mexican crisis of 1982.

---

[83] DANE: https://www.dane.gov.co/files/investigaciones/boletines/ipi/bol_ipi_abril_19.pdf

[84] http://www.dane.gov.co/

[85] CCB: https://www.ccb.org.co/informacion-especializada/observatorio/analisis-economico/crecimiento-economico/pib-bogota-y-colombia-2015-2022

Richard McColl

The Neo-Liberal Turnaround

Change started to come about with the election of César Gaviria in 1990. By that time the free-market wave had swept over the whole continent and Colombia could not remain unaffected. Protectionism was out of fashion, and the high-cost industries fostered by high tariff walls were increasingly uncompetitive.

The solution adopted by Gaviria, a former finance minister, was known as the *revolcón*, a complete turnabout in the direction of economic policy, presided over at the finance ministry by Rudolf Hommes, a US-trained economist. Free trade became the goal, and the country entered into a tariff cutting arrangement with neighbouring Venezuela that saw trade between the two countries surge from US$600 million in 1991 to almost US$2 billion by 1993.

Together with Venezuela, Colombia signed a free-trade pact with Mexico, forming the so-called Group of Three, which undertook to cut tariffs progressively from 1994. From Colombia's point of view, the Group was a springboard from which eventually to join the North American Free Trade Agreement (NAFTA), formed by the US, Canada and Mexico at the beginning of 1994.

Yet Colombia's liberalising, privatising revolution was much more cautious and partial than, say, Peru's. This was partly because the directly state-controlled sector in Colombia was much smaller. But there was no question of selling off the state-owned oil company Ecopetrol, for example, at least not at this time. Additionally, deregulation of prices and tariffs of public utilities were only slowly implemented.

But Colombia's economic managers optimistically liked to compare their policies with those of Chile, the shining example of economic success envied all over Latin America. Finance minister Guillermo Perry Rubio pointed out that, like Chile, Colombia had never depended on short-term foreign capital inflows to balance its budget and finance domestic consumption (unlike Mexico and Argentina), and was in a good position to escape the 'tequila effect' that followed the Mexican peso crisis of December 1994.

Steps were taken to set up an offshore stabilisation fund, along the lines recommended by the private economic think-tank *Fedesarrollo*, into which a proportion of oil export revenues were paid, to prevent the economy becoming too 'dollarised'. President Samper earmarked large quantities of the expected inflows for social and infrastructural investment.

Assisted by state incentives, non-traditional exports soared, leading to another export boom. The discovery of considerable oil deposits led to further investment, triggering a surge in private and public spending in the mid-1990s. Borrowing on a massive scale to cover this spending laid Colombia open to the risk of increased interest rates and taxes, which is exactly what happened following the 1997 Asian financial crisis.

Oil bonanza and fall-out

Vast new oilfields were discovered that promised to make Colombia the second-largest oil producer in Latin America, after Venezuela. The Cusiana-Cupiagua fields and the associated Volcanera gas deposits, which were developed by British Petroleum in partnership with Total of France, Triton of the US and Ecopetrol, are in the Casanare and Arauca departments. Part of the vast flat Llanos region, these backward and lawless piedmont grasslands east of the capital include large areas of the countryside formerly controlled by the ELN. These guerrillas regularly blew up sections of the existing pipeline from the Caño Limón field in Arauca to the Caribbean port of Coveñas.

Throughout its history, the pipeline has been attacked by guerrillas virtually on a weekly basis, causing an estimated loss of 66 million barrels of oil, and putting it out of action for about one third of its lifespan. As an alternative but costlier back-up, the Bicentenario pipeline was built to the port of Coveñas on the Colombian Caribbean coast, though it too has been targeted, causing further oil leaks. Total losses peaked at some 45,000 barrels a day in 2014, but they have eased off since the peace accord at the end of 2016.

Nevertheless, the pipeline attacks did not deter the BP-led consortium from continuing its operations. The Ocensa pipeline was also built, from the Cusiana and Cupiaguas oil fields to Coveñas, completed in September 1997 and capable of transporting up to 650,000 barrels per day. At their peak, these oil fields produced 440,000 barrels a day in 1999, but the pipeline made the headlines for all the wrong reasons. A group of farmers, whose land was crossed by the pipeline, took BP to court, accusing the company of damaging their land, crops and animals. Billed as the biggest-ever environmental lawsuit in UK legal history, the case was finally won by BP in 2014, with the judge rejecting the farmers' claims in their entirety and awarding the company compensation for their court costs. International energy companies found themselves caught up in a vicious triangle: between the government who needed their economic output and investment; armed groups, who targeted their vulnerable installations for propaganda effect; and local people who resented their intrusion on the land and their notoriously heavy-handed security personnel.

Despite declining oil production, by the turn of the 21st century, Colombia became the third largest oil exporter in Latin America, after Venezuela and Brazil. With a combination of learning from other people's mistakes (particularly those of neighbouring Venezuela) and long experience of successful economic management, Colombia's exploitation of its oil resources has been one of its best success stories.

Unfortunately, in recent years it has become over-reliant on oil, which now provides some 28 per cent of the country's total export revenue. And as global oil prices have fallen since 2014, this has had a detrimental effect on the economy. Increased terrorist attacks on oil pipelines and installations added to the country's woes and by the end of the millennium growth had slumped to its worst-ever levels.

Richard McColl

Extractives under Petro

Since assuming office in August 2022, President Petro has fulfilled an election campaign promise to halt licensing rounds for exploration acreage as part of a broader plan to accelerate the country's clean energy transition leading experts to suggest that the country will lose its energy independence unless this decision is reversed. Experts also warn that Colombia risks losing its international competitiveness because of changes to the oil and gas tax regime, including a decision to no longer allow companies to deduct royalty production costs from their taxable income.

Colombia actually has no need for fossil fuels for its own energy demand, given that approximately 80 per cent of its current energy supply comes from renewable sources, primarily hydroelectric. The problem is that, especially in the past four decades, the country has been heavily reliant on income from fossil fuel exports. In 2020, crude oil was the most exported commodity in the country, generating almost 6.9 billion euros for the economy, primarily thanks to trade with the United States. Essentially, oil has become a cornerstone of the Colombian economy. Thus, Petro's decision seems brave, all the more so in a country that borders Venezuela, which has suffered an economic collapse that has caused mass emigration, with millions of people leaving the country.

Then, there is the issue of an increase in gasoline prices.

Essentially, Petro inherited a terrible legacy from the Democratic Centre party under President Duque, who for a decade, plundered the state-run Ecopetrol using the company to pay unsustainable gasoline price subsidies and even paying itself special dividends from the company when they couldn't balance the budget. Duque did this twice causing an unsustainable situation.

Previously, Ecopetrol managed to offset the cost of the subsidy by producing low-grade, cheap gasoline and diesel (highly polluting) and do not meet US or EU emission standards.

It's *whataboutism* at its finest, but now Petro has to increase prices to pick up the broken pieces and risks more demonstrations against this decision, blockades by truck drivers and taxi unions bringing chaos to the cities and highways.

A New Criteria for Mining

The Petro government is scrutinising existing mining titles that were awarded without thorough consideration of environmental impact.

Colombia's mining industry is extensive. The country is the largest coal producer in Latin America and holds significant deposits of copper, gold, nickel and emeralds. In 2021, mining exports made up 24 per cent of the country's total exports and 2.3 per cent of the gross domestic product.

The proposals[86] include establishing a total environmental protection in the country that would impede future mining projects, the creation of mining districts or reserved areas for the use of strategic minerals for the energy transition and the legalization of illegal mining.

The new mining code will no doubt cause upset in the industry, but will honour existing contracts should they meet the appropriate criteria.

---

[86] Dentons Mining Law: https://www.dentonsmininglaw.com/change-is-on-the-horizon-for-miners-in-colombia/

Global partnerships

Colombia joined the OECD in 2018, becoming only the third Latin American country to join its ranks, alongside Mexico and Chile. OECD membership has provided Colombia with access to its economic expertise, network of regional cooperation, and global influence.

Critics, however, deride the OECD as a 'rich countries' club' that does not benefit developing member nations, but is tilted in favour of its wealthier core members, including the USA, France, Germany and the UK. In the words of Mario Alejandro Valencia, director of Bogotá-based labour thinktank, Cedetrabajo, "The defence of foreign investment is promoted over national rights, the economy is oriented toward the external market of commodities and the stimulation and protection of national companies is abandoned." Former president of Colombia Juan Manuel Santos takes a more favourable view of the OECD's influence on Latin America as a whole, highlighting its positive influence on the region's democratic standards. "It is a region that can benefit greatly from the concepts promoted by the OECD in the areas of governance, transparency and inclusiveness. Indeed, it is not easy to decide which is truer: more Latin America needs the OECD or the OECD needs Latin America."

Sustainable trade bodies, such as Rainforest Alliance and Fair Trade, have had a significant impact on specialist Colombian goods and products, particularly on coffee, cocoa and fruit. Rainforest Alliance offers farms a certification scheme, enabling them to use its logos in return for implementing a range of conditions, such as controlled waste treatment, protection of local flora and fauna, and the payment of fair wages to its workers. Comparison studies of certified and non-certified farms, carried out in 2010, showed appreciably higher scores of those using Rainforest Alliance practices.

Fair Trade uses a similar certification scheme, but focusses its attention on the working conditions and salaries of the employees. With regard to the coffee industry, Fair Trade is trying to raise typical workers' salaries of US$2 a day, and to redress the imbalance of an industry in which the middlemen - including the coffee roasters – soak up some 87 per cent of the profits. There is also the problem for both groups that the cost of certification is beyond the reach of small-scale farmers who make up the majority of coffee growers in Colombia. For small farms in Cundinamarca and Huila, for example, averaging respectively 5.3 hectares and 7.3 hectares in size, the average annual costs of certification were US$268 and US$224.

It is hard to come by precise figures of how much of Colombia's total agricultural produce is Fair Trade, but it is estimated that of the 12 million bags of coffee exported in 2009, one million bags were specialist organic or Fair Trade certified. During his mandate, Ivan Duque's government announced its aim to achieve Fair Trade coverage nationwide by 2027.

The Informal Economy

Like the drug economy, the 'informal' sector is, by its very nature, difficult to measure. Unlicensed factories, street hawkers selling smuggled cigarettes, backstreet workshops, windscreen washers and snacks sellers all work within the 'informal' economy, which is often closely linked to the 'formal' one of permanent employees enjoying paid holidays and social benefits.

These marginalised but highly visible working men, women and children are vital to the economies of all developing countries, even those with strong formal sectors. Some 52 per cent of all workers in Latin America are thought to be engaged in the informal economy; with Colombians ranking just below the average, at 48 per cent and falling slightly year on year.

The vicious cycle that has trapped medium-sized Colombian companies is that they are hit with disproportionately high corporate taxes, which gives excessive advantages to informal enterprises, thus encouraging more workers to set up their own informal small businesses instead. And so on. As the formal sector has cut back, the informal sector of casual workers and fly-by-night sweatshops has grown correspondingly - often because big factories sub-contract work to them for rock-bottom wages. Unemployment is high in Colombia, with official figures from DANE (June 2019) showing a rate of 9.4 per cent and 9.57 per cent in July 2023[87], another major factor driving many people to work independently by any means. Tax reforms and new legislation introduced since 2013 have alleviated the burden on smaller companies to some extent, and increased welfare benefits for the poorer members of society. The informal workforce is still shrinking, but whether this is as a result of recent government fiscal measures, is too early and complex to say with any certainty.

---

[87] Trading Economics: https://tradingeconomics.com/colombia/unemployment-

rate

Richard McColl

Alternative Crops

Since signing its historic Peace Accord in 2016, the Colombian government has been making concerted efforts to eradicate coca plantations and thereby wipe out or at least reduce the illegal drugs trade. Dramatic campaigns to destroy cultivated fields with anti-drugs crop-spraying planes have proved contentious due to the risk of the herbicide contaminating surrounding areas and poisoning water courses. There is also the danger to the pilots from armed traffickers on the ground, with numerous instances of fatal shootings and downed planes. Instead, authorities have been trying to offer local farmers positive incentives to cultivate alternative legal crops, such as cocoa and, more controversially, palm oil.

Colombia has been growing palm oil, on a modest scale at first, since the mid-1960s. In the last couple of decades, however, the agro-industry has been massively increased. Production has grown from 364,000 metric tonnes (MT) in 1995, whilst in 2020 Fedepalma (Federación Nacional de Cultivadores de Palma de Aceite) recorded 1,521,598 tonnes of palm oil extracted in the country. Today, although still only contributing a paltry two per cent of the global total, compared to Indonesia's 85 per cent, Colombia is the fourth largest exporter of palm oil in the world, and the largest in Latin America. Fedepalma, the national trade body, conscious of palm oil's impact on diverse tropical ecosystems, has claimed that Colombian palm oil is "unique and differentiated". According to Fedepalma, palm oil is not grown on deforested land, but predominantly on pastures that are already degraded and which do not harm the local biosystems.

The thriving industry has put to use some 44 million hectares of land, a significant proportion of which was formerly used for coca production. It has provided some 171,000 jobs, benefitting thousands of families, who are now engaged in safer and more viable livelihoods. On the other hand, by Fedepalma's own admission, only 14 per cent of Colombian palm oil was certified sustainable by the industry watchdog RSPO (Roundtable on Sustainable Palm Oil) in 2017, Perhaps the best argument in its favour is that it's the least harmful option compared to the coca crop it is intended to substitute.

Another alternative crop is cacao, with Colombian cocoa beans and chocolate highly valued by international trade bodies. The International Cacao Organisation rated 95 per cent of Colombian cacao in 2017 as being of "fine flavour". In total, some 57,000 tons of Colombian cacao were produced in 2018, a figure slightly down on the previous year, but which has been growing steadily for the last decade. Many cacao farms are small, family-run affairs, of only a few hectares, including some in former coca-growing regions. One project in Anorí, in the north-western department of Antioquia, is run by ASOMUCAN, a non-profit cooperative of 172 cocoa-growing families. It was set up in 2006 as a joint initiative of the government and the UNODC, helping families previously linked to coca production. Today, only 56 of the original families remain involved in Anorí, but its gourmet chocolate is sold throughout Colombia as well as competing at international trade fairs.

The drug economy

The illicit and widespread drug economy is, of course, an 'informal' one, with no registered companies or payments of social security contributions. Teenage *sicarios* (hit-men) are aware they have no job security or prospects, but can make a lot of money in a short time if they are very lucky. To give just one example, there seems to be some connection between the vicissitudes of the textile sector in Medellín and the increase in the number of guns-for-hire.

Bluntly put, the trade in illicit drugs permeates all levels of society given its economic benefits. Going back only a few decades, the successful presidential campaign of Ernesto Samper (president from 1994-1998) allegedly received funds of up to US$10 million from the Cali cartel. Former president Andrés Pastrana (1998-2002) strongly denied claims made in 2021 by members of the Cali cartel that his failed presidential bid in 1994 was also the recipient of funds from that cartel.

Álvaro Uribe (2002-2006 and 2006-2010) has been implicated in various scandals involving the drugs trade, not least during his tenure as the director of the *Aeronautica Civil* (Colombia's civil aviation authority between 1980-1982) and having supposedly used a helicopter belonging to Pablo Escobar amongst various other claims. A declassified DEA report from 1991 states that Uribe was close to Escobar and was linked to a business involved in narcotics activities in the United States and that he has links to the Medellín cartel.

Juan Manuel Santos (2010-2014 and 2014-2018) is accused by his detractors as having been one of the greatest allies to the FARC guerrillas and their cultivation of coca and production of cocaine by having suspended the use of glyphosate for aerial fumigations.

President Iván Duque's presidency was no less controversial. Marta Lucía Ramírez the then vice president had to field questions about her husband's business deals with a famed narcotrafficker called *Memo Fantasma.* Although Ramírez claimed to have known nothing of these business associations. It was revealed in 2020 that in 1997, her brother had been arrested smuggling heroin into the United States. Then, President Duque's ambassador to Uruguay, Fernando Sanclamente was found to have several cocaine laboratories on his family estate just outside of Bogotá. Further to these accusations, President Duque's pilot during his presidential campaign was also a pilot to members of the Mexican Sinaloa cartel.

The drugs business is no doubt one of the greatest tragedies to befall Colombia. Drug money is formalized through massive money laundering schemes in construction, restaurants and anything seen as a viable conduit. In facing up to the scourge of cartels and armed groups involved in the industry, the Colombian State is weak, whether it's due to an incompetence or its interests in this economy is anyone's best guess.

The Coca Market Collapse

Falling prices and high inflation have resulted in forced displacement and food insecurity for thousands of smallholders whose economic mainstay was growing the plant exclusively and selling coca paste. Why has this happened now?

It is difficult to get clear statistics for the coca market, but the newspaper El Espectador estimated that between 2021 and 2023, the average price of an *arroba* (12.5 kilos or about 28 pounds) of coca leaf has fallen by over 32 per cent in the department of Cauca, on Colombia's Pacific coast. Meanwhile, in the neighbouring southern department of Nariño, a kilo of coca paste — a later stage in the transformation of the leaf into cocaine — once cost $975, but today it sells for $240, according to estimates by the Colombian branch of the International Crisis Group think tank.

Few doubt that cultivation in other countries — such as

Paraguay, Guatemala, Honduras and Mexico – have exacerbated the issue, just as Fentanyl and other synthetic drugs gained ground becoming a primary concern in the US and pushing cocaine out of the frame. Then, there's the issue of transportation and this is where Ecuador comes in. Under President Correa[88], the US was expelled (2014) from the country and with them went Ecuador's ability (via US technology) to police the transhipment of cocaine through their territory. In addition to this, peace with the FARC in 2016 splintered the chain of command the different groups that moved cocaine.

The effects are far-reaching, including collective impoverishment and an acute social crisis for a good number of the 400,000 coca-growing families and people connected to the business in border departments such as Nariño, Putumayo and Norte de Santander, among others.

---

[88] BBC: https://www.bbc.com/news/world-latin-america-27165203

Corruption

How corrupt is Colombia? It's almost a throwaway question as corruption cases are rarely out of the news. Colombians are bombarded with stories on daily news shows, continually hearing about the corruption in the country and how it continues to stifle growth, businesses, progress, public works, politics, in fact just about every facet of Colombian life.

Transparency International, the worldwide body promoting transparency, accountability and integrity at all levels and across all sectors of society released its yearly report entitled the Global Corruption Barometer and Colombia never comes off well. In 2019, 94 per cent of Colombians polled believed that corruption in the government was a serious problem, and 52 per cent thought corruption increased in the previous 12 months. Colombia's corruption perception index remained stable at 39 points from 2020 to 2022[89]. However, according to the Capacity to Combat Corruption Index[90] Colombia slipped in the rankings in 2023. Colombia's ranking worsened compared to other countries, dropping to the 91st position out of 180 countries in the corruption perception ranking.

Corruption cases, including vote-buying, witness intimidation and campaign funding from nefarious companies and connections to shady characters haunt current President Iván Duque (2018-22) and former presidents Juan Manuel Santos (2010-18) and Álvaro Uribe (2002-10). In fact, the scandals extend much further back, but, that's for another book! Former mayors of Bogotá are by no means exempt either, Enrique Peñalosa (2016-19) is currently being investigated for allegedly squandering 1,400,000,000 pesos to ensure that his pet project of an elevated metro for Bogotá take precedence over previous mayor Gustavo Petro's (2012-15) more complete studies for an underground metro. Prior to that, mayor Samuel Moreno (2008-11) was suspended and stripped of his office for improprieties in awarding construction contracts in Bogotá. And then, there's the Odebrecht case. The *Lavajato* scandal which brought down a government in Brazil, implicated premiers, presidents and executives across the Americas and beyond, are epic in their proportions. In Colombia alone, payouts revealed so far, have taken down the former Minister of Transport Daniel García Moreno (allegedly having received US $6.5 million) and politician Otto Bula (Bula is also signalled as being the *"Ejecutivo de Cobros"* by US authorities for the *Oficina de Envigado* organized crime syndicate. Bula's criminal empire extends through Córdoba, Sucre and into the Montes de María). Accusations have been flung at both former President Juan Manuel Santos and his opponent in the 2014 elections Óscar Iván Zuluaga of having received funds from Odebrecht towards their campaigns. President Santos ordered a speedy investigation and Zuluaga's floundering political career took a nosedive before being indicted in 2023.

Odebrecht's tentacles reach far within businesses and politics in Colombia. Their sister company, Navalena, created to oversee the project to make the Magdalena River navigable once again, was also implicated in dirty business practices. Having received a loan from Colombia's Banco Agrario to the sum of COP 120,000 million (in 2015 when it was known that Odebrecht was in serious trouble) there are links in this carousel of corruption which should effectively rock the Colombian establishment to the core. At the time of the scandal, then Minister for Agriculture Aurelio Iragorri and then Finance Minister Mauricio Cárdenas were on the board of directors for the bank. It appears that no one is in the clear.

Having been accused of allegedly receiving up to as much as one million dollars in his presidential campaign kitty from Odebrecht, former President Santos has moved fast to quell all rumours. Whether he knew of the income remains to be seen, but, people cannot overlook the fact that the *Ruta del Sol* highway from the interior of the country to the Caribbean coast, the expansion of the Reficar oil Refinery in Cartagena (it has been said that Colombians are paying for this refinery 4 times over given the swindling which occurred), the dredging of the Magdalena River and more all took place under his watch.

For Colombia, theirs is a discombobulated country, staggering to its feet and showing the green shoots of economic and social growth against an inherent problem.

Hardly the type of information and negative publicity that the Government bodies involved in promoting and attracting international investment to Colombia enjoy seeing making the headlines both at home and overseas.

In 2023, the Odebrecht scandal came to the fore once again, Luis Carlos Sarmiento[91], one of the wealthiest men in Colombia and the main shareholder of Grupo Aval and its bank subsidiary, agreed to pay approximately US$80 million to settle corruption charges brought by U.S. authorities that alleged the conglomerate, along with a joint venture partner, paid at least $28 million to Colombian government officials to secure an extension of the Ruta del Sol construction contract.

And, as Colombia was assimilating this information, journalist Laura Ardila Arrieta, brought out her book: "*La Costa Nostra92*," a deep dive into the clientelism and corruption with its base in the Caribbean city of Barranquilla and overseen by the all-powerful Char family.

Ardila's investigations present a series of unpublished data that sheds light on the history and trajectory of the Char clan. The book delves into the contracting model implemented by Álex Char in Barranquilla, where mega contractors, with personal, family or political ties to Char, play a fundamental role. This contracting model opens the door to possible money laundering through state projects in addition to vote-buying scandals and a controversy worthy of soap opera including Álex Char and his mistress, the former politician Aida Merlano[93].

And there are so many "scams" that Ardila reveals in The Costa

Nostra that the book is intended to generate a broad public debate and shed light on the political and economic reality of the region in question.

And, who suffers the most, the Colombian people.

---

[89] Statista: https://www.statista.com/statistics/811556/colombia-corruption-perception-index/

[90] BNN Network: https://bnn.network/politics/colombias-anti-corruption-efforts-decline-in-latin-america-according-to-2023-index/

[91] Bloomberg: https://www.bloomberg.com/news/articles/2023-08-11/billionaire-sarmiento-s-companies-to-pay-60-million-in-us-graft-probe

[92] Rey Naranjo: https://www.reynaranjo.net/lacostanostra/

[93] Washington Post: https://www.washingtonpost.com/world/2019/10/03/watch-jailed-colombian-politician-escape-through-window-during-dentist-appointment/

Mixed prospects and Covid-19

Overall, Colombia's long-term economic prospects have been dampened recently by some credit ratings agencies downgrading it, citing domestic political tensions and the costs of ongoing migration from Venezuela as negative factors. On the other hand, the huge boost provided by the Peace Accord in 2016, has seen an upsurge in several sectors, not least tourism. So, in response to the original question of why the economy isn't doing better, maybe the short answer is that it could be doing a lot worse: two steps forward, one step back.

Then, in 2020 the Covid-19 pandemic struck, putting paid to any and all progress, unwinding advances made in the previous two decades and returning a vast population back to poverty. Tourism dried up, businesses such as hotels and restaurants closed and the outlook has been bleak as the government scrambled to offer low-interest loans to protect small and medium sized enterprises. Red rags were hung in windows where inhabitants lacked food and the veil was lifted further revealing the inequalities in Colombian society. The wealthy and the middle class were able to work from home and have their children attend school "virtually," but the large portion of the population not online, computer-less and working in the informal economy or the service industry were left to fend for themselves. According to the DANE the Colombian GDP contracted by 15,7 per cent in the second trimester of 2020 in comparison to levels in 2019, making it the worst in Colombia's history. Unemployment reached 20 per cent in mid-August 2020, an equivalent of four million lost jobs.

The question remains as to how Colombia can recover from this financial meltdown. The government announced its plan to provide economic incentives to business owners, economic aid for the most vulnerable and plunge money into infrastructure works. However, experts believe that there should be a greater emphasis on creating jobs. According to Andrés Giraldo, director of the Javeriana University's economics department: "in the second trimester we have seen a slight pick-up since there are businesses open, but the main problem is jobs, so if the government enacts a fast reactivation and provides the resources for this, there will continue to be improvements." Mauricio Hernández of the BBVA research team has predicted that the Colombian economy will not recover to 2019 levels until the end of 2022: "Growth will come from four sources: housing subsidies, infrastructure works, payroll subsidies and social support. These four points, in unison, will enable a creation of jobs and the management of household expenses."

PART 6.
Colombian Culture and Society

Culture: What does it mean to be a Colombian?

Colombians, generally speaking, can be divided up between those with clearly defined ideas of what it means to be from Colombia and then, those that don't. Both sets of ideas converge though and fall into a mixing pot of well-used stereotypes and generalizations to describe behaviours, personalities and outlooks on life. Inevitably, these will highlight the most negative aspects of behaviour without of course, delving into the core sentiment of what it means to be a Colombian.

Initially, we can focus on the importance of the complex geographical setting of Colombia to explain the soul of the country, the variety of climates, the diversity of styles of music and rhythms all, as if cultivated in the varied regions, just as we can focus on the enthralling yet painful social and historical difficulties encountered within these borders. The landscapes, made up of towering mountains, frothing rivers, wide valleys and inhospitable jungles, all of which are complex and diverse have combined to shape the soul of a Colombian, just as the individual's origins, the processes of blending races, migrations, habitat, the sociocultural context and external influences have all played their part as well.

What is Colombia? It's a confounding question and one to which a complete answer cannot be verbalized. Colombia is far more than the text penned in the Constitution, it's a collection of diverse communities with characteristics in common and which respect the cultural, historical, religious, racial or linguistic backgrounds as if they were one. However, this project of Colombia, this vision for a country, has been overwhelmed by complex social, economic, cultural and political processes which have taken place here and which could arguably lead us to think that the classical concept of what is a nation, has failed here.

Being Colombian means to struggle constantly to understand one's history, both personal and familiar, but also as the history of a nation and then to apply this knowledge to the geography, the towns, cities and populations in an immense effort to strive for a country which can be at ease with and within itself. Altruistic yet parochial, proud yet ashamed, Colombia is neither represented by the *vueltiao* hat of the Caribbean coast, the *ruana* of Boyacá, the *Currulao* of the pacific, the *Escobarian* memories rematerialized by Netflix's Narcos[94] and nor is it the yellow of the national football team jersey. She is all of these and more. Colombia is the culturally and racially diverse, coca producing country of well-read and educated citizenry, she is a country controlled by elites who have never set foot outside of their high-ceilinged apartments in Bogotá or Medellín and the family *finca* and who fail to understand that it is they who provided the context for magic realism. Being Colombian is to understand this and more of Colombia, within these contexts, and to possess the obligation of having to grapple with this meaning and to yearn for something better. Colombia could be several countries, but she is one, and she is all the richer, outrageous and extravagant for it.

---

[94] Netflix: https://www.netflix.com/co/title/80025172

The Population

Indigenous Colombia

Colombia is overwhelmingly mestizo or ethnically mixed (including Antioquia which thinks of itself as white); the Muiscas, Taironas and other indigenous peoples living in what is now Colombia at the time of the Conquest declined dramatically through a combination of war, disease, ill-treatment and intermarriage. Though some had highly-developed material cultures, they were neither as numerous nor as socially advanced as the peoples of the Aztec and Inca empires. Today, the indigenous population in Colombia consists of 115 different groups totalling slightly more than 1,9 million people and representing 4.4 per cent of the country's population.

The only substantial remaining groups of highland Indians are found in the region of Cauca and Nariño, south of Cali, where the Ocensa pipeline passes, Páez and Guambiano Indians have their reservations. This is an area of backward haciendas and patchworks of small farms and mountain towns of whitewashed walls and red-tiled roofs: the only part of Colombia similar in character and appearance to the Andean regions of Ecuador, Peru and Bolivia, further south, with their much larger Indian populations.

This otherness is at its most emphatic in Pasto, capital of Nariño, which sided with the Spanish during the wars of independence and then tried to join Ecuador when the post-war Gran Colombia federation broke up in 1830. It is also acknowledged in the popular image of the pastuso, the native of Pasto, who to other Colombians is proverbially and erroneously believed to be stupid.

Other notable Indian regions are the Sierra Nevada de Santa Marta, the scene of some of the most brutal confrontations between the traditional and modem aspects of Colombian society, and the and Guajira peninsula. Mestizo settlers and drug-traffickers, spurred by a mixture of land-hunger and greed, have been disputing control of the Sierra Nevada with the Kogui and Ika Indians for decades.

There are still some 395,000 Guajiro (Wayúu and Arhuaco) Indians, who make a hard living from their flat, sweltering peninsula on the Venezuelan frontier, where smuggling and the new open-cast coalmine at El Cerrejón are the only games in town. The Wayúu, who traditionally herd sheep and goats and dig salt, have shunned many of these developments and have kept to themselves. Poverty and a lack of clean water are taking their toll on the Wayúu community and more than 37 thousand[95] children suffer from malnutrition in that area.

Afro-Colombia

In the most recent census (2019), the Black Afro-Colombian, Raizal and Palenquera population numbered 2,9 million people, most of whom, who make up about 18 per cent of the total, are found along the Pacific and Caribbean coasts. Many were originally brought in from Africa to work the mines of the Pacific littoral that made the beautiful southern highland city of Popayan large and prosperous in the colonial period, before it was superseded as a regional centre by Cali in the mid-nineteenth century. An estimated one million black slaves passed through the port of Cartagena until the abolition of slavery in 1851. Many escaped from the mines and sugar plantations and formed free communities of cimarrones in the Cauca valley and on the isolated coast.

The separate identity and equal rights of their descendants are affirmed in the 1991 constitution and subsequent legislation, but black leaders remain sceptical that ingrained discrimination and disadvantage will be easily rooted out of Colombian society.

Anthropologist Jaime Arocha Rodríguez of the National University in Bogotá estimates that 10 per cent of the Colombian population are black and as many as 30 per cent are influenced by Afro-American culture (compared with two per cent indigenous Indians).

The first Afro-Colombian Vice-President

Francia Elena Márquez Mina was born in 1981 in Suárez, in the northern part of the Cauca department of Colombia. She was 15 years old when she decided to join the protests against the government of Colombia, which planned to deviate the river Ovejas toward the Salvajina dam. The huge project would impact the ancestral land of the African-Colombian communities very negatively, eliminating their ethnic and cultural identity.

In 2009 Márquez started a process of struggle and resistance to prevent 6,000 people of her communities from being expelled from the land, which the government had handed into a transnational enterprise for mining purposes. Márquez in 2015 received the Colombia National Prize. In 2018 in Paris, she received the Goldman Environmental Prize, for defying the illegal extraction and the construction of dams in her country.

In 2022, Márquez became Colombia's first Black vice president, winning on a leftist ticket with now-President Gustavo Petro. She became a symbol of hope for millions of Afro-Colombians, who saw in her the opportunity to have a seat at the table in a country where discussions of race and class are often cast aside for fantasies of a post-racial society.

European Migration

Independent Colombia has never been a country of large-scale European immigration, like Argentina in the late nineteenth century or Venezuela since the Second World War. The antioqueño colonisation that produced the modern coffee economy was given additional impulse by arrivals from Spain (particularly the Basque country), but many of the colonists were natives of Medellín who moved out in search of land to clear and cultivate.

Individual immigrant families from northern Europe have achieved prominence in various fields, such as the de Greiffs (from Sweden) and the Eders (from Germany) and Bogotá Mayor

Antanas Mockus was born in the capital because his Lithuanian parents arrived there as part of the United Nations resettlement programme for victims of the Second World War.

The other substantial immigrant group is from the Middle East, known collectively in Colombia as *turcos* although they are largely made up of descendants of Lebanese families leaving their lands during the era of the Ottoman empire. They are found everywhere, but particularly on the Caribbean coast, During the presidency of Julio César Turbay Ayala (1978-82), the 'emerging class' of nouveaux riches associated with the marijuana boom included many Turcos. Turbay is itself a *turco* name, and is ubiquitous in Colombian politics.

The Elites

Drawing on multiple interviews with oligarchic elites from Colombia, renowned academics Jenny Pearce and Juan David Velasco Montoyo produced a document entitled: *Élites, Poder y Principios De Dominación En Colombia (1991-2022)*[96]. This document discusses why it makes sense to use the term "oligarchic elites" and the constellation of families and elites in control of much of Colombia.

The authors use profound investigations to analyse both the failure to invest in the rule of law and also the elite preference for a fragmented security state whose permeability facilitates influence trafficking. The document explores how the elites have affected the nature of the state in Latin America, the diffusion of criminal violences, and the emergence of micro criminal orders in many parts of the country.

For any person interested in how the structure of power continues to this day through the different regions of the country, this study makes for essential reading.

---

[95] Human Rights Watch: https://www.hrw.org/world-report/2023/country-chapters/colombia

[96] London School of Economics: https://www.lse.ac.uk/lacc/assets/documents/PEARCE-VELASCO-ELITES-Y-PODER-EN-COLOMBIA-1991-2022.pdf

Music

One of the things you can't fail to notice in Colombia is the nation's love of music. It's not just the fact that music is ubiquitous and loud, but that everyone seems to know every word and sing or dance at every opportunity, including taxi drivers, people in corner stores, in their offices and even just people on the street. All too often the volume is set to "Colombian," which usually means that the speaker is blaring out distortion punctuated rhythms and nary a conversation can be had, but that's the point for, as it soon becomes clear in Colombia, the music is the protagonist, not the dancers, revelers or drinkers.

Colombia has produced its fair share of internationally successful artists, the likes of Shakira, Toto La Momposina, Bomba Estereo, ChocQuibTown and Carlos Vives all enjoy a fame beyond the frontiers of their homeland. It's worth noting that Colombians are fiercely patriotic when it comes to their music whether it's salsa, champeta or a local papayera.

Champeta

Originating on Colombia's Caribbean coast, Champeta is a style of music almost unchanged from its African roots. Though elements of rap and reggaeton can be heard in modern Champeta, it's more common for those genres to borrow from Champeta. The vocal stylings of the genre and the percussive elements are heavily influenced by African music. The sound relies on a strong snare drum and intricate guitar-work. Champeta is heard on both the Pacific and Atlantic coasts of Colombia.

Cumbia

Cumbia is one of Colombia's most important genres of music. Originating from the Caribbean region of the country. Its African roots are immediately obvious in the heavy use of percussion and the vocal style. The music began as a courtship dance practiced by the African slave population, but later mixed with European influence to arrive at the sound we hear today. The cumbia enjoyed at the Barranquilla Carnival finds its roots in the towns and communities along the Magdalena River.

Joropo

"Joropo," is a uniquely Colombian form of tap dancing blended with ancestral dance roots that are based firmly in Flamenco. Joropo music is undoubtedly the most authentic and representative music of the Colombian Savannah since it is a result of mixing the cuatro guitar introduced by the *colonos*, the harp brought in by the Jesuits, and small maracas which are a derivation of indigenous instruments. Like a bastard child from Andalucía, the music is played frenetically while the dancers seemingly try to keep up and the singers show their range.

Locally the word "joropo" means "party" and together with its regional variants blends machismo desires through big-hearted Colombian-style passion. The music, while led by the harp mixes an almost joyous declaration of regional pride, punctuated with string and percussion-based choruses.

Merengue

Merengue is a musical genre created in the Dominican Republic which is popular all over Colombia, and a frequent feature on dancefloors. Merengue is a fast, energetic style of music, and probably the easiest to dance to for foreigners too baffled by the footwork required for salsa. Musically and lyrically it is often very light-hearted.

Porro

Porro supposedly began in pre-Colombian times on the Caribbean coast of Colombia, with indigenous groups dancing and singing to African rhythms. What is certain is that it is a joyful, party-ready style of music closely aligned with Cumbia. Porro is very popular on Colombia's Atlantic Coast, as well as the Córdoba region. While it's not as popular as some other genres in places such as Bogotá and Medellín, it can still be heard in traditional bars.

Reggaeton

While some Colombians may tell you that they hate Reggaeton, it's likely you'll see that same person happily dancing to it in a club. Reggaeton isn't the most musically ambitious or deep music, but has an infectious beat and, more often than not, catchy choruses of debatable quality. While Reggaeton didn't originate in Colombia, it is currently by far the most popular genre on the dancefloors of Bogotá.

Salsa

Salsa doesn't originate from Colombia, but it has found a spiritual home all over Colombia but perhaps most of all in the southern city of Cali. Originating primarily in New York, Puerto Rico and Cuba (it is derived from a Cuban genre called son), it's a genre that is inherently tied to dance and, as such, is difficult to avoid in Colombian clubs. Musically the music relies heavily on percussion, with piano and horns also playing a major part. There is clear African influence in the music, most evident in the frequent employment of the call and response vocals.

Vallenato

Vallenato is considered to be a pure Colombian form of music blending Colombia's African, indigenous and European heritages. Popularized in the city of Valledupar, in the Caribbean region of Colombia, it started with local troubadours travelling from town to town and sharing the news and gossip through song as they played on the drum, guacharaca and accordion. Romantic vallenato, the genre's most recent evolution bears little similarity to the folksy beginnings of the original vallenato and the standard bearer for vallenato-pop is of course, Carlos Vives, once described as "vallenato in an Armani suit." You mainly hear the accordion-heavy Vallenato on the Caribbean Coast, but expect a great deal all over the country.

Sports

Football is undisputed king and when the national team or *selección* plays, the country comes to a standstill with virtually everyone wearing the yellow jersey of the *cafeteros* in support. While the domestic league in Colombia suffers from people preferring to watch readily accessible televised games from overseas and dwindling numbers in the stadia takes away from the atmosphere, local derby games such as the Bogotá clásico of Santa Fé vs Millonarios or Medellín's Atlético Nacional vs Deportivo Independiente Medellín are quite a sight to behold. Not dissimilar to much of the developing world, football is seen as a way to escape poverty and the dream is a big-money move overseas. In recent years the most successful Colombians in European leagues have been James (pronounced Hamez) Rodriguez once of Real Madrid, the ageing Radamel Falcao now playing out his days at Turkey's Galatasaray, Juan Cuadrado at Juventus and Yerry Mina formerly at Everton. Colombia's most successful World Cup campaign came in 2014 when the team fell to Brazil 2-1 in the Quarter Finals and the euphoria helped push away the painful memories of that fateful day in USA 1994 when team captain Andrés Escobar scored an own goal and went out in the group stage, an event which led to the player's murder – reportedly as retribution for his error – in a Medellín car park. Colombia again qualified for the World Cup in 2018 losing to England in the second round on penalties.

The only sport which can rival Football's hegemony is cycling and Colombia's riders are rightfully internationally recognized and respected. As Matt Rendell, author of *Colombia es Pasion, the Generation of Racing Cyclists who Changed their Nation and the Tour de France*, (Orion Publishing 2020) explains in his book: "… Colombia's cycling sons are not products of a rigorous sports system that nurtures them to the pinnacle of globalised sport.

They come from harder backgrounds, that surprise, shock –

even, at times, enchant." By winning the 2019 Tour de France, Egan Bernal became the race's youngest champion in 110 years and the first from Colombia. In the years prior to this spectacular success, Nairo Quintana won the Tours of Italy and Spain and very nearly the Tour de France. It's worth noting that Miguel Ángel López and Fernando Gaviria also made final podiums as well.

Perhaps it's their humble backgrounds and their individual stories of overcoming the hardships of poverty and violence which propel these world class athletes to inspiring a nation. Whatever the case, their achievements cannot be overlooked nor belittled as they resonate to lift a nation's spirits.

Finding its origins in rural Boyacá, Tejo is a national sport for the sportingly challenged. Originating in Turmequé over 500 years ago, today this humble farming community has a Campo de Tejo at its heart. Once known simply as Turmequé by the Chibcha people, this spirited throwing sport has evolved over time. Participants toss a small 2kg metal disk at a gunpowder detonator on a clay-filled target – all in the name of good fun and copious beers. Tejo takes place in a small circular area, fittingly and usually behind a local bar. The goal is to make the disk strike triangle-shaped mechas (gunpowder) in the middle of the target. Many professional tejo teams compete nationwide. Most are sponsored by beer companies because drinking is a vital part of the game. Tejo is played to nine or 21 points – or until players can no longer stand. The person who makes the most explosions is the winner – at which time the losers are obliged buy the next round.

Forgotten Histories

Jack Greenwell, Independiente de Santa Fe's Legendary English Coach

Winner of 13 awards in Spain with Barcelona, Espanyol and Valencia, Peruvian champions with Universitario of Lima and triumphing in the Copa America with Peruvian national side before arriving in Colombia and coaching Independiente de Santa Fe in Bogotá, Jack Greenwell of Crook Town, County Durham is arguably the most successful English football coach to have ever plied his trade overseas.

This begs the question, why does he remain an almost forgotten footnote in the archives of international football? There is so little recorded about Jack Greenwell's time in Bogotá, a mere two months, which perhaps makes the story even more enticing.

A rudimentary Wikipedia search brings up the obvious details, but this information is sufficient alone to snare even a fair-weather football fan or historian. For me, the search into the latter years of Jack Greenwell's life began with an innocuous mention on the BBC World Football phone in show where it was suggested that Greenwell was killed during the infamous Bogotazo of 1948 when the centre of the city was all but completely destroyed.

My research led me to discover that Greenwell was resident in the Pension Centenario (Cra 8a con Calle 16), a downtown area of Bogotá that has clearly seen better days and of course was largely razed to the ground in the chaos ruling for the days following Gaitan's murder.

But no, a swift visit to the Bogotá Archives was enough to prove that Jack Greenwell had passed away before this event, his name wedged between the Garcías and Guzmáns. To my surprise, the building where he lived survives while much around it was levelled in 1948, although, its use has evolved from guesthouse to that of bedsits, bookshops and the ubiquitous chicken eatery.

By my reckoning Jack Greenwell is absent from the football hall of fame due to the nature of his unceremonious demise in Bogotá on the 7th of October 1942 just as he was making a name for himself in the capital but before he could have his name cast into the hall of fame of Independiente de Santa Fe where he was coaching at the time.

Perhaps known only to a handful of die-hard Santa Fe *hinchas*, John Richard Greenwell known to everyone as Jack was the very definition of a journeyman football coach. It would be doing this native of County Durham a disservice to try and liken him to any contemporary figures since in reality no one comes close. Who can claim to have played in England and Spain and coached in Spain, Turkey, Peru and Colombia? Who else has a record with Barcelona only bettered by Johan Cruyff and Pep Guardiola.

A coal miner's son he began his playing career in his hometown of Crook and then moved on to Auckland Wanderers before making the amazing step of establishing himself with Barcelona where he made 88 appearances between 1912 and 1916 and scored 10 goals.

Greenwell had two stints as coach of Barcelona from 1917-1924 and 1931-1933 and in between spent time with Castellon, Espanyol, Mallorca and helped organize the Spanish national team for the 1920 Summer Olympics in Antwerp and then post 1933 he coached Valencia and Sporting Gijon before leaving the country in 1936 for Turkey due to the outbreak of the Spanish Civil War.

Little is known about Greenwell's stint in Turkey aside from him training up referees and the next we hear of him he has turned up in Lima coaching Universitario and preparing the Peruvian national side for the 1939 South American Championship in which they were victorious.

It was in 1938 that Greenwell savoured his first experiences in Colombia leading Peru to win the inaugural Bolivarian games in Bogotá. The Peruvian side defeated Colombia 4-2 and notched up a startling 18 goals in 4 games. The journeyman from Crook Town must have seen something in Colombia because he was back again in 1940 to help organise and prepare the Colombian national side for the *Juegos del Caribe* in Barranquilla.

The Caribbean city of Barranquilla must have been almost a homecoming for Greenwell since there was a large British community here at the time, and this city with its railways and port had been a key point of entry for the beautiful game to Colombia.

Whether he considered his two-year tenure in Barranquilla a success or not we cannot know for the *Juegos del Caribe* were abandoned for obvious reasons given the global geopolitical situation and he was drawn to Bogotá with a job offer from the *Federación Deportiva del Guayas*. This job never materialised and it was then that the directors of Santa Fe came calling.

Hired initially for a six-month period in 1942 by then Santa Fe President Enrique Santos Castillo (father of former President Juan Manuel Santos), Greenwell made his mark straight away with journalists from the national newspaper, *El Tiempo*, praising his discipline and tactics. Leading Santa Fe to their first amateur title for the state of Cundinamarca.

Greenwell's last game was a resounding 10 – 3 win over local rivals Deportivo Texas at the Alfonso Lopez stadium in the Universidad Nacional on October 5.

On October 7 having finished his morning training session in the *Quinta Mutis* in western Bogotá Greenwell was driven home by Rafael Urdaneta Holguín along with other Santa Fe players to his digs at the *Pensión Centenario* just below the *Séptima* avenue. According the obituary published in the Colombian national newspaper, *El Tiempo*, scarcely had Greenwell reached his room when he was taken gravely ill and various other residents of the *Pensión* called for medical assistance. Before the Doctor arrived, Jack Greenwell had passed away, his *Registro de Defunción* or Death Certificate, suggesting an aneurysm.

Buried in the British Cemetery in Bogotá, a reflection of Greenwell's life is not only astounding in its achievements but also the historical timeline in which he inhabited. He was in Barcelona for WWI and thus did not become a part of a lost generation, he had to leave Spain due to the outbreak of the Civil War, he moved to Peru and Colombia and was working diligently during WWII.

I spent several hours in the British Cemetery (Calle 26 No 17-19) thoroughly scanning each tombstone to try and locate Jack Greenwell's, but to no avail. His final resting place was not to be found nestled between members of Bolívar's Albion Regiment, natives of Kirkcudbride and Woking, Presidents of industry and banking. There were handfuls of weather-damaged slabs that could quite reasonably belong to Greenwell, the closest I came to his surname was a Greenwood as directed by the cemetery caretaker Edgar, but this was a child's grave.

Aged 58, Jack Greenwell passed away and his mastery of the beautiful game goes unrecognised by the vast majority of football fans. It has not been an easy task – the hierarchy at Santa Fe seemed ignorant of his tenure with them - that of tracking down his final resting place and his short life in Bogotá, it has been a trail that has taken me through the city archives, early Bogotá Notary offices – where he is listed as *entrenador de Foott Booll* - and unsuccessfully to the British Cemetery. But, hopefully, this can reawaken some interest in the history of the game here in Colombia and in this journeyman coach that made his mark globally in aiding leagues in their infancy get off the ground.

After much petitioning, Jack Greenwell was inducted into the Football Hall of Fame[97]

in April 2024.

---

[97] BBC: https://www.bbc.com/news/uk-england-wear-68833633

Colombian football, and why it matters

Dr Peter Watson[98]

A Twitter thread from @pipomadrid on 26th October 2022 perhaps best illustrates how much football matters to Colombia. In each video, we see Colombians clustered around television sets and laptops all erupting in joy as the Colombian goalkeeper dives to the left to save the crucial penalty against Nigeria. Boys and girls in classrooms, students, businesspersons, and people on board an airplane all begin cheering and dancing, hugging each other and celebrating wildly, actions mirroring the Colombian players on the pitch who with that save managed to qualify for the World Cup final. What makes this moment especially significant is that it is not the full men's *Selección* playing; this triumph was achieved by the Colombian U-17 women's national team. Fifteen years ago, even five years ago, such national celebrations would have been unthinkable for any women's team, let alone an under 17 team in a deeply conservative, *machista* country. The match would likely not even have been televised, given the relatively invisible nature of women's football in Colombia. However, given the men's team failure to qualify for the 2022 World Cup in Qatar despite the best efforts of Luis Díaz, a footballer from the Wayuu indigenous community in La Guajira, there was a need to celebrate women's football being good instead. Indeed, the U17 team built on the full women's team narrowly losing to Brazil in the Copa América final several months previously. A new Colombian hero was also born, young Afro-Colombian forward Linda Caicedo, who dazzled in both tournaments. Following the U17 team's victory, praise for the team flowed on social media; congratulatory tweets came from men's national team heroes such as James Rodríguez and Radamel Falcao. President Gustavo Petro tweeted that the women had made history, and now deserved not only the nation's admiration and recognition but also fair salaries, sponsorship, a women's professional league and the whole support of the government.

Such public, media and presidential attention is indicative of football's importance to Colombians. A 2014 study carried out by the Interior Ministry discovered that 94% of Colombians think football is either important or very important. Reasons for its importance included unifying the country, distancing young people from vice and violence and providing happiness. In a country where far too many national memories are related to violence, tragedy and death, many Colombians might admit to their happiest national memories being football-related. They would recall the last-minute equaliser scored by Freddy Rincón against West Germany (through the goalkeeper's legs, no less) in the 1990 World Cup, or the epic 5-0 thrashing of Argentina in Buenos Aires in September 1993 to qualify for the 1994 World Cup as being moments when the seemingly never-ending violence and misery of the Colombian conflict was briefly displaced by delight and a pride in being Colombian. Gabriel García Márquez, no less, apparently described the 5-0 win as one of the three most important moments for Colombia. On such occasions football finally provided the chance to celebrate being known for something other than being the home of Pablo Escobar. Despite the revelations of cartel involvement in football and the tragic murder of defender Andrés Escobar after his accidental own goal in the disastrous 1994 World Cup finals, the conviction remained that football somehow has the power to if not solve, then at least alleviate personal, local or national problems.

Sociologists and historians who research football in Latin America often describe it as being a 'zero institution'; football can be conceived as a kind of empty vessel of potential power that can be filled with a particular message or idea and then transmitted to the masses. Examples abound of politicians using football as a pacifying or distraction device from ongoing social problems, as a way of legitimising themselves and their regime by appearing with national footballing heroes at moments of triumph, or promoting a desired image of their country through hosting a major tournament. Most of these uses of football are temporary in impact, or can be dismissed as overtly populist demonstrations of patriotism or gesture politics. Such manipulations of football are present in Colombian history too; examples include the so-called El Dorado professional league being rushed into existence and supported by President Mariano Ospina Pérez as national violence spread and intensified after the assassination of liberal leader Jorge Eliécer Gaitán in 1948; the 4-4 'win' against the mighty Soviet Union in the 1962 World Cup was, according to incoming President Guillermo León Valencia, a 'triumph of democracy over totalitarianism', a victory over the forces of communism; the so-called Golden Generation of Carlos 'El Pibe' Valderrama, Faustino Asprilla, Andrés Escobar *et al* were lauded as presenting an image of the 'real' Colombia and a hope for the future by President Carlos Gaviria, who awarded them national honours for beating Argentina 5-0. In most cases, little concrete governmental support was provided and football's potential power was never fully activated beyond rhetoric and public displays of support.

In the last fifteen years or so, however, and most obviously during the presidency of Juan Manuel Santos (2010-2018), there has been a greater awareness in Colombia of the potential power of football, and of other sports for that matter. Perhaps inspired by symbolic moments such as Nelson Mandela's support for the South African rugby team or by ongoing developments and visibility of Sport for Development and Peace methodologies and projects in Colombia and worldwide, under Santos football became a key component of a consistent and multi-faceted strategy directed towards various domestic and external policy objectives. Foremost of these at a national level was the peace process with the FARC and accompanying national unity project, but football was also a feature of health and education campaigns. Internationally, football became a promoted element of Colombia's nation rebranding campaigns, attempting to change the identity and image of the country as well as enhance its positive visibility in the global gaze. It has also been an ingredient of diplomacy projects, creating sporting links and alliances with other countries, helping to establish common ground with Latin American neighbours and promoting the country as a venue for tourism and investment through the hosting of increasingly important football and multisport events. Such actions are not limited to the government; NGOs, transnational businesses and even anti-state actors (e.g. the FARC) have also deployed football to serve their own social, commercial and political projects. Football's use, therefore is no longer simply limited to political opportunism; it is increasingly deliberate, strategic, planned and wide-ranging.

The rhetoric is still present of course. It is obligatory for Colombian presidents to comment on national team performances, though it is a no-win situation. Congratulatory messages can be dismissed as jumping on the bandwagon or political appropriation of a non-political sporting success, but failing to comment would be unpatriotic or being accused as being out of touch. Santos, however, spoke about football and sport constantly, more than any other president, both in public speeches and on Twitter. He accompanied his praise of sporting endeavour with references to peace, national unity and how athletes were examples for the nation trying to move forward to a better future. His communications director acknowledged that this was a deliberate strategy attempting to use football as a way to unify the country with football linked to desired national values of peace, solidarity, reconciliation and working together as a team. The most salient example was after Colombia's best-ever performance in a World Cup in 2014, when they narrowly lost to hosts Brazil. In his first televised speech since his re-election, Santos wore the football shirt and told the watching Colombians that 'We can achieve everything, everything, if we work like the Colombian national football team – united for a country! This is the great lesson that those admirable Colombians left us, those great sportsmen and great human beings who represented us the World Cup 2014'.

Furthermore, Santos used similar speeches to readmit members of the FARC back into the national 'us' as fans of the national team. Previously demonised as being narco-terrorists and enemies of the nation, Santos recognised them as included members of the *hinchada nacional,* the national 'fangroup', telling the national team on their visit to the presidential palace in May 2014 that 'it doesn't matter what religion you belong it, it doesn't matter what the differences may be. Even those with whom we are negotiating to end the armed conflict, they will also be supporting you. All of Colombia will be supporting you'. FARC naturally, took the opportunity to legitimise themselves and show their patriotism and love of football by sending out their own messages of support to the national team, of course wearing the yellow shirt of the *Selección* with the hashtag #UunidosPorUnPais (united for a country) on the back.

Most importantly, this constant presidential rhetoric was supported by action. A series of laws originally contemplated to sanction and control fan violence in professional club football and around football stadia, expanded in range and vision to include aspects of football for coexistence and social development in their articles. Ensuing laws and public policies recognised and empowered the use of pedagogical and developmental projects around football, culminating with the continentally ground-breaking Ten-Year Plan for Security, Comfort and Coexistence in Football 2014-2024. Although not without flaws and not fully implemented, this public policy nonetheless provided a blueprint for a more holistic, participative and structured use for football towards addressing the causes of football and community violence. It helped promote spaces for collaborative work, socialisation and football for peace methodologies designed and developed by various Colombian NGOs such as Tiempo de Juego, Fútbol con Corazón and Colombianitos.

Such football for peace organizations have been present in Colombia since 1995 when Jurgen Griesbeck and Alejandro Arenas created a project in Medellín to attempt to reduce young people being caught up in gang violence. Similar programmes have mushroomed since then, to the extent that the Gol y Paz network was set up by organizations involved in the research and building of the Ten-Year Plan to improve cooperation and share knowledge of football for peace methodologies across the country. Governmental institutions such as Colombian Joven, the Ministry of Sport and the Agencia para la Reincorporación y Normalización have used similar sport for peace methodologies in their own projects. Foremost of these was the Golombiao campaign, a project supported by UNICEF, which was present at one time or other in each of Colombia's 32 regions. The Social and Community Sport department of the Ministry of Sport has also gained in importance and budget since 2010, changing a prior tendency to focus on elite-level sporting performance.

The most significant and visible use of sport for peace was in the FARC demobilization and reintegration camps following the signing of the peace treaty in 2016. Coaches were sent to the various camps across the country to provide sport and recreation opportunities for the former FARC guerrillas. The result was a series of highly-mediatised men's and women's football matches and tournaments involving members of the FARC, local communities, and the Colombian police and army. The most famous of these took place during the 2018 World Cup; the event held in Llano Grande in Antioquia took inspiration from the 1998 Sergio Cabrera film *Golpe de Estadio* which showed the FARC, soldiers and local villagers coming together to watch a Colombia match on the only television in the area. The 'Golpe de Estadio 2' event in Llano Grande had the same idea, as former FARC and paramilitary leaders, representatives of victims associations, the public forces and local community watched the Colombia vs Japan match together, before playing several football matches and giving speeches supporting the peace process.

Events such as these show that football really matters in Colombia, and can go beyond simply a passion for a club or national team. Although endowed at times with overly mythopoeic powers, football certainly has the potential to contribute towards addressing some of Colombia's social problems. At the very least it creates meeting spaces and can break down barriers between Colombians, providing shared moments, memories and experiences which could be built on for more transformative dialogues and processes towards remedying social and political disputes. With two young stars like Linda Caicedo and Luis Díaz at the forefront of the men's and women's national teams, given their Afro-Colombian and indigenous backgrounds and what they represent, there is grounds for optimism that more unifying and transformative moments lie ahead.

---

[98] Peter Watson PhD, Teaching Fellow in the Department of Spanish, Portuguese and Latin American Studies, University of Leeds.

Carnival and festivals

There may be a festival for every day of the year in Colombia if you include beauty pageants and the 18 public holidays. While you could enjoy the National Donkey Festival in San Antero in Córdoba or the Miss Petroleum pageant in Barrancabermeja, Santander, the most famous celebrations and festivals are well worth attending. The most famous is of course Barranquilla's carnival where revellers party all day and night in a bacchanalian form which rivals only that of the Carnival in Rio de Janeiro. Declared as intangible Cultural Heritage of Humanity in 2008, the Carnival retains, respects and protects its origins. The blending of various local traditions permeates numerous aspects of the carnival, particularly dances (as exemplified by the mico y micas from the Americas, the African congo and the paloteo of Spanish origin), musical genres (the predominant cumbia and variants such as the puya and porro) and folk instruments (tambora and allegre drums, maraca, claves, etc.). Carnival music is generally performed by drum ensembles or by groups playing a variety of wind instruments. The profuse material culture of handcrafted objects includes floats, costumes, head ornaments and animal masks. Groups of masqueraded dancers, actors, singers and instrumentalists delight crowds with theatrical and musical performances based on historical as well as current events. Contemporary political life and figures are satirized through mocking speeches and song lyrics that lend a burlesque atmosphere to the carnival.

Bogotá's biannual Iberoamerican Theatre Festival in March is of note as its innovative and decentralized style is designed to draw in the whole capital with thespian attractions and activities. Since its beginnings in 1988, the festival has included classical theatre, street theatre, performance art, circus acts, concerts, pantomime and other dance and performances presented in different settings from theatres to parks and plazas. Bogotá is not without other outdoor attractions and there are free of charge annual rock, jazz and salsa weekends held in the Parque Simón Bolívar.

Other national festivals and celebrations of note include:

January: Carnaval de Blancos y Negros, Pasto, Nariño.

March/ April: Semana Santa Holy Week processions in Mompós, Bolívar and Popayán, Cauca.

April: Festival de la Leyenda Vallenata, Valledupar, Cesar.

June: Festival de San Pedro, Neiva, Huila.

June/ July: Colombiamoda, Medellín, Antioquia.

August: Feria de las Flores, Medellín, Antioquia.

August: Festival de Música del Pacífico Petronio Álvarez, Cali, Valle del Cauca.

September: Festival Internacional de Jazz, Mompós, Bolívar.

October: Festival del Tatacoa, Huila.

December: Feria de Cali, Cali, Valle del Cauca.

Media

The onset of electronic media (television and radio) in digital form either from mobile phones, computers or tablets has become the norm in Colombia. Television remains as the most consumed media amongst Colombian citizens. Nevertheless, radio continues to be important and then is followed by the press. Third comes the Internet, which has been gaining ground and thanks to the convergence of other media, it is common to observe today that the main newspapers, television and radio are consumed online.

All of the media companies belong to private initiatives that use advertising and subscriptions as their main sources of income and the most important ones belong to large economic conglomerates of the country, some of them also owners of electronic and print media.

In this respect, at a television level, the private channel Caracol has the highest news audience followed by the private channel RCN (RCN, as well as the National Radio Network RCN belong to the magnate Carlos Ardila Lülle). For radio, the radio station Blu Radio, a subsidiary of Caracol television is the most successful. Both of these belong to the Santo Domingo family which also owns *El Espectador*, the second national newspaper in terms of circulation in Colombia. The second most listened station is La W, which belongs to the Spanish group *Prisa*. With regards to newspapers, *El Tiempo*has the highest national circulation followed by the free daily newspaper ADN, which is from the same publishing house, owned by Luis Carlos Sarmiento Angulo (owner of the *Grupo Aval,* part of the largest banking system in the country).

Whilst on paper, Colombia has a free press, the reality on the ground is far different and the country is an incredibly dangerous place for domestic journalists, in particular away from the main cities and working in the regional press who are routinely threatened by armed groups. The international press is given more leeway but pioneering journalists such as Adriaan Alsema of Colombia Reports[99] receives his fair share of threats for publishing articles unpopular with the Colombian establishment. Another worthwhile regional outlet, headed up by Joshua Collins is Pirate Wire Services[100].

According to the Reporters Without Borders (RSF), the world's biggest NGO specializing in the defence of media freedom: "Colombia continues to be one of the western hemisphere's most dangerous countries for journalists, who are still the frequent targets of death threats, physical attacks, abduction and murder. Coverage of such subjects as the environment, public order, armed conflicts, corruption or collusion between politicians and illegal armed groups elicits systematic harassment, intimidation and violence. Journalists also continue to be permanently threatened by "bacrims," gangs of former paramilitaries now involved in drug trafficking." The country ranked 139 out of 180 in RSF's press freedom index[101].

There have been widely publicized cases of "owner interference and influence" in the editorial decisions of their news outlets. The most impacting being the dismissal of popular columnist Daniel Coronel formerly at Semana magazine for critical and supported allegations against the government of President Duque in 2019. Then in August 2020, audio recordings of telephone conversations between Sen. Uribe, his lawyer and influential radio journalist Julio Sánchez Cristo of La W. surfaced during the former president's court case where he is alleged to have been involved in witness tampering, showing clear media bias and preferential treatment and throwing the industry's damaged reputation into further chaos.

For independent and investigative print journalism in Spanish on Colombia recommended are, *La Silla Vacia*[102], and, "*Los Danieles*[103]," Daniel Coronel's collaborative effort with renowned journalists and social commentators, Daniel Samper Pizano and Daniel Samper Ospina are a good place to start as is the podcast: "*A Fondo104*," with María Jimena Duzán, covering the most pressing issues in Colombia.

For political and risk analysis in both English and Spanish: Colombia Risk Analysis[105]

is a Colombia-based international outlet aimed to a business-oriented market and for a more international overview of goings on, the Washington Office on Latin America[106] (WOLA) offers keen socio-political insights.

For a weekly podcast in English addressing all topics falling under "Society and Culture," the "Colombia Calling podcast[107]," is available on all platforms. There are two English-language newspapers in Bogotá, the oldest being "The City Paper[108]," and then the alternative, "The Bogotá Post[109]."

---

[99] Colombia Reports: http://www.colombiareports.com/

[100] Pirate Wire Services: https://www.piratewireservices.com

[101] Reporters Without Borders: https://rsf.org/en/country/colombia

[102] La Silla Vacia: https://lasillavacia.com,

[103] Los Danieles: https://losdanieles.com/

[104] A Fondon: https://www.youtube.com/channel/UCXvLBn7NFhO9V48L05W-zyg

[105] Colombia Risk Analysis: https://www.colombiariskanalysis.com/

[106] WOLA: https://www.wola.org/program/colombia/

[107] Colombia Calling: http://www.colombiacalling.co/

[108] The City Paper: http://thecitypaperbogota.com

[109] The Bogotá Post: https://thebogotapost.com/

Press Freedom in Colombia

Adriaan Alsema director of Colombia Reports

Press freedom in Colombia deteriorated in 2023 amid persistent aggression and self-censorship

The freedom of the press continued to deteriorate in Colombia in 2023 as journalists continued to suffer violence and abuse by illegal armed groups, public officials and even their own bosses, according to Reporters Without Borders (RSF).

Particularly reporting on "the environment, public order, armed conflicts, corruption or collusion between politicians and illegal armed groups elicits systematic harassment, intimidation and violence," according to RSF.

Consequently, Colombia saw its suppression rate go up slightly and its position in the press freedom index drop to 139 of 180.

- Threat 1: illegal armed groups

Journalists continued to be "permanently threatened" by paramilitary groups that have been associated with the military, drug traffickers, "legitimate" businesses and politicians alike.

Additionally, "armed groups such as the ELN and FARC dissidents try to silence alternative and community media that cover their activities, leading to the creation of information "black holes," especially in rural areas," said the RSF.

- Threat 2: media bosses

"The media's close links to Colombia's business empires and political class undermines editorial independence and reinforces self-censorship," according to the press freedom organization.

The RSF has been monitoring media ownership in Colombia

since 2015 and found in 2018 that three corporations, the Ardila Lulle Group, and the Santo Domingo and Sarmiento families accumulate 57 per cent of the market.

This interdependence particularly between newspaper *El Tiempo* of Luis Carlos Sarmiento and the government of President Iván Duque became particularly evident last year when the two exchanged executives.

"Media groups and companies also often financially support electoral campaigns. Their support for one candidate then again has influence on the media coverage of those elections. On the regional level, this phenomenon seems to work as a trait – the winning candidate puts the public advertising into the media outlets, which supported his election."

Reporters Without Borders

Press freedom foundation FLIP warned last year that the increasingly blurred lines between mass media and government threatened the democratic character of Colombia.

- Threat 3: President Iván Duque (until 2022)

The RSF confirmed that the government has increasingly become a threat to the freedom of press.

"Since conservative politician Iván Duque's installation as president in August 2018, journalists and media outlets have been the targets of harassment and intimidation campaigns and espionage after reporting that members of his government had been involved in fraud, corruption and human rights violations."

Reporters Without Borders

With the help of government officials, followers of former President Álvaro Uribe have regularly embarked on smear campaigns against journalists, particularly after the Supreme Court began investigating Duque's far-right political patron over alleged fraud and bribery.

The military has been accused of terrorizing journalists of

weekly *Semana* who were investigating corruption and human rights violations inside the military.

Literature

Colombian literature with its heterogeneously blended racial backdrop of Spanish, Indian and African influences is perhaps the perfect example of the lively and continual struggle for an identity between heritages and the situation inherent in this country.

Obviously with such a colourful and conflicting history, this has enabled Colombia to inspire a nation of writers and poets either escaping the realities of the contemporary Colombian condition or directly expressing vitriolic discontentment with a political situation.

The most recognized Colombian author is of course the magic realism specialist Gabriel García Márquez (1927-2014) whose literary efforts, in particular, *100 Years of Solitude* (1967) which won him the Nobel Prize in 1982, journalistic works and short stories have made him an international household name. There is no doubting his strong influence on contemporary Colombian literature which in many cases struggles to step out from his long shadow. Gabriel García Márquez has addressed almost every era dating from the period of independence with *The General in his Labyrinth*(1989) to the sinister themes of the current day in *News of a Kidnapping* (1996) but this is not to say that there is not a vast reservoir of other scribes and poets to instill further delightful imagery to hasten the visitor to Colombia.

Pre-Colombian Period

Proving that the literary tradition in Colombia dates back significantly one need only reference the oral traditions of the Kogui tribe of the Atlantic coast and their beliefs in *Creación* or indeed the *Chiminiguagua: creación del mundo*, of the Chibcha or Muisca people from the country's central highlands. *El Diluvio* from the Chocó, Colombia's lush Pacific coast that stretches up to the borders with Panama, recreates life as the

Embera tribe knows it in the tangle of jungle found there.

Chronicles and Poetry of the Spanish Dominion

Gonzalo Jiménez de Quesada (1495-1579) the founder of Bogotá, discoverer and conqueror of all but small parts of Nueva Granada is also a noted chronicler and while neither copies of his *Relación de la Conquista del Nuevo Reino de Granada* nor *Compendio Historial de las Conquistas del Nuevo Reino* exist we have been left with his insightful take on and refutation of the Italian Archbishop of Nochera, Paolo Jovio's, anti-Hispanic writings of the era in his recognised tome, *Antijovio* (1567).

19th Century National Emancipation

Correctly, much has been made of Antonio Nariño (1765-1823) whose works of journalism embrace an honest desire for liberty justice and equality. A native of Bogotá, Nariño dedicated his life to improving the quality of life of his compatriots and in turn translated from French into Spanish the *Declaración universal de los derechos del hombre y ciudadano* (1794). His efforts landed him in prison in Cádiz on more than one occasion before he returned to Colombia in 1820 and was named a Senator.

Born in either Cali or Quibdó, depending on which biographer you read, Jorge Isaacs (1837-1895) is remembered as a distinguished writer, politician and soldier. From 1867 he led the editorial team in the recently formed conservative newspaper La República. However, it is his masterful work *María* (1867) that epitomises the romantic literary movement in Colombia at the time known as *costumbrismo* and it is this single work of Isaacs' that has become one of the cornerstones of Latin American romanticism.

The poet Candelario Obeso (1849-1884) differs somewhat from the previous two authors since he is of a mixed-race background and is considered as the forefather of black Latin American poetry. Born in the wetland area of the *Depresión Momposina*, a place famed for its heat, colonial architecture and mestizo roots, Obeso's most striking poem, *Cantos Populares de mi tierra* embodies the struggle of the local mestizo class written in their voice. This work gained him posthumous fame as his brief life ended in suicide.

Modern Literature and Poetry

The new wave of Colombian literature found itself between two literary fashions, Costumbrismo and Romanticism which ran parallel to political events at the time such as civil wars and the independence from Spain still fresh in the memory. Tomás Carrasquilla (1858-1940), known for such works as *En la diestra de Dios padre* (1897) and *La Marquesa de Yolombó* (1928) was particularly affected by the goings on around him in Colombia at the time and only gained famed for his writing later on in his life at age 68. Perhaps Carrasquilla's reputation suffered somewhat amongst his peers as often his historical novels blurred the line between costumbrismo and romanticism leading his writing to fall into both categories but specialising in neither.

José Eustacio Rivera (1888-1928), after travelling and witnessing with his own eyes the atrocious treatment and quality of life under which the rubber plantation workers barely survived in Casanare, bordering Venezuela, wrote La Voragine (1924) or the Vortex. Recognised as one the most important novels to come out of Colombia, Rivera was elected to a government position and while in New York to oversee the translation of the novel and the adaptation for the film version, he passed away.

While Gabriel García Márquez (1927) is known for his works of magic realism one must address the Grupo de Barranquilla that consisted of a number of writers and artists from or who gravitated to the Caribbean port city of the same name and nurtured one another's writings in a bohemian haunt of *La Cueva*. During the 1940s and 1950s they produced and edited the magazine *Crónica*, and cemented their fame as hawkish purveyors of culture throughout the region.

There is never too much written of Gabriel García Márquez and Barranquilla and the Colombian coast remain constant as key influences in his writing. *Memorias de mis putas tristes* (2004) recalls a Barranquilla of the 1930s and his autobiography *Vivir para contarla* (2002) is thick with memories of his hometown of Aracataca, his courtship of Mercedes his wife and his travels in the Colombian Caribbean.

Having criticised Gabriel García Márquez for his use of magic realism Laura Restrepo (1950) blends tough realities with fiction pushing readers to read between the lines in her novels, in particular *El Leopardo al Sol* (1993), a wretched tale of two families killing one another and their links to the drugs trade, while never actually mentioning the word "drugs" in the text.

Politically charged as a one-time member of the Socialists Workers Party in Spain, as part of an underground resistance movement opposing the dictatorship in Argentina and as a mediator in the Colombian peace talks, Restrepo's writing often includes as one would imagine, political themes and struggles making Colombia an ideal backdrop for this writer.

The filmmaker and writer Fernando Vallejo (1942) presents a far bloodier and far less glamorous image of Colombia. Vallejo goes to great lengths to debunk the myths and misplaced style of the narco-culture that is embedded in Colombia's psyche. Reading the *La Virgen de los sicarios* (1994) leaves one in no doubt of the damage wrought upon Colombia by the drugs trade.

Colombian literature and literature about Colombia explore every facet to life in the South American nation and takes on predictable but no less interesting variety of topics of magic realism and the armed conflict with all the different off-shoots of corruption, identity, status, feudalism, corruption and beyond. This is after all a country with a grand literary tradition, a notable annual book fair in Bogotá and the Hay Festival in Cartagena attended by world famous authors and public speakers.

A Prophetic voice

Richard McColl

The Solitude of Latin America

What does it mean to be alone? Is it possible for an entire part of the world, one containing over half a billion people, to feel alone? It's an intriguing question, and there may be nobody better suited to answer it than Colombian author Gabriel García Márquez, author of the literary classic One Hundred Years of Solitude.

Gabriel García Márquez

In 1982, García Márquez was awarded the Nobel Prize in Literature for his numerous novels and short stories that collectively helped define the distinctly Latin American genre of magical realism. In his acceptance speech, entitled "The Solitude of Latin America," García Márquez used the themes of his novels to highlight the unique place of Latin America within the world. So, how can 600 million people feel isolated in an increasingly globalized world?

Let Gabriel García Márquez explain.

Background

Before we can get into García Márquez's speech, we need to understand the world in which he wrote it. In the early 1980s, Latin America was spiralling through a pretty rough decade.

The 20th century began with revolutions across this region, many of which resulted in the rise of dictators and tyrants. After World War II, popular rebellions reappeared, but the world was different. From roughly 1950 through 1991, the world was entrapped within the global struggle between capitalist and communist powers known as the Cold War.

Latin American rebellions in the Cold War were actively managed by both the USA and USSR, each trying to sway the economic ideologies of the region. The result was a perpetual rise and fall of military leaders, many of whom drastically violated the human rights of their citizens and some who even undertook ethnic genocides against Amerindian populations. All the while, the rest of the world continued to view Latin America in terms of their own interests. It was in this world that Gabriel García Márquez wrote One Hundred Years of Solitude in 1967, and "The Solitude of Latin America" in 1982.

Themes of the Speech

When Gabriel García Márquez won the Nobel Prize in Literature, he drafted an acceptance speech that managed to contextualize the genre of magical realism within the contemporary struggles of Latin America as a region. That's what "The Solitude of Latin America" is really focused on: the unique isolation of Latin America within a globalizing world. García Márquez explains both magical realism and Latin American struggles through a few major themes.

The History of Latin America

García Márquez begins his speech by examining the global fascination with Latin America as a place of magic and wonder. He cites authors ranging from Magellan's sailors to 19th century missionaries who told tales of cities of gold, magical creatures, and mythical riches. He also explores the region's more recent history, including the Mexican president who held a state funeral for his amputated leg and the Ecuadorian president whose well-dressed corpse continued to sit in the presidential throne after death.

In his acceptance speech titled The Solitude of Latin American he explained why Latin America being conceived as a magical land since the times of the colonies, cannot be explained using North American or European logic.

The point is to illustrate that Latin American history had been defined, to both outsiders and locals, by a degree of madness. The result was two-fold. For one, it encouraged a devoutly creative collective Latin American culture, one obsessed with tragedy and magic simultaneously. At the same time, the global understanding of Latin America as a place of fantastical oddity had let the world look the other way as genocidal dictators, poverty and inequality claimed the lives of millions.

One of the reasons for his message to continue to be significant for the generations of the 21st century is that the novel may be perceived as a deep insight over the history of America and its contact with the east, and a story of progress and civilization.

Repeatedly in these speeches he discourses on the "tragedy" of Latin America, whose wars, military coups and thwarted political idealism make it the "immense homeland of deluded men". Márquez spoke from experience. His father, Gabriel Eligio García, had worked in Colombia in the 1920s for the United Fruit Company, which succeeded in reducing Honduras to such a state of corruption that it earned the original title of "banana republic". In an extraordinary speech to a gathering of Colombian military in 1996 Márquez explains that his fascination with the corrupting tendency of power is "almost anthropological" in its obsessiveness and rigour. His mid-1970s masterpiece The Autumn of the Patriarch, about a vile Latin American despot, remains one of the great fictional explorations of power gone mad.

Gabo and Peace

"Gabo, the great absent presence on this day, who was the shadow architect of many peace efforts and processes, could not make it to live this moment, in his beloved Cartagena, where his ashes rest. But he must be happy watching his yellow butterflies fly above the Colombia of his dreams, our Colombia, finally reaching, as he said, 'a second chance on earth'."

So, proclaimed Colombian president Juan Manuel Santos in honour of author Gabriel García Márquez at the September 26 signing of the Colombian peace accords with the FARC – an agreement that just days later would be voted down by the Colombian people.

FARC guerrilla leader Timochenko, also cited Gabo, as García Márquez is affectionately known in Colombia, ending his speech by welcoming this "second chance on earth".

Gabo, the communist, the writer and the atheist, here, representing a common thread between opposing sides signing a peace agreement. I'm sure, had he lived to see this, he would have laughed at the juxtapositions between his life, his literature and the Colombian reality.

Gabo, I suspect, would not be surprised by what happened on October 2 when the referendum failed. He knew Colombia to be a place of extremes. In One Hundred Year of Solitude, he scrutinises the many aspects of Colombia's fratricidal conflict in the political field. Colonel Aureliano Buendía, he writes, "promoted 32 armed uprisings and he lost all of them". At the end, he recognised that pride, or "something that means nothing to anyone," is the only reason for fighting.

However, Gabo also recognised that Colombian hearts are usually unwilling to forgive and to make real change.

We have to admire García Márquez for his great capacity to capture Colombia's reality; indeed, what he wrote in yesteryear is still apt today, and perhaps remains a prophetic voice for what will come tomorrow.

Gabo's magical realism could only have emerged in just such a country, a place of fierce contradictions, surprise endings, pain, grief, and exuberance.

Throughout his speech he constantly appeals to emotions to get his point across. From Latin America being an absurd and "magical" place to making martyrs out of the communists that where prosecuted by Right wing Dictatorships; nevertheless, the emotional is the strongest when he speaks about his ideologies. García Márquez was a renowned anti-imperialist and constantly criticized the United States for interfering in Latin American politics. This critique is recognizable as he speaks about the coup that resulted in the death of Salvador Allende, the socialist president of Chile overthrown by his general Augusto Pinochet with the support of the CIA as a part of what is now known as Operation Condor. About Allende, García Márquez says the following: "A promethean president, entrenched in his burning palace, died fighting an entire army, alone", he also gives a similar account on the death of presidents Jaime Roldós and Omar Torrijos when he said "and two suspicious airplane accidents, yet to be explained, cut short the life of another great-hearted president and that of a democratic soldier who had revived the dignity of his people", both dead in plane crashes, under similar circumstance and in both cases the United States is a suspect.

It is interesting to find a speech like this in stage like the Nobel Academy because those in attendance are some of the most important and powerful people of that time including presidents, scientists, doctors, economists, insurgents, revolutionaries, pacifists, philanthropists, physicists and others. Although it is common for the laureate to choose to address a social issue it is not common for him/her to make accusations against a superpower like the United States. One would expect a speech like The Solitude of Latin America to receive a great deal of media coverage, and that it would still be a talking point, but unbelievably it never reached the level of fame that speeches by other authors achieved; nevertheless this speech surpassed its main goal, and this was to provide guidelines for the way Latin American culture should be studied because it meant to inform people all around the world that in order to understand Latin America it was necessary to change the lens through which this continent was viewed.

The idea of Latin America being a land full of supernatural places and animals makes people question the way they think of it, which was the authors main objective, this means that although the speech was not quite famous it was highly effective and represents a jewel of Latin American literature. By fronting the continent's tragic history with the unquenchable fiesta of his style, Gabriel García Márquez was most definitely a prophetic writer.

Colombian cinema

Colombian cinema and filmmaking do not make a standalone genre per se, but neither does it conform to type. It's too small to consider an industry since the annual output is quite low, less than Hollywood and most European countries, but, at the same time, a leader within Latin America. Exploring Colombian cinema permits a great investigative tour of the country in terms of history, tradition, and roots, the relationship that man has with nature and a nation that war has splintered.

Colombia's tortured past and present have constantly preoccupied its filmmakers and writers. In the narrative of feature-films of the 1980's and early 1990's the historical political and social violence is reflected. For example, in the film *Condores no entierran todos los días* (1984), directed by Francisco Norden, and based on the novel by Gustavo Alvarez Gardeázabal, the political killings of the pájaros is fictionalized. The pájaros were hired killers, who were found especially in southwest Colombia, during *La Violencia*. The Conservative party and some government members mostly supported them. Don León María Lozano, El Cóndor was the most notorious pájaro and the novel by Gardeázabal tells the story of this simple store-clerk who became one of the most feared assassins of his time.

Confesión a Laura (1990), directed by Jaime Osorio is based on the assassination of the Liberal Party leader Jorge Eliécer Gaitán, on April 9, 1948, which sparked the "Bogotazo," one of the bloodiest days in the history of the country in which approximately 2,585 were killed in one day. The destruction of the symbols of Conservative power in downtown Bogotá, the looting and the bloodbath, placed the Colombian society in a state of crisis.

Canaguaro, (Dunav Kusmanch, 1981) also shows the violence in the eastern plains, sparked by Gaitán's death. *María Cano* (Camila Loboguerrero, 1989) tells the story of the union leader

María Cano and the violent struggles of the workers. *Rodrigo-D, No Futuro* (Víctor Gaviria, 1991), displays the violence in Medellín as a consequence of drug trafficking. In *Rosario Tijeras*, the narrator explains the situation of violence in Colombia, especially in Medellín, in very poignant terms:

"Rosario's fight isn't so simple, it has very deep roots, from long ago, from earlier generations. Life weighs on her with the weight of this country, her genes drag a long a race of sons of plenty and sons of bitches who with the blade of a machete cleared the pathways of life. They're still doing it. They ate with the machete, they worked, shaved, killed, and settled differences with their wives with a machete. Today the machete is a shotgun, a nine- millimeter, a chopper. The weapon has changed but not its use. The story has changed too, has become terrifying. Once proud, we are not ashamed, without understanding how, why and when it all happened. We don't know how long our history is, but we can feel its weight. And Rosario has borne it since time immemorial, for that reason, when she was born, she didn't come bearing bread under her arm, but misfortune" (32-33).

The first and most constant narrative of magic realism is one that has been reproduced by a cinema that nurtures and exaggerates the fantastic and improbable. The second narrative, that of the long-running conflict is created with a predominant realist aesthetic and few melodramatic traces and is always anchored to the facts and reality. There are hundreds of films to choose from, but here we list a place to start with just twelve.

La vendedora de rosas (1998)

Los viajes del viento (2009)

María (1922)

El abrazo de la serpiente (2015)

Los colores de la montaña (2010)

Paraíso travel (2008)

Richard McColl

La estrategia del caracol (1993)

Cóndores no entierran todos los días (1984)

Jardín de amapolas (2012)

Sumas y restas (2005)

Confesión a Laura (1990)

Perro come perro (2007)

Architecture

Colombia's cities and towns are a melting pot of architectural styles that range from opulent to humble and that can ideally reflect the political ideologies and intellectual desires of the time. One may be wandering through an innocuous town only to spot an art deco theatre or some of the best-preserved colonial architecture in the western hemisphere. Colombia is a regionalist country and this is well displayed through the variations between anything from wooden Caribbean structures to the paisa architecture of the coffee zone. Sometimes it seems that every style of architecture has descended upon the nation in a hurry with neoclassical and gothic being mixed with no particular order and this disorderly situation is not bettered with the country's rapid urbanization from population displacements - forced and unforced – from the countryside that has added to Colombia's pre-existing urban chaos.

Main traditional styles

Pre-Columbian style

While the term Pre-Columbian architecture refers to the period prior to the 16C it can usually be applied to any structures constructed in a fashion that represents the image and ambience of the indigenous communities that existed before Spanish colonisation or conquest. It would be naïve and ill-informed to judge this architecture as primitive since here in Colombia and throughout the region indigenous practices such as the use of bahareque and guadua were widely adopted in Spanish building patterns in the New World. While most dwellings consisted of oval or rectangular malocas it is interesting to note that the Muisca people, located in the regions of Bogotá and thereabouts, never employed the use of stone despite the prevalence of this building material. Most Pre-Columbian styles incorporated products such as palm and fronds for roofing and ran straight to the ground. Today this building style can be seen when trekking to the Ciudad Perdida or visiting Tayrona National Park both of which are close to the city of Santa Marta.

Colonial style

There are fine examples of colonial architecture in Colombia, perhaps best seen in the towns of Mompós, Popayán and Barichara and in the cities of Bogotá and Cartagena. Notable for the thick walls, clay baked roof tiles, internal patios situated around cloister-style low buildings, colonial architecture is inimitable. A fine example of a religious building in this style is the church of the Santo Domingo Convent (1578) in Cartagena with its austere façade and high ceilings dating back to the 16C. In order to see preserved versions of colonial dwellings there is no better place than the town of Mompós found further inland and heading to the Calle Real del Medio where one can view unaltered colonial houses, majestic ironwork windows and skilled carpentry on the roofs. A further place of interest is the imposing Plaza de Bolívar (1539) in Tunja with its cathedral, official buildings and Casa de la Cultura.

Neoclassical style

With its Doric façade, cornices and carved stone there is no doubting the neoclassical credentials of the Teatro Colón (1892) in Bogotá's Candelaria district and then just down the hill from this in the Plaza de Bolívar, the regal Palacio de Nariño (restored in the 1970s after the 1948 Bogotazo). With its columns, stonework and Louis XV salon it certainly fits the bill for the seat of Government. In towns throughout Colombia including Bucaramanga with its Club del Comercioand Cartagena with the Edificio Banco Bolívar, one can also spy out other versions of neoclassical design; formerly perhaps they were ornate and played a central commercial role but now have been incorporated into the sprawl of urban centres.

Republican style

With the industrial revolution ticking over so came Republican-style architecture to a Colombia crying to break out from the mould of the Spanish colonial regime. In Cartagena the Republican architecture was more or less placed on top of the old colonial buildings in particular in the sought-after barrio San Diego, increasing their size from single storey to three storey and opening out spaces in order to proclaim an architectural independence not only a political one. Demonstrating the city of Manizales' desire to step out from its image of a provincial town to that of a coffee wealthy elite, Republican edifices such as the Palacio de la Gobernación de Caldas and the Edificio Manuela Sanz sprang up here too.

Gothic revival style

There are whole host of neo gothic churches in Colombia ranging from the Iglesia del Señor de las Misericordias (1921) in downtown Medellin to the most striking and recognised as a wonder of Colombia, the Santuario de Las Lajas (fifth and final stage completed in 1949) close to Ipiales in the south of the country. With huge flying buttresses and ornate windows this is a popular site for pilgrims from all over Colombia.

Mudejar revival style

There are a few versions of Mudéjar revival architecture in Colombia such as the tower to the San Francisco (1751) church in the centre of Cali. Its unmistakable blend of hispano-arabic styles as if plucked from the Iberian Peninsula in Andalucía are employed in both the tower section of the church and the lateral doorway. This style really came about in the late 19C and 20C when a Mudéjar revival hit Europe and the most striking example of this architecture in Colombia could be the Santa Maria Bull Ring in Bogotá constructed in 1931. Even the city of Cartagena, better known for its Colonial and Republican architecture is not exempt from Mudéjar edifices, and has a fine example of this with its smooth curves and high entrances in the form of the Casa Covo (1931) in the well-heeled barrio of Manga.

Art deco style

While not striking the visitor as the most scenic place to visit, the Caribbean port city of Barranquilla houses more than its fair share of Art Deco buildings including the Cristobal Colón Theatre and the Romelio Martínez Stadium. But it is not just in Barranquilla, one can see representative structures of this style dotted all over the country from the smallest towns to the major cities.

Colombian Urban Context

Urban Planning

Colombia's urban structure has undergone a transformation of jaw-dropping proportions in the last 50 years and much of this can be blamed on the problems raging on in the countryside. Between the late 1930s and early 1970s Colombia's urban population increased from 30 per cent of the national total to nearly 60 per cent. It is safe to say that the nation was in no way ready for this population explosion in urban areas and the cities were placed under immeasurable pressures and construction was uncontrolled and disorderly. This chaotic shambles of roads, poorly constructed buildings and poverty can be seen today and are an example of when politicians mistake themselves for urban planners and focus on building their way out of problems rather than addressing the root causes.

It would be remiss to believe that much of Bogotá urban "renewal" took place as a result of the Bogotazo on 9 April 1948, when a great number of historic buildings in the downtown area were burned to the ground in the violence following the assassination of the Liberal presidential candidate, Jorge Eliécer Gaitán. Changes were already well afoot and four-time mayor of Bogotá during this era, had a significant role in the urban changes effected on the capital. More than an urban planner, Mazuera oversaw construction and sought to bring Parisian, he had lived extensively in France, style to the Andes. Demolitions were undertaken and large boulevards constructed in this era of "automobilization" when owning a vehicle meant high class, exclusivity and economic affluence. Mazuera oversaw the extension of the Carrera 10, the Avenida de la Americas – at one point suggested the removal of the Cementerio Central to create a further North-South avenue in the city and admitted to dictatorial tendencies when it came to expounding urban growth in Bogotá.

Since Mazuera, each Mayor has sought to improve or ignore the problems facing Bogotá and despite promises being made for a metro for the city in the 1950's, one has never materialized. However, in 2019, Chinese firm China Metro (an amalgamation of two companies: China Harbour Engineering Company LTD. (Chec) y China Communications Construction Company Ltd. (CCCC)), involved in other infrastructure projects in Colombia, was awarded the contract with work to begin in 2020 and an estimated conclusion in 2028.

Of course, second city Medellín's metro, built in the 1990's, has been a cause for celebration and contributed to the urban regeneration of much of that city, not least a source of mirth to the paisas that they have one and the capital does not.

While Medellín rightly enjoys international applause for the work done in renovating and regenerating down at heel areas of the city, the metro, the tram system, the escalator in Comuna 13 and the cable car connections, all of which bring the working-class neighbourhoods closer to the centre, Bogotá is slowly attempting to pick up the slack. Truly the jewel in Colombia's crown for integrated and inclusive public transport Medellín's urban planners came up with the novel idea of connecting the metro and integrating it with a cable car service that rides up and over the hills to the poorer barrios located beyond the actual city limits. In itself, this cable car system has become a tourist attraction.

The metro cable (cable car) in south Bogotá and the plans to link the city on existing railway lines with the Regiotram commuter lines will be a major step forward for the capital.

In terms of civic-minded and socially aware city mayors, there are two notable examples, the first being the former mayor of Bogotá Antanas Mockus (1995-7 and 2001-03) and the former mayor of Medellín Sergio Fajardo (2004-07) who deserve special recognition for their work in their respective cities for incorporating inclusive ideas based on civic pride and education. Later politicians have attempted to emulate the work of both but have been found wanting.

The capital Bogotá seems a mess of uncontrolled transit with buses and taxis all competing to knock over motorcyclists, cyclists and pedestrians, but slowly and steadily city politicians have been addressing this problem and since 2001 the TransMilenio bendy bus system has been taking further vehicles off the roads as commuters opt for public transport. The TransMilenio though has outlived its usefulness in the absence of other major public transport infrastructure and that Colombian politicians – such as two-time mayor Enrique Peñalosa - betting heavily on this system, it has left Bogotá well behind in terms of integration, affordable and flexible public transport.

But not all plaudits go to Medellín since in 2006 Bogotá was awarded the Golden Lion Award for Architecture, as a recognition for having addressed "the problems of social inclusion, housing, education and public space especially through innovations in transport", for having "applied Mies Van der Rohe's dictum 'less is more' to the automobile: less cars means more civic space and more civic resources for people", and for providing "a model for streets which are pleasing to the eye as well as economically viable and socially inclusive".

During the worldwide pandemic of 2020 when Covid-19 devastated parts of Bogotá, the city's new mayor Claudia López, sought out a solution to social distancing and the eternal problem of overcrowded public transport system by extending and increasing cycle lanes on principal avenues. To tame traffic after pandemic lockdowns, the Colombian capital has embarked on a bike-lane building spree that could a be model in Latin America. In February, López announced that the city's development plan for the next four years would add a total of 280 additional kilometres of bike lanes to the existing 550-kilometer network. Currently, almost seven per cent of overall trips in Bogotá are on bicycles, more than in any other city in Latin America. But the city is aiming much higher: The long-term goal is to have 50 per cent of total trips made on bikes or other micro-mobility alternatives such as scooters.

Modern Architecture

Colombia has more than its fair share of skyscrapers and modern buildings and there are more architects making a name for themselves by creating interesting and sustainable buildings in all corners of the country. The Torre Colpatria in Bogotá was the tallest building in the country with 50 storeys until the ill-fated construction of the Escollera Tower in Cartagena. This Escollera Tower was to be the tallest building in Colombia but resulted in being de-constructed and redesigned due to serious structural foundation flaws. The mantle of Colombia's tallest building now goes to Bogotá's Edificio BD Bacatá completed in 2016.

Perhaps what it is most striking is Colombia's infatuation with the brick. Buildings from Bogotá to Cali have been constructed in brick to great effect; one need just look at the Torres del Parque (completed in 1970) in Bogotá in the Macarena district above the Plaza de Toros.

The architect Rogelio Salmona (1927-2007) responsible for the Torres del Parque wished to create open spaces in these towers designed specifically for apartments, and the curve of the brick construction to turn with the mountains situated to the immediate east of the building. Less subtle and more extravagant is the Maloka Museum that resembles a kind of Colombian Epcot centre and this has driven forward architectural designs – which for so long have attempted to imitate Salmona's creations - with its futuristic shape. The boulder-like constructions that make up the Biblioteca España in Medellín are truly a sight and have pushed forward optimism in this city for the future despite their current structural difficulties.

Continuing in Medellín, the Museo Casa de la Memoria (House of Memory Museum) created in 2006 – as a project of the Victim Assistance Program of Medellín City Hall – with the aim of contributing to the memory of open and plural dialogues, critical and reflective, to understand and overcome the armed conflict and the violence of Medellín, Antioquia and Colombia. This phenomenal example of modern architecture has been designed to be inclusive, representative and educational on all levels and certainly makes an impression.

Fashion

Fashionistas from around the world will be all too familiar with the creativity and styles on display in Colombia's chic couture boutiques found in upmarket shopping malls in Bogotá, Barranquilla, Cali, Cartagena and Medellín as the designs of many have graced the catwalks at the most glamourous international fashion events. Beyond the arts, crafts and jewellery, Colombia's designers have rightly been lauded on the global stage and through their unique brands and designs one can appreciate a certain wave of decolonialization of the industry. Bogotá Fashion Week[110] (held annually in May) and Medellín's Colombiamoda[111] (July) represent perfect windows on to the country's up and coming designers seeking to include and incorporate traditional heritage into contemporary fashion.

This celebration of the traditions of design and craft so inherent in Latin American heritage, from the audacious use of gold and the spiritual indigenous influences, to the vibrant colours represent a break from the perpetuated stereotypes and fetishism of the exotic so often forced on the region by European designers is, happily, becoming something of the past.

Some of the most famous designers, who have made their mark on the international stage are the Bogotanos, Amelia Toro and Haider Ackermann, Silvia Tcherassi, Hernán Zajar, Lina Cantillo all bringing their Caribbean roots to the world and Olga Pedrahita from Medellín.

---

[110] Bogotá Fashion Week: https://www.bogotafashionweek.com.co/

[111] Colombia Moda: https://colombiamoda.inexmoda.org.co/

Graffiti

Graffiti

All major cities in Colombia have breath-taking urban art scenes, political, humorous or just whimsical and you can gain a true insight into the turbulent waters of the country and gauge the public sentiment, just by engaging in the street art. Bogotá and Medellin are the main two locations and enthusiasts should head to Bogotá's la Candelaria and Chapinero districts and in Medellín to the Comuna 13 and the centro.

At street level, Bogotá possesses a distinctly DIY appeal, an ambiance of change being propagated by a new generation. While this undercurrent may feel noisome like metal, it's the graffiti on display that catches the eye, making this city one of the world's great centres for expressive street art.

If ever there was a city more suited to being "punk rock," it would be Bogotá, with her haphazard blend of social cliques, political motivations and variety of architectural styles, all of which provide an ideal canvas for some of the most poignant graffiti murals found in South America. Bogotá is often referred to as the "Athens of South America" and "2600m closer to the stars" by intellectuals and academics, due to her well-educated citizenry and the lofty altitude of the city. Want to plunge into another world of discord and hope? Then take a stroll through the downtown colonial neighbourhood of La Candelaria or a drive down the infamous and brutalist Calle 26 en route to the El Dorado airport to take in the urban artwork with its messages in favour of indigenous rights, the environment and commemorating the lives of people killed in the conflict.

Perhaps the messages displayed up on high overlooking the rooftops and city divisions are not clear to visitors who aren't familiar with Colombia's turbulent politics, but this can be quickly remedied by signing up for a highly-rated "graffiti tour" which, led by the street artists themselves, aims to educate visitors about the capital in a way that Netflix's popular "Narcos" series cannot.

To take a step back and really look at this city is to examine the dirt beneath her nails, to trip on the uneven and cracked pavement, to breathe in the dark fumes from the buses and to feel yourself snarling, all the while being watched over vigilantly by the city's huge murals, cleverly political stencils and paste-ups.

The graffiti tour "guides" remain philosophical about their work and its longevity, and opinions are divided among the artists regarding the "legality" of where they work and with whose permission. Previously, urban art was illegal in Bogotá. Now, it's simply "prohibited," which may seem confusing and indeed contradictory, but, it means that the authorities can have the final say in where artists can paint.

One wonders what local artists such DjLu, Guache, Erre, Lesivo Bestial, Ledania and Ceroker (and the estimated 8,000 street artists of Bogotá) make of such measures to control where they work and perhaps mute the rebellion and protests in their compositions. Whatever the case, it seems that the voices from an underground movement have transferred to the mainstream, on glorious display for both locals in the know and enthusiastic visitors alike.

The artwork pictured on the cover of this book was done by a collective and artist Chirrete Golden kindly gave his permission for its reproduction.

Fine Arts and Crafts

Much is made of Colombia's literary offerings but a much overlooked and incredibly wealthy facet of the country's cultural heritage and contemporary situation is that of the wide range and variety of Fine Arts and Crafts. From intricate Pre-Columbian offerings to a master class of religious Baroque styles, murals, overweight and exaggerated sculptures, photography, jewellery and street art. One could spend years researching and investigating Colombia's artistic legacy but your best bet is to enjoy small portions from an enormous buffet and keep an eye out for special exhibitions and of course the excellent permanent displays!

Painting

Pre-Columbian Period

Colombia's painting inheritance spans all the way back to the tombs and remains found in Tierradentro in the Cauca department where primitive artwork can still be seen and visited in this complex funeral center (see San Agustin) displaying patterns that date between 600-900AD. But by no means are these the only examples of "primitive" art in Colombia as new discoveries in Chimita, Santander have revealed petroglyphs dating to 1300BC and then there are supposedly dozens of cave paintings in lesser known and visited Departments in the country. For example, in the departments of Guaviare and Caquetá in the Sierra de Chiribiquete there are the remnants of artwork done by the Guayabero tribe, known as the Mural Guayabero that dates to 300BC. Not too far from here is the Cerro Azul, also in Guaviare, a large rock as if completely defaced by indigenous graffiti about which little is known due to previous issues of security and accessibility.

Colonial Period

Early Religious Art 1530-1650

To begin with, most of the art that was on show in the years directly following the arrival of the Spanish was of course that brought from Seville, displaying fully the one-dimensional religious style of Christian images that was the fashion at the time. But there was also the artwork that caused ripples of interest and devotion from the indigenous Muisca population such as the Virgen de Mongui in Boyacá which, as legend has it was sent over to the New World by Philip II. Examples of home-grown religious art are visible still in churches, specifically in Tunja and Villa de Leyva and all through the regions of Cundinamarca and Boyacá and are notable in that they were created not by artists but by craftsmen and copied from examples from the motherland. To be expected since carpenters and shoemakers were the artists of the time, the artwork still on display in fine houses and old churches today is such that there is a blend of mediaeval, renaissance and even indigenous symbolism that these voyagers have picked up over the years. These religious offerings continued to be defined this way while the nation of Colombia came about and started to find its identity.

Perhaps the first example of religious art native to Colombia or New Granada comes from the work of Alonso de Narváez (born Seville 16C died Tunja, Colombia 1583) and his Nuestra Señora de Chiquinquirá, painted onto cotton fabric and supposedly, according to fervent Catholics, a self-restoring piece of artwork.

Baroque Religious Art 1650-1750

Gregorio Vasquez de Arce y Ceballos (1638-1711) is probably the most notable and notorious of the of the Latin American Baroque movement. Considered the great master in his method his paintings such as the Holy Trinity, as a being with several faces, was considered entirely controversial and to some heretic, can be described as nothing more than an elaborate Creole interpretation inspired by European masters and works coming out of Cuzco and Quito. Another Creole, contemporary and possibly a teacher of Gregorio Vasquez was Baltasar de Figueroa

(1629-1667) "el Viejo" the inventor of the Colombian Baroque. In 1658 he was commissioned to do 20 paintings for the Convento de la Concepción, a contract which he never completed and in 1660 he signed on to paint all the images for the Iglesia de Nuestra Señora de Chiquinquirá. He did not complete this work either, but, he did leave many notable works including the Coronación de la virgin (1663) notably strong, as was his style, on delicate facial features. Possibly done by Baltasar de Figueroa or possibly by the Ecuadorian Miguel de Santiago, the twelve canvases of the Arcángeles de Sopó, remain in the Church of the Divine Savior in Sopó and stake the claim of being the most representative of the Colombian Baroque movement. Despite the question mark that hangs over their creator, they are indicative of expressionist emotionalism that appealed to a more humanitarian viewer in the wake of the Counter Reformation. Just as the Spanish Enlightenment came about in the 18C, with it came political change which in turn affected artistic output. The warmer more colourful style came in and Joaquín Gutiérrez, "Pintor de los Virreyes", in addition to painting aristocratic portraits of the Virreys also produced 26 strong series of la Vida de San Juan de Dios (1750). Many of his works can be seen in the Museo de Arte Colonial in Bogotá and he was also prolific throughout the City and surrounding areas.

Republican Period (early 19C to early 20C)

As is the norm upon the advent of independence and the struggles for it, art takes on a romantic notion to display and justify the heroism of the leaders and of the battles fought. Colombia is no exception and works of this nature are no better illustrated than by José María Espinosa Prieto (1796-1883). Having fought in the campaigns of Antonio Nariño, the artist was well placed to compose portraits of Simón Bolivar, however his most famous collection may be his memoirs in the painted word, Memorias de un Abanderado (1876). Self-taught, Ramón Torres Méndez (1809-1885) is famed for his works such as Señora Desconocida and Cristo se aparece a la Magdalena, before gaining notoriety for creating a gallery of religious artwork rescued from property belonging to religious orders expelled from the country and ensuring therefore that these pieces were not destroyed. Ricardo Acevedo Bernal (1867- 1930) was a faithful witness to an inhospitable time in Colombia's history and his paintings followed religious motifs, landscapes and topics of a patriotic matter. His paintings have been declared as paternalistic, classist and even racist as they portray the white Spanish Bogotano upper class always as finely dressed in the day's fashion, a result of the impressionist schooling he had received in the United States and Europe. This Republican period was not only one of searching for a national identity it also represented the great age of exploration in an attempt to understand the boundaries and riches within the frontiers of Colombia and so artists were often contracted on scientific missions. Manuel María Paz (1820-1902) was one such artist and he accompanied the famous Agustín Codazzi in his expeditions mapping New Granada. Focussing on landscapes and portraits Manuel Maria Paz charted all levels of society in New Granada. Although Venezuelan, Carmelo Fernández Páez (1809-1887) was called upon by Codazzi to accompany him on several expeditions and he contributed greatly to the Comisión Corográfica Colombiana.

Modern Painting

Straddling the Republican styles but not quite fully embracing the modern period is Fidolo González Camargo, (1883-1941) whose portraits and landscapes ably reflect a French romanticism. It is worth looking out for his drawings in the Museo Nacional de Bogotá, in particular his charcoals of Tipo Callejero and the Sirvienta Bogotana.

Muralism 1920-1940

Pedro Nel Gómez (1899–1984) is without question one of the greatest muralists of the 20C and his name rings alongside that of the Mexican Diego Rivera. There is no dearth of Colombian muralists but given his output, the 11 murals in the former Palacio Municipal de Medellín now the Museo de Antioquia, and his three frescos: "De la Bordadora a los Telares", "el Problema del Petróleo y la Energía" and "el Trabajo y la Maternidad" tell the whole story of his quality.

Modern Styles

There are simply so many contemporary painters in Colombia to mention and so we focus on but a few of the bigger names. With the advent of the 20C you could say that at long last national artists started searching for a uniquely Colombian style and started to use geometrically abstract forms such as cubism to define the new era of this nation's art. With a certain colombianisation of art the shackles of the colonial and republican legacies of religious artwork from Spain were finally dropped and these artists started discovering styles to define themselves.

Alejandro Obregón (1920-1992) was one of Colombia's big five artists including Grau, Villamizar, Botero and Negret and whose work was fully inspired by a cultural and artistic manifestation of the events that had taken place at the end of the 1940s in Colombia. Clearly influenced in part by Picasso his works such as the Estudiante Muerto that commemorates the death of a political agitator still create an impact today. Obregón is considered as the founding father of modern Colombian painting.

Enrique Grau (1920-2004) is a distinctly surrealist and tropical artist, whose studies were mainly of mulatas and of his beloved Cartagena. He placed a strong emphasis on the subject of flowers in his imagery, flowers being one of the principal products for exportation from Colombia. His voluptuous generosity given afforded to the color in his artwork is unmistakable and to see a work of art that will stay with you, just step into the Teatro Heredia in Cartagena and take a look at the backdrop to the stage that Grau painted. It is spectacular, kitsch and profoundly

Colombian in its symbolism.

Another artist also affected by the political troubles of the 1940s was Marco Ospina (1912-1983) who is recognised as being Colombia's first abstract painter. Using his abstract style Ospina was able to order his painted elements in order to allow the viewer to enjoy the art. His was an art style that displays, through watercolours, a picturesque and provincial reality.

Contemporary Painting

Attitudes towards art have changed significantly and an acceptance of modernity blended with the métissage of backgrounds, indigenous, European and African have allowed for a diversification of what is now known as Colombian art.

Juan Cárdenas (1939-1991), is a figurative and introverted artist whose art has often been likened to the labyrinthine literature of Borges. Cárdenas' world appears as if in sepia and his paintings seem reminiscent of yesterday and are as much an intellectual study as they are a piece of art. His desire to create the truth in the painting allows for no romanticism and his paintings can at times feel empty and two dimensional but are far from it.

Carlos Jacanamijoy (1964) is considered as one of the shining talents of current South American artwork. His pieces embody much of his ancestral heritage through abstract landscapes. Jacanamijoy is from the Inga tribe in and was born in the Amazon region of the Putumayo department in southern Colombia. Son of a shaman his work displays what is often referred to as a unique "indigenous character" and he has become a recognised name. His abstracts while influenced by his upbringing in far off and tropical lands (he now lives in New York) reflect an interior landscape as well as if everything is being recalled from an earlier date.

David Manzur (1929) defies the literary and the narrative in his art and embraces antiquity albeit cloaked with a modern spirit. Manzur's dynamic works show his willingness to try various styles that could lead to it being called hyperrealism making him one of the most important Colombian artists today.

Sculpture

Pre-Columbian Period

There are plenty of sculptures dotted around Colombia to know that the pre-Columbian period prior to the arrival of the Spanish was one that was prolific in this art form one need only look at the vast areas in the departments of Huila and Cauca where the San Agustín and Tierradentro cultures are found. Here you can visit the most well-known and recognised pre-Columbian cemeteries in the country with the anthropomorphic and zoomorphic carvings.

But there are more examples that are not so widely known such as the hollow ceramic figures of animals and plants of the Chorrera culture (15000-500BC) found in the region. The La Tolita – Tumaco (500BC-300AD) culture was also recognised for their stone work and ceramic. This culture that ran from Ecuador into the Colombian Pacific left everyday occurrences carved into their sculptures and there are many representations of disease and medical disorders. In the regions around Bogotá, the Muisca (1000-1550) left us some interesting artefacts in the tall phallic carvings at El Infiernito near to Villa de Leyva.

Colonial Period

To begin with, sculptures and Early Religious Art in Colombia during the colonial period were either imported or heavily imitated versions of pieces back home done by Spanish settlers. The Capilla Mancipes in Tunja is a particularly good example of Spanish sculpting as the work was done by Juan Bautista Vázquez (1510-1588) who was also responsible for impressive works in the cathedrals of Toledo and Seville. Also, in the cathedral in Tunja one can make out anthropomorphic figures near to the altar which are no doubt imitations of work done by the Dutch renaissance artist Vredeman de Vries (1527-1607). Perhaps the most celebrated Colombian sculptor of the 17C was Pedro de Lugo Albarracín who worked on the Cristo Caído, better known as el Señor de Monserrate located at the highest point in Bogotá and a destination for many pilgrims.

Later as the Baroque movement swept through the colonies again it was the city of Tunja that would arguably most benefit from religious sculptures. The Capilla del Rosario that makes up part of the Iglesia Santo Domingo is often referred to as the Sistine Chapel of Latin American Baroque art in particular due to the eight polychrome wooden relieves done by Lorenzo de Lugo. Regarding the Rococo movement in Colombia, the best examples can be seen in Cathedral at Tunja, the Templo de San Ignacio in Tunja and Bogotá's Cathedral, all of which was done by Pedro Laboria (1700-1770).

Republican Realism

By the 19C, Colombian sculpting, religious and baroque artwork took on a more realistic and academic edge but all the time following the same lines created in the colonial period. Bernabé Martínez and his son Toribio Martínez created what can only be described as a small dynasty of religious sculptors.

Modern Sculpture

While Santiago Martínez Delgado (1906–1954) and Pedro Nel Gómez (1899–1984) were mentioned extensively in the introduction on Colombian painting it is worth mentioning them both again here since their legacy in the art world is considerable. Martinez worked on the considerable carving on the façade of the National Palace in Cúcuta and Gomez working with various materials created from wood, Mujeres Emigrantes, from bronze, Cacique Nutibara Fountain in Medellín and from marble the Barequera melancólica.

In the sphere of modern Colombian sculpture there are many variations on a style ranging from Academic to Abstract and Nationalist. One notable Academic sculptor was Gustavo Arcila Uribe (1895-1963) as any visit to the capital means that you will see some of his work as he is responsible for the illuminated Virgen Milagrosa (1946), visible by day and night on top of the Cerro de Guadalupe above the colonial Candelaria district. In the Abstract field look no further than Hugo Martínez González (1923) with his smooth lines and careful movement somehow transposed onto his works such as Cabeza de Mulata and La Huida.

Considered as one of Colombia's finest living sculptors, Édgar Negret (1920) started out in stone modernism before moving into metal constructivism. Using doubled up aluminum such as in the Cabeza de Bautista he is able to create a feeling of space all the while using bright colors of red, blue and yellow which are supposedly drawn from inspiration from pre-Columbian art. Eduardo Ramírez Villamizar (1923) recognized alongside Negret as one of the masters of Colombian sculpture, can be regarded as traditional in spite of the abstraction and the breath which traverses the constructivism of his work.

With regards to Nationalist Sculpture, a fine example of this is the Monumento a la Raza by Rodrigo Arenas Betancur (1919-1995) in Medellín made from bronze and concrete and reaching up to a height of 38m. He also made the enormous Monumento conmemorativo de la batalla del Pantano de Vargas at Paipa.

Contemporary Sculpture

A great deal is made of the works of Fernando Botero but there are plenty more sculptors worthy of recognition. Doris Salcedo (born 1958) with her strong feelings and emotions – all of which developed and experienced in Colombia - towards the themes of racism and borders has had her works described as mental and political archaeology. She was the eight artists commissioned to produce something for the Turbine Hall in the Tate Modern in London and provided the city with the unforgettable Shibboleth. Her most recent work was Fragmentos an "anti-monument," in her words made from 37 tonnes of weapons surrendered by the FARC. Resembling a metal floor, the idea has been to change the concept of a monument in the hierarchical sense and provide a new platform upon which Colombia can walk.

Nadin Ospina (1960) has taken an interesting and relatively controversial look at the contemporary capitalistic consumerist culture in which we inhabit. She gained significant international recognition for her sculptures of contemporary cartoon characters such as Bart Simpson and Goofy made in a pre-Columbian fashion, following principally the style of the sculptures in San Agustín.

Fernando Botero

Fernando Botero (1932-2023) is currently Colombia's most famous artist, known for being the sculptor and painter who creates rotund people and animals. Botero had an interesting upbringing which has undoubtedly affected his interpretations and delivery of his art. As a young man he was sent off to train as a Bullfighter and this time has been ably reflected in his series on the Corrida. We cannot say that he has been more of a social commentator than an artist nor vice versa but he has focused a great deal of time and energy on highlighting injustices inherent in Colombian society and society in general.

By the 1960s he had found his corpulent style after having studied in various countries in Europe and then in New York. Most of his work involved themes such as family, animals and every day pursuits but beneath the pleasantries you can make out the strains of Botero reaching for the Colombian national identity. His religious composition Our Lady of Colombia is flying the national flag and even a piece like Marie-Antoinette and Louis XVI, clearly depicting the French 18C royalty, seem to be set in a Colombian village street.

A visit to Botero's home city of Medellín will bring you up close and personal to a large amount of his works. In front of the Museo de Antioquia and in the Parque Berrío there are 14 of his large corpulent bronze figures out front including La Mano, Cabeza and Adam and Eve.

Quirky in tone, most Botero paintings seem lighthearted, with a love for simple joys. Yet Botero has a knack for shaking up the viewer with the occasional piece that reflects cutting social commentary or a sober reflection on the dark side of Colombian life. So, just as you're getting used to smiling at the carefree women looking at themselves in the mirror, or the young couple holding hands in the park, a Botero painting like Carrobomba or Secuestro shakes your notions of Botero as a naive, simplistic artist. Nowhere is this more impacting than in his highly stylized portrayal of notorious drug kingpin, Pablo Escobar, being gunned down by government troops.

But it is the Bird of Peace sculpture in the Parque San Antonio in Medellin that really brings the Colombian situation up close. In 1995 a huge bomb was placed at the feet of this sculpture and 23 people lost their lives, Botero was asked if he wished to replace the sculpture but he declined deciding instead to create an identical Bird of Peace and place it alongside the destroyed one to show the futility of the action.

Perhaps his most impacting social commentary has been a series criticizing the treatment of prisoners at the infamous Abu Ghraib prison in Iraq.

Gold and Silversmithery

Pre-Columbian Period

With pre-Columbian communities and tribes based all over what is now referred to as Colombia and with archeological accounts from expeditions as well as finds by grave robbers we have a pretty god idea of the range and spread of gold craftsmanship through this land. Of course, the Spanish would have spent far less time here had there been neither precious metals nor the legend of El Dorado.

Most of the best preserved and interesting pieces of gold can be found in the Museo del Oro in Bogotá such as that of the Calima culture (200AD-1200AD) in particular the pectoral ornaments and breastplates made from hammered gold sheet. For the Tolima (1200BC-1500AD) culture gold was a symbol of power and hierarchy and their ornaments such as the human headed bird, the avian pendant and the ornamental Tumi knife are some of the most representative of pre-Columbian gold craftsmanship from the region. The Quimbaya (500BC-600AD) placed a strong importance on fertility and from digs and findings in the region of Cauca have yielded zoomorphic figurines, nose rings and assorted jewelry and the intriguing ceremonial poporos with their smooth and symmetrical surface.

Urabá was chosen by the conquistador Alonso de Ojeda to create the first Spanish settlement on the South American mainland and it is not hard to figure out why since it is clearly an important trading route given its geographical location and calm waters. The Urabá people used this area as a route up into Panama left behind gold ornaments portraying female figures as well as pendants and flasks. On the Pacific side in the Chocó, the pre-Columbian tribes with access to greater gold deposits created masks with feathers as worn by shamans. In the Tayrona area, between 900AD and 1600AD finds from the Sierra Nevada have produced hammered nose plates and breast plates as well as gold figurines of animals. From the highlands of Cundinamarca and Boyacá where the Muisca (600-1600AD) people were in power comes the legend of El Dorado in Lake Guatavita. Gold offerings were made to the goddess Guatavita and were tossed into the lake creating the infamous legend. Typically, Muisca gold resembles anthropomorphic figures and a predominance of man and bird figures.

Filigrana Momposina

Filigrana Momposina is some of the most intricate and sought-after jewelry in Colombia. Delicately coiled gold or silver is painstaking melted and manipulated into shapes to create earrings, pendants, necklaces and bracelets. Named thus, it comes as no surprise that it is from the town of Mompós, Bolívar, a few hours from Cartagena. The styles have become slightly more contemporary and international in recent years with the influx of foreign tourists, but on the whole, the jewels are created with traditional designs in mind. Since Mompós lies along the banks of the River Magdalena and has been central to Colombia's growth and has always and a mix of ethnic backgrounds this has become reflected in the jewelry. You can find a mix of Hispanic, indigenous, African and Arabic influences in the designs.

Textiles

Colombia is an incredibly regional country and crossing from East to West could lead you to believe that you have actually left one nation and entered another the variations in cultural habits are so strong and in the country's textile heritage is no exception.

In the chillier highlands of the Andes and in particular through the rural departments of Boyacá and Antioquia the Ruana, is a traditional and frequently worn type of sleeveless poncho used to fight off the cold and damp.

Voted once as the symbol of Colombia, the Vueltiao hat is a wide-brimmed hat made from the woven fibers of the arrow cane palm tree. The tradition comes from Zenú practices from the Caribbean coast and the town of Tuchín, supposedly having some significance with their cosmology. The finer the weave and the ability to fold or roll up the hat, the higher the quality and the more it will cost.

The Wayúu people of the Guajira peninsula on the Caribbean coast bordering Venezuela have become famed for their fine knitwear in particular their chinchorros or hammocks and their mochilas or shoulder bags. Brightly colored and tightly woven these products last forever and have become incredibly fashionable both nationally and internationally.

In the region of Urabá that spreads down from the autonomous Panamanian territory of the Kuna Yala and San Blas islands is territory of the Kuna or Tule people. Their Molas are hand knitted products with animal and cosmological references and are brightly colored.

Cartago embroidery from the Valle del Cauca has its origins in the Hispano Arabic heritage brought over from Andalusia and for this reason often bears floral and Andalusian designs. Here in Colombia the designs mainly focus on the wildlife and nature of the department of the Valle de Cauca.

On the road from Cartagena to Mompós you will pass the town of San Jacinto, known locally as the capital of the hammock and all sort of trinkets, musical instruments or woven goods. Just off the highway, one can find cotton hammocks of every type of shape, color and size.

Basketry

In the village of Guacamayas, Boyacá in the ancestral homelands of the ancient settlement of Lache and Tunebo (U'wa) Indians, the local people have continued the indigenous practices of basket weaving making products from straw and fique. These practices involve elaborate spiral basketwork where rolls of straw are created and then fastened by fique threads. Once the desired shape is made the fibers are dyed in a natural process. Products such as baskets, dishes, place mats and bowls can all be found made from straw and fique.

On the Pacific coast in Pichimá, Chocó the Wounaan Indians have created an exotic and tasteful form of basket known as the Wérregue. Each basket, depending upon its size, can take between 30 and 60 days to make and it is believed that this tradition came from Africa given the form and symmetry involved. The fiber used is from the Wérregue palm and is rolled up in a spiral fashion and then attached to a wooden base making for a unique and beautiful basket.

Ceramics

Given that large parts of Colombia are effectively enormous burial grounds for semi nomadic pre-Columbian populations it is no wonder that mountains of ceramic offerings have turned up. Originally the ceramics pulled from tombs by grave robbers was of little importance since these looters were principally looking for precious metals but later ceramics came into fashion and the whole sacking process recommenced.

Obviously, since the pre-Columbian tribes made offerings to deities and their lives were largely controlled by the elements and the seasons it seems clear that they should create ceramic offerings that bore certain significances to their beliefs. So, all though Colombia you can find ceramics that represent fertility such as those from the Calima culture (1500BC-100AD) during the Llama period which bear the recurring theme of maternity.

In Cauca and following the maternity theme, the Quimbaya culture (500BC—600AD) has thrown up some curiosities in the shape of uterine or pregnant woman shaped funeral urns. Death and the afterlife were of major importance and significance to the indigenous tribes and these feature heavily in the symbolism.

The Tolima culture (1200BC-1500AD) from the Magdalena Valley around the current site of Ibagué has provided us with some spectacular funerary urns and some small funerary seats.

One thing to look out for and study when viewing some of the pre-Columbian ceramics is the painting and artwork since there are several styles. In the Tierradentro culture there are funerary urns decorated with figures of snakes and lizards and their plates, pots and tripods were usually painted black, coffee brown and dark red. The Nariño culture (600BC-1500AD) used positive and negative styles to painting, often black negative cups on a red background and creamy colored cups with red and white designs.

Another key facet to pre-Columbian pottery is the abundance of anthropomorphic shapes and designs. By no means is this habit constricted to any one tribe, in fact it was practiced by most groups, but we can see fine examples of this in the ceramics unearthed belonging to the Muisca (600-1600AD). The Muisca are also recognized for the prevalence of zoomorphic references especially including frogs and snakes.

All of these pre-Columbian peoples would relate and repeat the subjects around them and what was natural to them such as the practices of the Zenú (200BC—1600AD) on the Caribbean coast who would paint various representations of the local fauna such as waterfowl and crocodiles.

Contemporary

In the department of Boyacá is the town of Ráquira which is the epicenter of ceramic pot making in contemporary Colombia and in the indigenous Chibcha language the town's name means "city of pots". This Andean pot making practice has led to a certain fame for Ráquira as much of the pottery gets exported. Originally the vases and urns were used for fermentation and storing provisions and there are various forms of clay and ceramic production done here. There is the black clay with high levels of charcoal, white, yellow and red clay.

In the Andean region of Tolima and in the town of La Chamba local artisans create a black pottery that is fetching and is in keeping with indigenous traditions. The clay is pulverized and molded into shape before being left to dry for 30 days before being baked and then later it is buffed to give it its shiny finish. These pieces of ceramic are all hand made from the local micaceous clay and some archeologists have reported that in the immediate region of La Chamba is home to the oldest pottery produced in the Americas.

Art Exhibitions

At any given time in Colombia, you will most certainly encounter high quality exhibitions in one of the dozen or so world class museums or galleries dotted around the country. Art lovers and indeed buyers are encouraged to visit Bogotá during the capital's Art Week, held at the end of October. In addition to the widely publicised ARTBO[112].

held in the city's immense Corferias convention centre, there's a growing number of fairs and events that display all kinds of visual and performing arts around the city, all concentrated in the same month. Hosted in various private houses in the colonial Candelaria, Barcú[113], focuses on bringing people to the centre to eyeball works by exciting new prospects in the Latin American art scene. A young but outrageously successful event is the Feria del Millón[114] – Art trade fair created to showcase some of the youngest and most exciting new talents in Colombia. Each piece of artwork costs in the region of a million pesos ($260 or GBP200) and each artist has to compete in a rigorous selection process. In 2019, the Feria was held in the decaying classical buildings of an abandoned hospital and prior to that in a re-designed textile factory in an industrial area of the city.

---

[112] ArtBo: htttps://www.artbo.co/

[113] Barcu: https://barcu.com/

[114] Freia del Millón: https://feriadelmillon.com/

Richard McColl

Colombian Photography

Colombian interest in historical photographs is relatively recent and began really in 1981 when an exhibition was being planned in Medellin entitled "100 Years of Photography". This awoke a national interest in the subject and since then efforts towards rescuing, cataloguing and preserving Colombia photographic heritage has really taken hold and is led for the most part by the Biblioteca Pública Piloto de Medellín para America Latina. This library and archive of photographs was created in 19952 by UNESCO and houses over a million examples some of which date back to 1849.

Alberto Urdaneta (1845-1887) was the first Colombian to really promote the new art form of photography and with his colleague Demetrio Paredes (1830-1898) created the journalistic publication Papel Periódico Ilustrado in 1881. Julio Racines Bernal (1848-1913) was a major contributor as well and together they compiled images and portraits of some of the most important characters of the time. With Urdaneta's passing the Papel Periódico Ilustrado folded and with it one of the golden eras of Colombian photography. But this was merely seeing out the 19C and in the 20C came a new and different take on the art form.

Luis Benito Ramos (1899 - 1955) having studied in France and learnt from and befriended Henri Cartier-Bresson returned to Colombia and in 1938 and inaugurated an exhibition celebrating the 4th centenary of the city entitled, "50 aspectos fotográficos de Colombia". His photos marked notably the nationalist sentiment in Colombia at the time but he also did studies on the countryside and the hunger suffered by poor campesinos and was critically acclaimed for being able to capture the emotion of these times. Melitón Rodríguez (1875 - 1942) also focussed on social images of the day but mainly in his native Medellín and Antioquia with an emphasis on artistic composition and showing the differences in the social strata of the population.

Perhaps the most impacting photographer of recent times to have come out of Colombia is Juan Manuel Echavarría Olano (1947). His efforts as an artist and photographer have been to record and publicize the lack of peace in his native land, given that since his birth the country has not seen one year of peace. He deals with the fallout from the violence inflicted by the guerrillas, paramilitaries, government and drugs cartels and gets the viewer to associate with the people afflicted by this violence.

A child of a country-dwelling family displaced by the violence in Antioquia, photographer Jesús Abad Colorado's work has been rightly lauded internationally and at home. His 2019 exhibition in Bogotá, El Testigo, displayed 500 of his images curated by him and accompanied a documentary by the same name. His photographs have captured the suffering in the rural context of Colombia's conflict and tell the story of the lives those people pictured have led.

Food and Drink

From the hearty stews served in the highlands to the seafood soups ladled out along the Caribbean coast, you'll find distinctive regional cuisine everywhere. Beef is popular everywhere as is chicken and most dishes will come adorned with the doughy staple of the arepa – Colombia's distant cousin (although don't mention this to a Colombian for fear of insulting them) to the tortilla but heavier, thicker and varying from region to region. Bogotá's most traditional dish is ajiaco, a thick chicken and potato soup garnished with capers, sour cream, and avocado. On the Caribbean coast you're more likely to dip your spoon into a cazuela de mariscos, a seafood soup with cassava or fried fish accompanied by coconut-infused rice and plantains. On the islands of San Andrés and Providencia, the local favourite is rondón, a soup made of fish and snails slowly simmered in coconut milk with yucca, plantains, breadfruit, and dumplings. Expect hearty food in Antioquia where people from Medellín and the surrounding areas expect healthy portions of beans and rice with every meal and the signature traditional dish is the heart-attack inducting Bandeja Paisa which includes, pork scratchings, ground beef, plantains, rice, beans, arepa and for good measure, a slice of avocado. In the department of Boyacá just outside of Bogotá, the cheesy roadside arepas are definitely worth trying and you'll discover an interesting selection of locally-made chorizos.

Do try some of the piangua clams, which are harvested from the roots of the mangroves, on the Pacific coast. Stuffed pork known as lechona and the haggis-like pepitoria in Santander make for filling meals and don't forget to try some of the salty toasted fat-bottomed ants from San Gil and around known as *Hormigas Culonas*.

A trip to a traditional market is recommended if you are a foodie and wish to try the plethora of fruits cultivated from Colombia's different and fertile regions. Vendors will be happy to talk to you and explain each one.

Whether you are knocking back multiple bottles of beer during an afternoon playing tejo with the locals or planning on a night out dancing, you'll find a tipple of choice for your taste in Colombia. The main international breweries produce light beers such as Club Colombia, Aguila, Poker but there is also an interesting micro-brew start-up scene taking hold.

International wines are expensive due to importation taxes and locally produced win from Boyacá still has some way to go to meet international standards. Try the rum and a few shots of the local aguardiente firewater if offered as well and in Bogotá's Candelaria colonial centre you can find places selling the indigenous fermented corn drink of Chicha if you are so-inclined to try it.

Other traditional dishes

Carne a la Llanera – a BBQ in the style of the people from the Llanos.

Fritanga - plate of deep-fried sausages stuffed with pork loin, yuca, potatoes, corn.

Mondongo – a cow's stomach lining, stewed up and served as a soup.

Mote de queso is a coastal soup made with a base yam with cubes of the salty costeño cheese inside.

Mute - thick soup made with beans, corn, garbanzos, potatoes and various meats.

Mute Santandereano – a typical dish from Santander, containing everything from pumpkin to eggplant, as well as pork, various corns and pasta.

Pandebono: Using yucca starch and cornmeal as staples in the recipe, in Boyacá bakers have created an almost addictive afternoon snack in the Pandebono.

Colombia has been undergoing a restaurant renaissance of

late and there are world class options for the discerning visitor in most major cities. Ask around for favourites and enjoy contemporary Colombian cuisine from some of the most adventurous and exciting young chefs in the continent.

Restaurants in many cities often close for a few hours between lunch and dinner (roughly 3 to 6). Appropriate attire in restaurants is comparable to U.S. or European standards--- dressy for the more formal places, casual everywhere else.

PART 7.
Geography and the Land

Richard McColl

Overview

Colombia sits atop the South American continent, benefiting from both Pacific and Caribbean coastlines and boasting a total surface area of 1,138,914 sq. km (707,691 sq. mi). Its high cordilleras that mark the beginnings of the Andes run diagonally parallel down the length of the nation, drawing the tectonic plates together and then smoothing the way for vast savannahs, depressions, topographical anomalies, coralline islands, coursing rivers and of course the mighty Amazon.

If ever a country's geography reflected and conditioned its society and politics it is Colombia's. The Andean mountain range splits into three near the Ecuadorean frontier to the south, after marching up the west coast of South America for thousands of kilometres from the icy wastes of southern Chile. Any cross-country journey in central Colombia, where most of its 50 million people live, involves a succession of climbs and descents that are impressive and exhaustive in equal measure.

A bus journey from the capital, Bogotá, to the big industrial city of Cali in the hot valley of the Cauca river 280km away to the south-west takes you first across the flat green expanse of the Sabana de Bogotá, the lush, mountain-girt basin that surrounds the capital on three sides. This is followed by a climb over the mountains ringing the city, a descent into the hot Magdalena valley at Girardot, an ascent to the Quindío pass (3,350m above sea level) over the Cordillera Central, the middle of three Andean spurs, a winding descent through the coffee-growing mountains around Armenia, and finally a long run through the baking sugar-cane fields that gave Cali its original raison d'etre.

Until quite recently, geography made Colombia more like a collection of city-states than a unified country. Regional identities have always been a powerful force in Colombian life, and it lingers on in the psychology of the people. This is particularly true of Medellín, Colombia's second city, high up

(1,480m) in a valley surrounded by the mountains of Antioquia, almost 500km to the northwest of the capital. The city's two and a half million people see themselves as almost a race apart and are resentful of what they regard as the overbearing arrogance of the distant capital. Medellín, like Sao Paulo in Brazil or Guayaquil in Ecuador, likes to regard itself as the real heart of the country, where wealth is generated and talent is nurtured, only to be appropriated by undeserving bureaucrats and politicians of Bogotá.

Given that Colombia has such a great variety of landscapes and shares borders with Panama, Ecuador, Venezuela, Peru and Brazil, it takes no stretch of the imagination to realize that just about every microclimate is represented within its borders. Those visitors drawn to high-altitude adventures will be just as pleased as those searching for white sandy Caribbean beaches or the verdant cornucopia of the fertile coffee zone. With such great natural riches comes a great responsibility, that of protecting their fragile ecosystems. Colombia has an extensive network of carefully controlled and administered national parks and natural reserves that allow the visitor to enjoy sightings of rare birdlife, interesting flora and fauna, and explore curious topographies.

Geology and Hydrography

The westernmost portion of the Guiana Shield falls within the country's borders at the Chiribiquete Plateau in central southern Colombia, completing the largest expanse of tropical rainforest in the world. This rainforest thins out to become a topography of broken rocks, terraces and streams. Vast fluvial plains splay out from this region that over time have created some of the most interesting and most ancient geological regions of Colombia. These include the Serranía of Macarena, a narrow mountain range 30km (19mi) wide and 120km (74mi) in length and that merges with the Amazon and the Orinoco rivers. The algae and mosses that create the yellow, blue, green, black and red colours that enflame the Caño Cristales River in the Parque Nacional

Natural Sierra de la Macarena almost seem otherworldly and unnatural, and have led to claims that this is one of the world's most beautiful rivers.

Colombia's incredible array of rivers does not end here though, and just one department to the West, in Guaviare runs the river by the same name, forming the geographical border between the Amazon rainforest and the humid savannahs of the Orinoco basin. Heading back from the Guaviare River one can trace the blue line snaking on the map extending to the Vaupés River and then the Guainía River that is more often known outside of Colombia as the Río Negro. Forming part of the border between Venezuela and Colombia, the Río Negro then flows east, connecting with the Solimoes in Brazil to join the Amazon River.

The Andes mountains

The Andean region of Colombia is a massive wedge of land that cuts diagonally through the country from the border with Venezuela all the way to Ecuador in the west, rising to heights of 5770m, while at the same time containing the most populous and economically active regions of the country. At the border with Ecuador the Andes form one cordillera, and then tracing the jagged line north it breaks into three, the Oriental, Central and Occidental ranges, all of which have mountains permanently covered with snow. The three cordilleras form a network of canyons, valleys, plateaus and of course the mighty Magdalena and Cauca rivers.

On the mountainsides, thick with vegetation and draped in moss, are the Andean Highland Cloud forests. It is here that Colombia can stake its claim to being the country with the greatest number of species of orchid (the national flower).

The Paramos

The paramos or high-altitude plateaus are bleak areas of peat and glacially formed valleys. With the three cordilleras running the length of Colombia, it should come as no surprise that this country contains roughly 50 per cent of all the world's paramos. Comprising of an area of 178,000 hectares, the paramo of Sumapaz, only 50km south from Bogotá, is the largest in the world. It is largely unspoilt due to guerrilla incursions, and has become the perfect habitat for the endangered spectacled bear. Beyond the snowline in Los Nevados National Park in the departments of Tolima, Quindío and Risaralda, is a habitat and environment known as an altitude desert. In addition to scree slopes and high peaks, there are glaciers where only the most well-adapted flora and fauna can survive.

The Sierra Nevada

Often erroneously considered to make up part of the Cordillera Oriental, the Sierra Nevada, located on the Caribbean coast close to the city of Santa Marta, is actually an isolated mountain range separate from the Andes chain. It hosts the two highest mountains in Colombia, the Pico Cristóbal Colón and Pico Simón Bolívar, which rise to approximately 5,700m (18700ft). It is from here that snowmelt from the world's highest coastal range runs into an array of rivers including the River Magdalena.

Pivotal to the creation and development of modern-day Colombia, the Magdalena River runs through 18 departments between the Oriental and Central cordilleras from its source in the southern region of Huila to the Caribbean at Barranquilla.

Converging with the Magdalena is the River Cauca, another key waterway in Colombia. This major river runs northeast from the southern highlands, passing the imposing Puracé and Sotará volcanoes and then irrigating the lush sugarcane fields of the Valle del Cauca department.

Coastal Colombia

Colombians proudly state that theirs is the only country in South America with coastlines on both the Pacific and the Caribbean, a staggering 3,208 km in total: 1,760 km on the Caribbean and 1,448km on the Pacific. The Pacific and Caribbean coastlines show marked differences.

The Caribbean lowlands extend south from the jungles and

humidity of Panama into arid semi desert. The northern most area of the lowlands at the of the Gulf of Urabá bears little resemblance to the same coastline further along the coast to the southeast passing the cities of Cartagena, Barranquilla and Santa Marta, as the fauna rapidly changes in the approach to the highlands of the Sierra Nevada.

The Caribbean Coast

Although famed for its crystalline turquoise sea and white sand beaches around Tayrona National Park close to the city of Santa Marta, the Colombian Caribbean coast is actually a mixture of complex landscapes. Beginning at the Darién Gap bordering Panama, the landscapes undergo dramatic changes. Around Montería and Sincelejo in the departments of Córdoba and Sucre, vast coastal savannahs are set aside for cattle grazing. Close by, in the resort destinations of Tolú and Coveñas, and further west near Cartagena, there are thick and protected meshes of mangrove swamps replete with birdlife that act as formidable barriers from the sea.

Travelling northeast from Cartagena towards Barranquilla, passing the mouth of the Magdalena River, there is a long stretch of hot, dry desert. By the town of Ciénega, the waterways replete with fish open out into a vast area of marshes and wetlands, the ideal habitat for many species. There are many inland swamps, as well as land ideal for supporting the ubiquitous banana and cotton plantations found here.

To the east of Santa Marta, one quickly leaves behind the lush vegetation encountered in the shadow of the snow-capped Sierra Nevada Mountains, replaced by arid desert-like conditions. The Guajira peninsula that borders Venezuela is merciless with its cruel thorn trees and xeric scrub offering scant shade and meagre rainfall – the lowest in Colombia - averaging out at only 300mm per year. The land here seems fit only for the herds of goats bred by the local Wayuú people.

The Pacific Coast

From the northern reaches of Colombian territory bordering Panama on the Pacific coast to the frontier with Ecuador in the south, Colombia's coastline alters only slightly. Both the Pacific and Caribbean sides share the Darién Gap, an almost impenetrable cornucopia of jungle known for its lawlessness.

The Atrato wetland or swamp is a muddy quagmire measuring 65km (40mi) that has until now prevented engineers from developing any effective ground transport through the region from the Chocó to Panama.

The tropical rainforest that extends through the departments of Chocó, Valle, Cauca and Nariño is one of the wettest, most bio-diverse places on earth, thanks to the heavily laden rain clouds blown in from the ocean. The mangrove forests in and around the municipalities of Guapi, Tumaco and Buenaventura are known for the piangua mollusc that grows beneath the water on the roots of the plant and is a staple food for locals.

Pacific Tropical Piedmont

Descending from the nation's most narrow mountain range, the Pacific Baudó range, into the ecologically magnificent regions that are predominantly made up of virgin jungles and swamps brings one to the Pacific coast. Fertile alluvial forests have been created in the flood plains of several rivers including the Atrato, San Juan and Baudó. While the Baudó range is relatively low, it is the Andean piedmont that rises up and creates a huge natural barrier dividing the Pacific from the rest of the country. This is an area of outstanding natural beauty where the tangled jungle, in this one of the wettest places on earth, seemingly tumbles directly into the sea. Despite the area's obvious attractions this is a relatively unvisited region due to its inaccessibility.

The Llanos and Orinoco Basin

The open savannahs, directly South of Bogotá, that constitute the Llanos Orientales in Colombia, an area that occupies just under 30 per cent of the total national area, is a vast region of grasslands that is largely uninhabited. Characterized by a continual cover of sturdy grass that measures between three and six feet high, the Llanos Orientales or Orinoco Basin expand and cover the four enormous departments, Arauca, Casanare, Meta and Vichada. The savannahs are kept well-watered by the annual flooding of the Orinoco and Arauca rivers and their respective tributaries and of course all this water permanently on the ground through the flood season inhibits the growth of trees.

The Amazon Basin

A stranger to no one's imagination, the sprawling, tumbling, immense snarl of foliage, vegetation and rivers that make up the Amazon basin, accounts for roughly 35 per cent of Colombia's territory, some 403,000 square kilometres in total. The Amazonian tropical forest, with its unparalleled biodiversity including, according to the WWF (the World Wildlife Fund), no less than one in ten known species in the world, is at its centre. Then as the topography changes to the north to include rolling lowland hills so does the flora, whilst a slight change in altitude brings is a marked difference, with a prevalence of broadleaved and fern-like herbaceous communities springing up on sandstone surfaces.

Insular Colombia

As a further addition to Colombia's already exuberant geographical offerings there are the coral islands in the Caribbean. 46km (28.5mi) southeast from the coastal city of Cartagena there are the ringed Islas del Rosario, a popular day trip from the city. There are 43 islands in this chain, making up part of a protected marine area popular with divers.

The former pirate islands of the San Andrés archipelago, Providencia and Santa Catalina, are a Colombian anomaly since they are located 775 km (480 miles) to the northwest of the Colombian mainland and are in fact closer to the coast of Nicaragua. This location has often given rise to disputes over ownership between the two nations. Politics aside, these small

Caribbean islands – San Andrés measures only 12km (7.5mi) in length and only 3km (1.85mi) in breadth – are ringed by white coralline sandy beaches fringed with windblown coconut palms. Providencia, the smaller island of the two, differs in that it is volcanic and at its highest point reaches 363m (1190ft). The tiny island of Santa Catalina is connected to Providencia by a causeway.

On the Pacific side of Colombia, some 35km (22mi) from the coast near the municipality of Guapi is the former prison island of Isla Gorgona. Now a national park, the volcanic island hosts a small number of tourists who come to glimpse endemic species and the annual humpback whale rituals that take place within view from the shore.

Even further out to the west in the Pacific is the island of Malpelo. With steep cliffs of volcanic rock 490km (304mi) from the Colombian mainland, Malpelo is uninhabited yet permanently protected by the Colombian Navy which ensures that this area is free from illegal shark fishing and that the huge colony of birds remains untouched and protected.

Climate

With so many microclimates and geographical variations, it is impossible to say that Colombia has a single climate. From region to region, extending from arid semi-desert on the Caribbean coast to the cold barren plateaus in the cordilleras and then down into the rain forests such as the Amazon, tropical Caribbean jungles and mangrove swamps of the Pacific, the climate can show extreme changes. Colombia is often perceived as being a steamy tropical country, but its climate varies greatly with altitude. Along the Caribbean Coast temperatures are an average of 82F (28C); in changeable Bogotá, the average is a chilly 54F (12C). The valley cities of Medellín and Cali have pleasant weather. Seasons don't really exist in Colombia, but rainfall and brisk weather is common from October to November and April to June. The dry season usually runs from December to

March in mountainous areas, mid-December to April and July to September in low-lying coastal regions.

Environmental challenges

Colombia's natural habitats are under constant threat on three fronts: natural disasters arising from the country's location close to many tectonic fault lines; drastic climatic shifts, and man-made dangers.

Given that so much of Colombia's geography and economy is defined by the three cordilleras that make up the Andes Mountains, much of the land that is situated on and around the Pacific Ring of Fire - the circum-Pacific Ring of Fire, where the Pacific Plate meets many surrounding tectonic plates. The Ring of Fire is the most seismically and volcanically active zone in the world - is unstable and constantly under threat from seismic movements. Most recently in January 1999, the city of Armenia, located in Colombia's coffee zone, suffered a catastrophic 6.2 earthquake that levelled the city and left more than a thousand casualties.

There is also the ever-present threat of volcanic eruptions as Colombia sits firmly in the northern volcanic zone. The Galeras volcano in the department of Nariño is considered Colombia's most active threat, but it is the 1985 eruption of the Nevado del Ruiz volcano that remains in the collective memory after it wiped out the town of Armero, Tolima and left an estimated 23,000 dead.

On 1 April 2017 a landslide dragged massive amounts of water, dirt and mud downhill, and buried 17 neighbourhoods of Mocoa in the departmental capital of Putumayo, killing more than 300 people. Poor land management, deforestation and aggressive cattle farming over decades have been seen as the causes for this disaster.

Dry weather conditions resulting from the El Niño phenomenon have been hitting Colombia's agriculturalists in recent years. 2010 was particularly damaging, when coffee production in the south of the country was ruined due to the lack of rain. While the Caribbean coast, during El Niño affected years, generally suffers from a lack of rainfall, the Pacific coast suffers from terrible floods. These dramatic swings in the normal climate patterns also bring with them further problems such as disease carrying mosquitoes, notably malaria and dengue.

On 5 November 2022, President Petro signed Colombia up to the Escazú Agreement[115].

Man-made dangers

It is estimated that between 1.5 to 2.2 million acres are deforested in Colombia every year, mainly in the Amazon and in the Chocó. Deforestation on this scale will deplete the nation's forest reserves within 40 years and cause the extinction of much flora and fauna, as well as severely upsetting the social dynamic and habitat of indigenous groups living in the affected areas. This deforestation arises from several causes and market-led drivers: logging for timber both legally and illegally, clearing the land for agricultural purposes, coca plantations, and mining. The cultivation of coca and the production of cocaine has also led to major chemical contaminants being released into water systems and into the atmosphere from the fumigation and eradication flights.

Overcrowding and poor drainage has led to disastrous consequences for the people near to the cities of Cartagena and Ciénaga, where water purity has been affected and effluent runs openly into the sea. In Bogotá the use of low-grade fossil fuels and gases from vehicle emissions stifle the clear high-altitude air. The local government in the capital attempted in the late 2000s to implement some recycling practices into the waste habits of the capital's populace in an attempt to minimize some of the mountains of refuse, but little has been achieved.

Fracking

For over a decade Colombians have been debating whether or not to allow oil companies to use hydraulic fracturing or fracking in the national territory. A basic regulatory framework was created in 2008 and has since been updated to reflect new practices and regulations internationally as well as local studies. A two-year study was undertaken in 2014 to understand the environmental impacts of shale development and incorporate them into regulations. Yet in 2018, Colombia's high court provisionally suspended the previous rules used to regulate fracking, citing concerns over its effect on the environment and human health, and since then its legal status has been in limbo. Colombia's conservative president Iván Duque was ambivalent in his position on shale development during his electoral campaign but has since sought to strike a balance by taking the stance that fracking could be done safely with sufficient monitoring. When he was been in power, the probability of fracking being "approved" increased, with a move to permit the process for "research and scientific" purposes under strict environmental guidelines in four parts of the country.

Communities where fracking was been proposed demonstrated against the practice, and there was a strong anti-fracking sentiment in the nationwide demonstrations that paralyzed Bogotá and other main cities in late 2019. One of President Petro's first actions when he came to power in 2022 was to ensure that fracking be completely outlawed.

Mining

Gold, silver, platinum, nickel, emeralds, coal, salt, tungsten and coltan are just some of the minerals mined in Colombia, making extractive industries a key source of employment. The biggest mining sectors are in coal and gold, and a boom in gold mining in recent years has been driven not only by large international mining corporations but also by unregulated small-scale mining. This is often controlled by illegal armed groups who have seen the opportunity to boost their income and influence. As a result, the value of illegal gold exports from Colombia in recent years has surpassed the value of cocaine exports, becoming the country's largest illicit export - up to 80 per cent of Colombia's gold exports are estimated to be produced illegally. In some cases, armed groups directly operate mines themselves, while in others they enforce extortion fees and incite terror on communities where unregulated mining is taking place.

---

[115] Cancilleria de Colombia: https://www.cancilleria.gov.co/newsroom/news/presidente-gustavo-petro-sanciona-ley-aprueba-acuerdo-escazu

Where to Go

Principal Cities and destinations nearby

· Bogotá

Bogotá sits firmly in a category of South American cities which are in a constant state of flux. Although various barrios and districts may display the architecture and polite mannerisms of a suburban borough of London or the modernity found in suburban living in the US or Canada, the Colombian capital is very different. Stroll south one block or three blocks west from the neo-classical columns of the central Palacio de Nariño and Plaza de Bolívar and you are confronted with some classic Latin American barrios of misery and human suffering.

Blend together the districts south of the Calle de los Comuneros, west of the Avenida Caracas, into the middle class Chapinero, from the well-heeled tree-lined streets of Rosales and El Chicó, the developments of the Cuidadela Colsubsidio and north way up into the suburbs stretching out to Chía and up the Cerros Orientales of Lijaca, and you will get some sense of the *sancocho* of Bogotá.

Outsiders may say that *"Bogotá es una ciudad de todos y de nadie,"* but this statement is becoming something of the past, as the thousands of families that resettled here generations ago, are now becoming Bogotanos rather than staking a claim to herald from outlying departments. The idea promoted by younger generations for this new Bogotá is to highlight the city by unearthing forgotten anecdotes, reclaiming untold histories and telling the story truthfully, be it focusing on the unmarked graves of Matatigres, the car workshops of the Siete de Agosto, the Tattoo Parlours of Lourdes, Chapinero's culinary revolution or the chic bars of Parque 93.

Near to Bogotá: Boyacá

In addition to the widely visited destination of Villa de Leyva, just three hours from Bogotá, the department of Boyacá is steeped in history and scenic small towns which make for wonderful daytrips from a central base in the region. Choose from Tibasosa, Monguí, Iza, Nobsa and Ráquira and be sure to visit the tropical looking Laguna de Tota.

Heading North: Santander

Barichara

Widely considered as one of the most beautiful towns in Santander, if not in Colombia, Barichara is now an artsy, bohemian destination with more than a touch of class. Founded in 1705 by Francisco Pradilla y Ayerbe (1673-1748), the town is a national heritage monument and its cobblestone streets, whitewashed walls and elegant colonial rooftops have been carefully maintained permitting Barichara to remain charming and scenic. Situated on the top of a bluff that allows for views of the sweeping valley carved here by the River Suárez, Barichara is a town that has embraced tranquillity and permits the visitor to wander its ornate streets in an unhurried fashion. Linking the town to Guane some 9km/5,6mi away is the old Camino Real that, prior to the Spanish arrival, was a key pathway created by the indigenous Guane people. In recent years, Barichara has attracted a wealthier crowd which has seen fit to provide the town with boutique hotels and upmarket handicrafts stores ensuring that this corner of Santander is a key point in which to rest and relax after adrenalin pumping activities enjoyed in nearby San Gil.

- **Medellín**

Nestling in the narrow Aburrá Valley, this north-western city of almost three million people is the capital of Antioquia province. The industrious *"paisas,"* as natives of the province are called, built the successful coffee and textile industries that have enabled Medellín to prosper; today it is Colombia's second city. Modern and affluent, Medellín has the country's only elevated train system. It also has several interesting museums, respected universities, and wide, tree-lined boulevards in addition to having spear-headed noteworthy urban renovations projects such as the escalator and cable car system connecting more humble barrios. But Medellín also has thousands of impoverished citizens whose shanties appear on the city's edges. Although local and international intervention has lessened the drug trade, the city remains violent and unpredictable in parts.

Near to Medellín: Antioquia

There's a long tradition of the people of Medellín exploring their own back yard and the small towns in Antioquia are special with their ornate beauty intact, strong Catholicism and welcoming inhabitants. Choose any from Santa Fé de Antioquia, Santa Elena, Jardín, Jericó, Tamesis and immerse yourself in coffee and flower growing towns.

Near to Medellín: The Coffee Zone

With easy access to the three principal cities of the Eje Cafetero or Coffee Zone, Armenia, Manizales and Pereira, this region of rolling verdant hillsides, attractive villages, volcanoes and welcoming people should be everyone's list of places to visit in Colombia. Tourists throng to Salento and use this as a springboard when exploring the Valle de Cocora, home to Colombia's national tree, the towering wax palm. There are less visited nearby towns such as Filandia and Pijao where you can escape the throngs. A little further adrift but well worth visiting is the ornate town of Salamina. Do visit a working coffee farm and try the local produce and for those seeking more adventurous activities, options for horse-riding, hiking and mountaineering abound.

- **Cali**

Located in the fertile Valle de Cauca, Cali is a lively provincial capital and an important agricultural centre, responsible for a hefty portion of the country's sugar, coffee, and corn exports. The city's elevation at 3,000 feet contributes to the year-round spring-like temperatures. Many people visit during the Christmas-New Year festival, when the city unapologetically devotes itself to merrymaking. The mountains near Cali contain some of the country's most important archaeological sites, such as the enigmatic statues of San Agustín and the painted tombs of Tierradentro. Within the rapidly expanding city (it has grown fourfold in the past 40 years) you'll find a small colonial quarter, some interesting museums, and many leafy parks. In the centre is the Paseo de Bolívar, a large park on the north bank of the muddy Río Cali. To the south are the main sights, including most of the interesting old churches in the district of San Antonio. The nearby town of Buga has long been a destination for religious pilgrims seeking to ask favours of the "miraculous Christ" in the church.

Near to Cali: Popayán

Founded in 1537 by Sebastián de Belalcázar, Popayán quickly became an important administrative centre of the Viceroyalty of New Granada because of its position on the Cartagena to Quito gold route. Although the town was largely destroyed by an earthquake on Good Friday in 1983, its colonial buildings have all been painstakingly rebuilt and the result is an ornate and picturesque setting. Hotel rooms must be booked months ahead of time for Semana Santa, the week between Palm Sunday and Easter, when the streets are filled with colourful religious processions.

· Barranquilla

Colombia's main Caribbean port and capital of the department of Atlántico, Barranquilla is the country's fourth largest city and a true cultural melting pot strategically positioned at the mouth of the Magdalena River. Home to the second largest Carnival celebration in the Americas, birthplace of Colombian songstress Shakira and fundamental to the writings of Gabriel García

Márquez, Barranquilla is a contemporary cultural heartbeat on the Colombian Caribbean coast. For a glimpse of traditional Barranquilla that belongs to the people of Afro-Colombian descent you should head to the Centro. Low houses with high pavements that protect the locals from the street floods in the rainy season and a village-like feel have created this community within the city and it is here that the real ambiance of Carnival is created.

Many residents feel that this is the real heart of the festivities and the essence of Barranquilla away from the shiny new shopping centres and high-rise apartment complexes. Enjoy fine dining sophisticated shopping, the spectacular Museo del Caribe and literary haunts here in La Arenosa (the sandy city) located between Cartagena and Santa Marta.

Near to Barranquilla

Puerto Colombia is just 14km (8.5mi) along the coastal highway from Barranquilla. Puerto Colombia has been immortalised in the novel *Memories of my Melancholy Whores* (2004) by Gabriel García Márquez. In 1888 the jetty at Puerto Colombia was created by the Cuban engineer Francisco Javier Cisneros, which at 2km (1.2mi) was reputedly the second largest in the world at the time of its construction. Extending out into the Bay of Cupino this jetty was created to resolve the problem of boats crossing the agitated waters of the Bocas de Ceniza.

Thousands of immigrants disembarked here in search of a better life, Puerto Colombia was, if you like, the Colombian version of Ellis Island. Over time Puerto Colombia fell into disuse but recently it has become a tourist attraction and weekend escape for visitors.

· **Cartagena**

The first Spanish city on the South American mainland, Cartagena, founded in the sixteenth century is Colombia's Caribbean colonial jewel. La Heroica or Cartagena de las Indias as she is sometimes known is a UNESCO World Heritage Site of tall republican era buildings constructed on top of colonial architecture. Brightly painted homes made from hard stone and coral that hide inner courtyards and high colonial roofs, line the narrow streets that snake into breezy and shaded plazas and alongside ornate and opulent churches and palaces. Sacked by European pirates, a formidable city wall of 11km (7mi) was built to protect the city and at the entry the impregnable Castillo San Felipe. Cartagena is now a city of international and domestic tourism and it shows, designer boutiques line the colourful streets, exclusive hotels have pushed out traditional communities and prices are the same as you would encounter in many major world cities.

Near to Cartagena: Mompós

Follow the Magdalena River 248km (154mi) inland and you will find yourself as if in a fairy-tale of an elegantly decaying colonial wonderland. You are in Mompós, also spelt Mompox, a town of roughly 45,000 inhabitants founded as a safe port along the river in 1537 by Alonso de Heredia, brother of Pedro, the founder of Cartagena. This is a land of legends, history, Masonic influences and folklore and was key in Simón Bolívar's missions to liberate this region of New Granada. A key port on the river transporting the gold and silver from Ecuador up to Cartagena, Mompós grew exponentially in the colonial era, becoming a cultural and commercial centre. Gradually Mompós' importance waned when the river began to silt up. While considered to be difficult to be reached by some, it is this relative isolation that has enabled the town to remain intact as a preserved colonial relic.

- **Santa Marta**

Situated in an extraordinary geographical location, on one side beneath the Sierra Nevada Mountains that reach almost 6000m (19,700ft) in altitude and on the other side the Caribbean ocean, Santa Marta is blessed with incomparable natural riches.

Populated first by pre-Columbian cultures and then later becoming a bastion of Royalist support during the colonial era, Santa Marta is steeped in history. As the capital of the department of Magdalena it is a major port and commercial centre and due to its tropical climate and beaches has become a major national and international tourist destination for holidaymakers keen on hiking its parks, sunning themselves on the beaches, immersing themselves in the history and bird-watching in the mountains. Santa Marta has undergone a complete makeover with serious investment pumped into its colonial centre and it now offers small exclusive hotels, chic restaurants and boutiques.

Near to Santa Marta: Parque Nacional Natural Tayrona

By far the busiest national park in Colombia, Tayrona's beaches are legendary and are amongst the most scenic and breath-taking in the world. Perhaps it is this blend of glorious stretches of white sand with the obvious influences of indigenous Tayrona culture and extreme biodiversity that makes this park so special. The beach of Arrecifes is stunningly beautiful and a snarling current throws up surf that crashes on immense sun-bleached boulders. There are good hikes to be enjoyed here in the park that can lead you to the pre-Columbian ruins at El Pueblito that resembles a miniature Ciudad Perdida and to the archaeological Museum at Chairama. With more time you can hike out to further beaches with fewer tourists such as Bahia Concha and Bahia Neguanje.

Near to Santa Marta: Ciudad Perdida

Within the lush Sierra Nevada and the reward for a tough yet not gruelling 5-6-day 40km (25mi) hike is the unforgettable Ciudad Perdida or Lost City. Constructed around 700AD (600 odd years before the construction of Machu Picchu) Buritaca or Teyuna as it is known by local tribes is a collection of levelled terraces cut into the foothills of the Sierra Nevada. The Arhuacos, Koguis and Asario have all declared that the surrounding area and the constructions are of sacred importance to their beliefs. To say that the Ciudad Perdida is a collection of ruins would be inaccurate because all about here are indigenous dwellings and populations and, on the trek, you have the opportunity to pass through traditional villages and interact with the local people. The terraces at the Ciudad Perdida, all found between 950m and 1300m above sea level (3120ft-4265ft) are better described as living ruins. The Ciudad Perdida itself is believed to be a political and economic centre for the indigenous tribes here and its population apparently fluctuated between 1400 and 3000 inhabitants all spread over the 250 terraces thus far uncovered.

Near to Santa Marta: Aracataca

The birthplace of Gabriel García Márquez lies some 88km (55mi) or an hour and half drive from Santa Marta and at this moment in time is a destination for the discerning literature fan.

It is not without its charms and any visitor will receive a warm and friendly welcome, be shown around and will be able to observe the inspiration for the fictional town of Macondo of "100 Hundred Years of Solitude". Nothing of colonial interest remains, the old movie house is a hardware store but the Colombian government has created a museum in Gabo's grandparents' home dedicated to the author. This museum was also victim to a bit of magic realism since its opening was delayed due to an internal political argument whether it should resemble the home of Garcia Marquez' grandparents or the Buendía family of the novel.

There are spots to swim in the nearby Aracataca River and take in the new era of environmental exploitation: where once there were bananas now there are African palms.

Near to Santa Marta: Minca

Just a 40-minute drive up into the foothills of the Sierra Nevada mountains are the breath-taking views and trails around the town of Minca. The town itself is a mix of old and new as bohemian Europeans and Colombians have taken up residence alongside the traditional locals and made Minca a destination for hikers, yoga aficionados and birdwatchers. The cool breeze from the mountains takes the edge off the stifling Caribbean heat as do the pristine rivers and natural pools in which you can bathe.

Near to Santa Marta: Palomino

If you are keen on tuning out and lazing away your days on sandy beaches in the shade of towering palms, your destination should be Palomino. Located just inside the Guajira department a few hours' drive from Santa Marta, the town itself is little more than a rest stop on the highway to Venezuela. However, it's here, away from the main road and towards the shoreline that a community of eco lodges, luxury resorts and backpacker haunts have sprung up to cater to all types of bohemian travellers seeking time away from the hoi polloi. It's recommended that you book in advance for high season dates and European holidays as places fill up fast.

- **The Caribbean Islands**

San Andrés and Providencia

The island of San Andrés is long and narrow and is made up of three urban centres the principal being the disorderly El Centro or North End where the majority of the hotels and businesses are located and the beach of Playa Spratt Bight also known as Bahía Sardina.

More or less in the centre of the island is La Loma, a traditional Caribbean village of brightly painted wooden homes situated on the top of the island's hill. San Luis is far less hectic and much more laid back that El Centro and those who wish to get away from it all, lounge on a beach, and empty their minds of all stress are advised to come here. Little volcanic Providencia located 90km (56mi) north of San Andrés, is so dull, islanders will tell you, that you will arrive here as a couple and leave as three! While this may be true, there is plenty more to do on this the Caribbean's best kept secret whether it be for lounging on a beach, scuba diving, hiking, fishing, exploring or attending a beachfront horse race. For the true Caribbean experience, Playa Manzanillo on Providencia is not to be missed. The water is calm, lapping gently at the sand, the beach is shaded and your own amateur photos look as if they have been sprung from the pages of a holiday catalogue. For the more adventurous visitors to the island there are trails that take you up to The Peak at 360m above sea level (1180ft).

The Pacific Coast

Wrongly overlooked by the vast number of travellers visiting Colombia, the Pacific region is slowly but surely gearing up to receive manageable numbers of environmentally conscious visitors. The awe-inspiring geography that in the north bordering Panama includes the impenetrable tangle of the Darién, an area recognised for its lawlessness inasmuch as its ecological diversity then continues south through bays of crystalline waters, favoured areas for the migrating humpback whales, along through protective mangrove swamps and the important ports of Tumaco and Buenaventura before reaching the frontier with Ecuador. This area is one of the rainiest on earth with an annual rainfall averaging in some parts to more that 5m (16ft) and it is this fiercely tropical climate and ecosystem combined with the problems of the armed conflict here that has seriously inhibited the successful development of a capable and inclusive infrastructure.

However, the Pacific is gradually being placed on the map as a tourist destination with national parks as Gorgona (a former penal colony), Sanquianga and Utría receiving more visitors every year and the local populations, mainly of Afro-Colombian descent as well as indigenous tribes have been setting about creating eco-lodges to benefit the local traditional communities. Surfing and scuba can be enjoyed in Nuquí.

Whale Watching

From July through October Bahía Solano becomes one of the key focal points in Colombia for tourists eager to witness the breaching and crashing of the formidable humpback whale and its young. Boat tours that go out into the bay and beyond can be organized through any hotel.

Deserts

La Guajira

The northern most point on the South American mainland, Punta Gallinas is basic and breath-taking and has that end of the world feel. The Ranchería (settlement) here is sparsely settled and feels as if raised up from the water. Public transport is available as far as Cabo de la Vela but to get to Punta Gallinas you are strongly recommended to hop onto an organised tour as it may be days before a car passes to give you a lift and of course you could be confronted with the very real possibility that some of the people you encounter only speak Wayuú and not Spanish. If you have come this far – 75km (47mi) north from Cabo de la Vela – then it makes sense to visit the flamingo colonies in the small inlets and around the islands and to take a boat trip to the stunning beach of Bahia Hondita frequented by shrimp fishermen. Be sure to visit the vast dunes at Punta Taroa that slide from great heights directly into the sea at sunset, and then indulge your inner child by taking a tumble down the sand and into the surf.

Others

Parque Nacional Natural el Cocuy

The Vuelta al Cocuy may someday become as famous as the Inca Trail in Peru or the Ciudad Perdida in northern Colombia, as this demanding five-day trek (walking about 8 hours per day) inspires and continues to entice a growing number of international visitors every year to this region. The route, which follows the base of the Sierra, can be done either north-south from Güicán to El Cocuy (accessed in an overnight bus from Bucaramanga) or the other way around, and unveils most of the park's natural attractions. During a goodly portion of the trek, you will enjoy almost uninterrupted views of snowy peaks and icy summits, and given the distances that are being covered, you will traverse a great variety of terrain and have an opportunity to do some mountain climbing. The park is often closed due to weather and restrictions on tourist numbers to protect the environment, so check beforehand.

http://www.parquesnacionales.gov.co

San Agustín

Declared a UNESCO World Heritage site as far back as 1935, San Agustín plays host to the relics of an advanced pre-columbian culture that thrived in the area for more than seven centuries. This Agustinian culture is now protected and cherished and on show for all in parks in the environs of San Agustín where the visitor can stroll back through the centuries marvelling at anthropomorphic sculptures representing symbols of fertility, maternity and the alter ego.

Further ideas

The Tatacoa desert (Huila) and Los Estoraques (Norte de Santander) are two smaller arid desert regions, ideal for stargazing and birdwatching respectively. The Tatacoa is reached through Neiva and the town of Villavieja where modest but charming accommodation can be found. Los Estoraques is a small but perfectly formed area of outstanding national beauty located on the edge of the Playa de Belén colonial town.

Amazon, the Llanos and beyond

Leticia

Traditionally the Colombian gateway to the Amazon, Leticia is the quintessential frontier town with a bustling trade in provisions passing through the shared border with Brazil's Tabatinga and Peru's Santa Rosa. The real sights are beyond Leticia, and trips can be organized from the town itself or beforehand.

The Llanos

Stretching across the departments of Casanare and Meta, the Llanos has charm, style and substance and oozes all of them and anyone wishing to experience adventure, bird watching and authenticity. This is Colombia's big sky cowboy country where vast open plains, savannahs and wetlands can provide the ultimate Colombian safari. Stay in a Hato – as the rural haciendas are known – and rise early on horseback to see anacondas, bird life, capybaras, alligators and if you're lucky track down an elusive jaguar. Daily flights into both Villavicencio and Yopal from Bogotá make the llanos eminently accessible.

Guaviare

Lying to the south of Bogotá and Meta in an almost straight line, the department of Guaviare is a destination for nature lovers and those seeking out ancient rock paintings. For so long off-limits, Guaviare is slowly opening up with a focus on community-led tourism showing off the curious rock formations, colourful rivers and exotic species, all of which inhabit this region where the savannahs meet the amazon.

Caño Cristales

Caño Cristales is a phenomenon and is rightly known as, *"el rio mas bonito del mundo".* This anomaly of nature is produced by a blossoming of the tell-tale burgundy and red *Macarenia clavígera* plants found just beneath the water level. The best time of year to visit is from June to November when the plants are in full bloom. Aside from the obvious, amazing hikes, photographing this glorious river, bathing in the naturally formed pools carved out of the Guyanese Shield over millennia, there is plenty more to see and do over a few days in the town of La Macarena.

PART 8.
Further Information

Further Reading

There is an embarrassment of riches on offer to those seeking out Colombian literature in its original Spanish or translated into English and this curated list is by no means complete, blending history, politics, 19th century love stories, contemporary horrors and magic realism. But, hopefully it provides a starting point for a love-affair with Colombia. Obviously, no collection of books on Colombia would be complete without a couple of works by Gabriel García Márquez, but we have tried not to overwhelm you with his astonishing back catalogue.

Héctor Abad Faciolince and Juan Gabriel Vásquez could easily provide you with a healthy insight into Colombia's reckoning with her past and her struggles for an identity. In terms of journalistic style reportage on the cocaine trade, war correspondent Toby Muse has written the most complete first-person narrative based on direct research. There are plenty of stories of those kidnapped and held by one armed group or another, but none is more harrowing than that of former presidential candidate Ingrid Betancourt.

For a sociological look at the changes taking place in Colombia, Matt Rendell uses the lens of Colombia's awe-inspiring cyclists to show how soft diplomacy can make a difference.

Themes of patriarchy and nationhood run deep in all literature devoted to Colombia and William Ospina, Pilar Quintana and Laura Restrepo pursue these ideas profoundly. For photojournalism, look no further than offerings by Carlos Villalon, Stephen Ferry and Malcolm Linton.

For the sake of coherency, the list has been put in alphabetical order by author and sectioned up between Drugs, Politics and Conflict, Fiction and Non-Fiction. Clearly, there are places where the themes intersect and overlap, but, these can be debated at a later date!

Drugs, Politics and Conflict

Ardila Arrieta, Laura. La Costa Nostra, 2023.
Ballvé, Teo. The Frontier Effect: State Formation and Violence in Colombia, 2020.
Bowden, Mark. Killing Pablo: The Hunt for the World's Greatest Outlaw, 2008.
Britto, Lina. Marijuana Boom: The Rise and Fall of Colombia's First Drug Paradise, 2020.
Brodzinsky, Sibylla. Throwing Stones at the Moon: Narratives from Colombians Displaced by Violence, 2012.
Burnyeat, Gwen. Chocolate, Politics and Peace-Building: An Ethnography of the Peace Community of San José de Apartadó, Colombia, 2018.
Bushnell, David. The Making of Modern Colombia: A Nation in Spite of Itself, Berkeley 1993.
Castillo, Fabio. Los jinetes de la cocaína, 1987.
Dudley, Steven. Walking Ghosts: Murder and Guerrilla Politics in Colombia, 2003.
Fals-Borda, Orlando. Subversion and Social Change in Colombia, 1969.
Farnsworth-Alvear, Ann, Palacio, Marco and Gómez López, Ana María. The Colombia Reader: History, Culture, Politics, 2017.
Fattal, Alex. Guerrilla Marketing: Counterinsurgency and Capitalism in Colombia, 2018.
Fattal, Alex. Shooting Cameras for Peace / Disparando Cámaras para la Paz, 2021.
Feiling, Tom. Short Walks from Bogotá: Journeys in the New Colombia, 2013.
Ferry, Stephen. Violentology: A Manual of the Colombian Conflict, 2012. (photojournalism)
Galeano, Eduardo. Open Veins of Latin America: Five Centuries of the Pillage of a Continent, 1971.
García Robayo, Margarita. The Armies. New Directions 2009.
Guillermoprieto, Alma. Looking for History: Dispatches from Latin America, 2002.

Gutierrez Sanin, Francisco. Clientelistic Warfare: Paramilitaries and the State in Colombia (1982–2007), 2019.
Henderson, James. Cuando Colombia se desangró: una historia de la Violencia en metrópoli y provincia, 1942.
Idler, Annette. Borderland Battles. Violence, Crime, and Governance at the Edges of Colombia's War, 2019.
Kaplan, Oliver. Resisting War, How Communities Protect themselves, 2017.
Karl, Robert. A. Forgotten Peace. Reform, Violence, and the Making of Contemporary Colombia, 2017.
Kirk, Robin. More Terrible Than Death: Drugs, Violence, and America's War in Colombia, 2004.
Kline, Harvey. F. Between the Sword and the Wall: The Santos Peace Negotiations with the Revolutionary Armed Forces of Colombia, 2020.
Linton, Malcolm. Metamorphosis, 2019. (photojournalism)
McFarland Sanchez-Moreno. There are No Dead Here: A Story of Murder and Denial in Colombia, 2018.
Molano, Alfredo. The Dispossessed: Chronicles of the Desterrados of Colombia, 2005.
Muse, Toby. Kilo: Life and Death Inside the Secret World of the Cocaine Cartels, 2020.
Otis, John. Law of the Jungle: The Hunt for Colombian Guerrillas, American Hostages, and Buried Treasure, 2011.
Palacios, Marco. Between Legitimacy and Violence: A History of Colombia, 1875–2002, 2006.
Paternostro, Silvana. My Colombian War: A Journey Through the Country I Left Behind, 2007.
Pécaut, Daniel. En busca de la nación colombiana, 2017.
Rempel, William. C. At the Devil's Table: The Untold Story of the Insider Who Brought Down the Cali Cartel, 2011.
Salazar, Alonso. No nacimos pa' semilla, 1990.
Sánchez Baute, Alonso. Líbranos del bien, 2011.
Serrano, Enrique. Colombia: Historia de un olvido: Tras siglos de un pueblo que surgió sin tirar una piedra, 2018.
Serrano, Enrique. ¿Por qué Fracasa Colombia? 2016.

Steele, Abbey. Democracy and Displacement in Colombia's Civil War, 2017.
Tufano, Sara. Colombia: Una Herida que no Cierra, 2023
Villalon, Carlos. Coca. The Lost War on Drugs. 2018. (photojournalism)
Zuleta, Estanislao. Colombia: violencia, democracia y derechos humanos, 1991.

Fiction

Alvarez Gardeazábal, Gustavo. Cóndores no entierran todos los días, 1985.
Behar, Olga. Noches de humo. Los protagonistas, 2010.
Bibliowicz, Azriel. Rumor Del Astracán, 2013.
Caicedo, Andrés. ¡Que viva la música! 1977.
Castro Caycedo, El Karina, 1998.
Delgado Lopera, Juli. Fiebre Tropical, 2020.
Escobar, Melba. House of Beauty, 2021.
Franco, Jorge. Rosario Tijeras, 1998.
Gamboa, Santiago. Return to the Dark Valley, 2017
García Márquez, Gabriel. One hundred years of solitude, 1967.
García Márquez, Gabriel. News of a Kidnapping, 2008.
García Márquez. The Scandal of the Century: And Other Writings, 2019.
Hincapié, Juan Fernando. Mother Tongue: A Bogotan Story, 2018.
Isaacs, Jorge. María, 1867.
Litwicki, Mark. Bogotano por Accidente, 2019.
Mutis, Álvaro. La Última Escala del Tramp Steamer, 2002.
Ospina, William. Ursua, 2010.
Pachico, Julianne. The Anthill, 2020.
Pachico, Julianne, The Lucky Ones, 2017
Restrepo, Laura. Delirium, 2008.
Rivera, José Eustacio. The Vortex (La vorágine), 1924
Rosero Diago, Evelio. The Armies, 2009.
Quintana, Pilar. The Bitch. US: World Editions 2020
Vallejo, Fernando. La virgen de los sicarios, 2017.

Vásquez, Juan Gabriel. The Sound of Things Falling. 2014
Zapata Olivella, Manuel. Changó, el gran putas, 1983.

Non-Fiction

Abad Faciolince, Héctor. Oblivion, 2013.
Arana, Marie. Bolívar, American Liberator, 2014.
Bennion, Neil. Dancing Feat: One Man's Mission to Dance Like a Colombian, 2014.
Betancourt, Ingrid. Even Silence has an End: My six years of captivity, Penguin Press 2010.
Birenbaum Quintero, Michael. Rites, Rights and Rhythms: A Genealogy of Musical Meaning in Colombia's Black Pacific, 2018.
Chao, Ramón The Train of Ice and Fire: Mano Negra in Colombia, 2010.
Davis, Wade. One River. Explorations and Discoveries in the Amazon Rain Forest, 1997.
Davis, Wade. Magdalena: River of Dreams: A Story of Colombia, 2020.
Doherty de Novoa, Caroline. Was Gabo an Irishman?: Tales from Gabriel García Márquez's Colombia, 2015.
Feiling, Tom. The Island that Disappeared, 2017.
Ferry, Stephen and Ferry, Elizabeth. LA BATEA, 2019.
Fitzgerald, María. F, Los Nombres Que Olvidamos. 2023
Gonsalves, Marc. Howes, Tom. Stansell, Keith. Out of Captivity: Surviving 1,967 Days in the Colombian Jungle, 2009.
González Toledo, Felipe. Crónicas bogotanas, 2008
Hart Dyke, Tom and Winder, Paul. The cloud garden, 2004.
Jacobs, Michael. The Robber of Memories: A River Journey Through Colombia, 2013.
Kellaway, Victoria and Lievano, Sergio. Colombia a Comedy of Errors, 2014.
Kevin, Brian. The Footloose American: Following the Hunter S. Thompson Trail Across South America, 2014.
López González, Alejandra. El vuelo del flamenco, 2017.
López-Pedreros, A. Ricardo. Makers of Democracy: A Transnational History of the Middle Classes in Colombia, 2019.

Martínez, Enrique. Quinta Sión: Los judíos y la conformación del espacio urbano de Bogotá, 2018.
Max Wills, Barry. Better than Cocaine: Learning to grow coffee, and live, in Colombia, 2023.
McColl, Richard. Bogotá through the 5 Senses, 2017.
McMullen, Miles. Field Guide to the Birds of Colombia, 2013.
Nicholl, Charles. The Fruit Palace, 1998.
Ospina, William. Pa que se acabe la vaina, 2013.
Rendell, Matthew. Colombia Es Pasión! The Generation of Racing Cyclists Who Changed Their Nation and the Tour de France, 2020.
Rendell, Matthew. Kings of the Mountains: How Colombia's Cycling Heroes Changed Their Nation's History, 2003.
Reyes, Emma. The Book of Emma Reyes: A Memoir in Correspondence, 2012.
Rojas Contreras, Ingrid. Fruit of the Drunken Tree, 2018.
Various Authors. Voices of Bogotá: A Short Story Collection 2018.
Young, Rusty. Colombiano, 2019.
Zanetti, Luca. Colombia: On the Brink of Paradise, 2018.

Basic Health & Safety

There are obvious pieces of advice to follow such as, for the most part you can drink the water in all major cities but always err on the side of safety. Should you find yourself in a smaller more remote town then only drink bottled water. Colombia's pharmacies are well stocked, although you should bring some basic supplies to combat diarrhoea, just in case.

Some people experience dizziness and headaches upon arrival in Bogotá because of the thin mountain air. Until you acclimatize you should avoid alcohol and caffeine, get plenty of sleep, and drink a lot of water and juice to keep hydrated.

Immunizations against the following diseases are recommended at least three months in advance of your trip: hepatitis A and B, tetanus-diphtheria, measles, typhoid, and yellow fever. The decision whether or not to take malaria pills should be made with your doctor. In rural and tropical regions special care should be taken to avoid getting dengue which can be rife depending on the season. Chikungunya and Zika affected Colombia during the spike in cases 2015 but cases have since abated.

Avoid the illicit industries

Violence perpetrated by the drug cartels, the various armed groups involved in the civil conflict, and gangs of delinquents are a fact of life in Colombia, but with common sense you can avoid most problems. Decades-old civil conflict and the drug trade have left some areas off-limits.

Avoid black-market money changers or any dubious transaction offering a better rate of exchange - counterfeit bills are a very real problem. Have nothing to do with drug dealers, because many of them freelance as police informers. Possession of cocaine or marijuana can lead to a long sentence in an unpleasant Colombian jail. Don't accept gifts of food, drink, cigarettes, or chewing gum from strangers; there have been reports of travellers being drugged and relieved of their valuables.

In short, use your common sense.

Key Sources

The contents of this book are meant to provide a broad overview of Colombia, her history, people, politics and challenges. By no means is this an exhaustive and complete history of a country and there will be details which have been overlooked, but it is a compilation of essays and collection of writings and research which I have undertaken since 2007 and written for various outlets and for my own enjoyment and understanding of a complex country.

So much knowledge was gleaned first-hand as a travel writer working on the only Michelin Green Guide to Colombia to date, traipsing around the country for Bradt, then as a specialist in Conflict Resolution before embarking on a PhD and providing political analysis on Colombian politics for international entities.

This said, interviews done on the Colombia Calling podcast and for the LatinNews podcast have been pivotal in providing in-depth information for academic and social backgrounds to the country and with this in mind thanks need to extended to the following people:

Sergio Gúzman of Colombia Risk Analysis, Adam Isacson of the Washington Office on Latina America (WOLA), Elizabeth Dickenson of International Crisis Group, the people at Insight Crime and the scores more who have been interviewed and with clarity and comprehension are setting the record straight on happenings here.

I strongly urge people to visit Colombia having read as much as possible from the reading list provided and to come to the country with further understanding and empathy.

About Fuller Vigil

Fuller Vigil is a boutique family-run editorial company based in Bogotá and London with the aim of publishing a couple of books a year in English and Spanish to better cover the subject of Colombia and the region.

Unsolicited manuscripts from first-time authors with an interest in Central and South America are welcomed.

www.fullervigil.com

Also by Richard McColl and Published by Fuller Vigil

Richard McColl is the author of various guidebooks about Colombia, his forthcoming book which is a deep look at his time restoring colonial houses and opening small hotels with his wife, Alba:

"The Mompós Project: Lifting the Veil, a Story of Love and Hotels," will be released in the second half of 2024.

Better than Cocaine: Learning to Grow Coffee, and Live, in Colombia (2024)

by Barry Max Wills.

Was Gabo an Irishman?: Tales from Gabriel García Márquez's Colombia (2015),

various authors.

Printed in Great Britain
by Amazon